I0795847

IMAGES
of America

ARKANSAS COUNTY

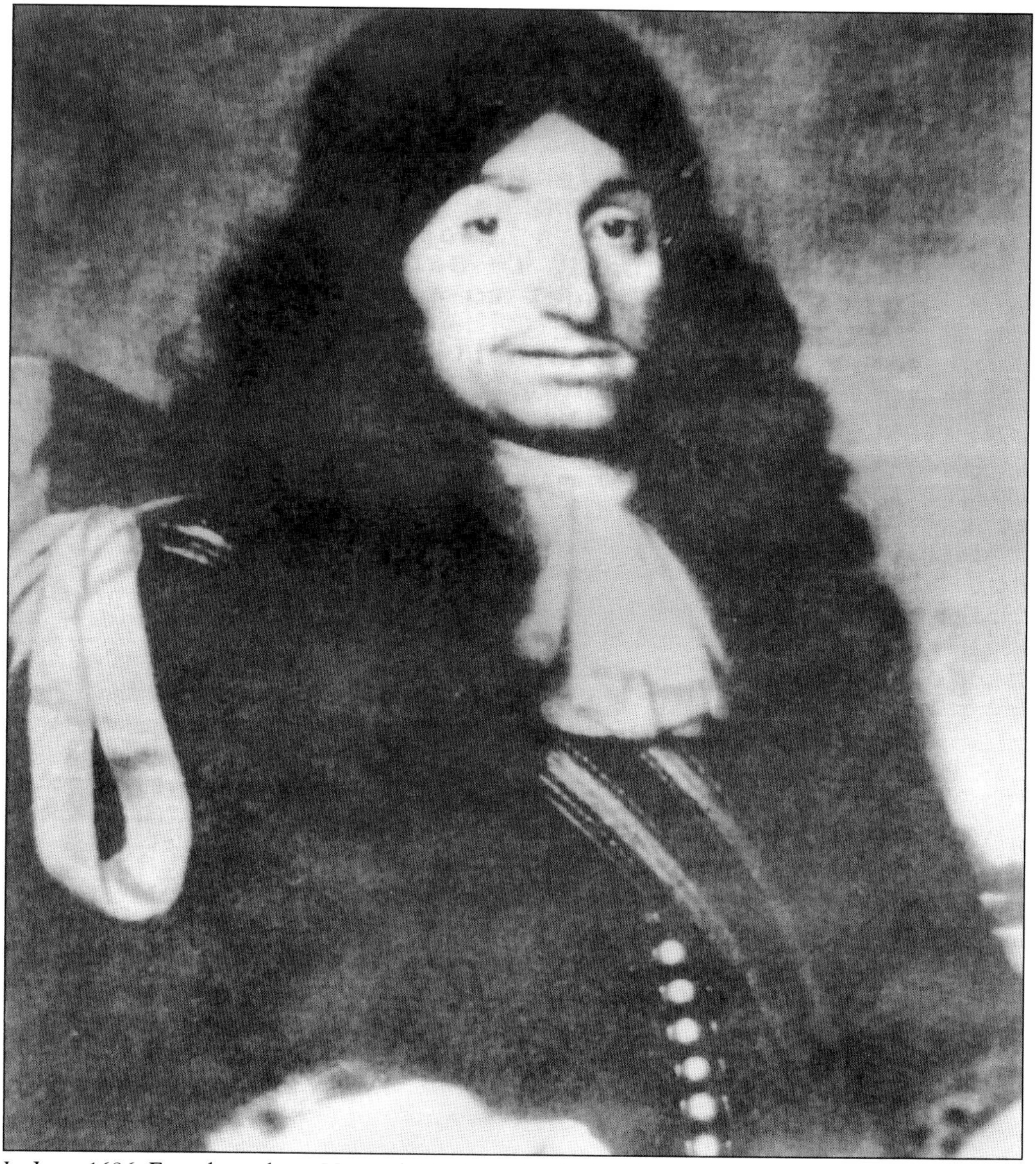

In June 1686, French explorer Henri deTonti established a Native American trading post on the Arkansas River about 30 miles from its intersection with the Mississippi, and a team of six men built the first house there. Known in French as *Poste de Arkansea*, the tiny Arkansas Post was the first semi-permanent European settlement in the Mississippi River Valley. Located in what would later become Arkansas County, it would play a key role in the long struggle between France, Spain, and England for dominance of the lucrative fur trade.

ON THE COVER: Horse- and mule-drawn equipment had previously provided all the available power for planting and harvesting crops like rice. But with the introduction of the first Case traction engine, initially sold in Stuttgart in 1906, mechanization had its start on the Grand Prairie. The huge steam-powered iron machines, which could pull all manner of equipment through the sometimes deep mud, allowed for the rapid expansion of rice farming. This photograph was taken near the tiny hamlet of Rule, southeast of Stuttgart, in 1909. (Courtesy of Ray Hanley.)

IMAGES
of America

ARKANSAS COUNTY

Steven and Ray Hanley

ARCADIA
PUBLISHING

ISBN 978-0-7385-5340-5

Published by Arcadia Publishing
Charleston, South Carolina

Printed in the United States of America

Library of Congress Catalog Card Number: 2007935871

For all general information contact Arcadia Publishing at:
Telephone 843-853-2070
Fax 843-853-0044
E-mail sales@arcadiapublishing.com
For customer service and orders:
Toll-Free 1-888-313-2665

Visit us on the Internet at www.arcadiapublishing.com

We dedicate this book to all those in Arkansas—and especially in Arkansas County—who are committed to preserving the history, architectural legacy, cultural heritage, and rich wildlife that make our state a special place to call home.

Contents

Acknowledgments

This book has been made possible because of a collaboration between the authors and the Museum of the Arkansas Grand Prairie in Stuttgart. Headed by Pat Peacock, the museum is ranked within the top 10 free attractions in the nation and is without question one of the finest regional museums we have found. Thanks go to Pat and her staff—Gena Seidenschwarz, Ann Prislovsky, and Frances Camp—who helped us access photographs and information on Saturdays.

We would like to thank Jim and Gail Craig of Stuttgart, who were kind enough to look at a century-old postcard and then help us locate the restored home of pioneer Dr. W. H. Moorehead, and who also gave us a fascinating tour of the older part of Stuttgart. We owe thanks to Karla Sigala of the National Park Service's Arkansas Post National Memorial for assisting with photographs. We are grateful to have obtained from the estate of Daisy Dixon of Versailles, Illinois, the postcards and images she received over several years from her sister Maude Brierton, a Stuttgart resident whose correspondence gives an insight into early life in Arkansas County. We would last like to credit Diane Hanley for editing the final manuscript and for performing the detective work with Maude Brierton's correspondence.

All uncredited photographs come from the authors' personal collections.

FOREWORD

Arkansas County, the center of the Grand Prairie, boasts a very rich heritage as the oldest county in the state. This book is written in an effort to preserve the history of the largest grain-growing area in the state and possibly even in the entire South.

The reader will notice that the authors are not just historians with a love of their state; their interest also seems to lie in a diverse variety of perspectives on the area. Arkansas County, being larger than most counties, has many stories to recount, and the Hanleys have done this in diligent form, in hunting down facts and photographs.

From the first days of the settlers at Miller Plantation to the later groups at Gum Pond, and from the naming of the largest town on the prairie (Stuttgart, for their hometown in Germany) to the first county seat of DeWitt, the authors have exercised their quest with honesty and determination to the fullest.

I hope that you, the reader, will learn through this book to appreciate the heritage of the Grand Prairie and its great leaders—both past and present.

—Pat Peacock
Director, Museum of the Arkansas Grand Prairie, Stuttgart, Arkansas
August 2007

INTRODUCTION

Located in the heart of the Grand Prairie, Arkansas County is the oldest in Arkansas and is adorned with a colorful history. Though unusual, the county has a dual seat, with courthouses in DeWitt and Stuttgart. The oldest records in Arkansas are in the Stuttgart Courthouse; they date from 1796 and are written in Spanish. These records begin the tale a century earlier, with the arrival in June 1686 of French explorer Henri deTonti, who established a post for trading with the native population near the juncture of the Arkansas and Mississippi Rivers. *Poste de Arkansea*, or Arkansas Post, was the first semi-permanent European settlement in the long Mississippi River Valley.

Over the years, the settlement was relocated from time to time because of flooding on the Arkansas River. Its position was consistently strategic for the French, Spanish, Confederate, and Union military. In April 1783, during the American Revolution—in which Spain sided with the colonies—Capt. James Colbert led a band of British partisans and Chickasaw Indians in an attack on Arkansas Post. The engagement was the only battle of the American Revolution fought west of the Mississippi River.

Created by the legislature of the Missouri Territory in 1813, Arkansas County comprised about two-thirds of what is now the state of Arkansas, along with part of eastern Oklahoma. In 1819, more than half of the state's counties were carved off of this original county when the Arkansas Territory was created. Arkansas Post was named the capital of this new territory.

On November 20, 1819, less than a month after arriving at Arkansas Post, a 23- year-old New York native named William Woodruff published the inaugural issue of the *Arkansas Gazette*, the first newspaper of the Arkansas Territory. Post residents celebrated with a barrel of whiskey donated by two local merchants. Woodruff printed the paper at Arkansas Post until November 24, 1821; when the capital moved to Little Rock, Woodruff brought his office there.

The most important battle fought in Arkansas County during the Civil War was the capture of Fort Hindman at Arkansas Post by Union forces in January 1863. The Confederate government had built the huge earthen fortress as a base for harassing enemy efforts on the Mississippi River and to help guard Little Rock, 117 miles upstream. Destroyed in the fighting, the town of Arkansas Post was never rebuilt. Today the site is a national monument.

After the war, the towns of Crockett's Bluff, Casscoe, and St. Charles became thriving river ports, thanks to the return of steamboat traffic to the White River. Railroads eventually connected the towns of Stuttgart, DeWitt, Gillett, Almyra, and Humphrey with the outside world and hauled the Grand Prairie's bountiful harvest to distant markets.

Stuttgart, the largest town in Arkansas County, began as a dream of Rev. Adam Buerkle, a Lutheran minister who immigrated to the United States from near Stuttgart, Germany, around 1852. By 1877, Reverend Buerkle was seeking a "certain spot" to establish a colony of his fellow German immigrants. He realized he had found just the spot when he visited the Grand Prairie region. The town he founded was named for the city in his homeland.

With the introduction of rice to the area in 1904, the region's agriculture was changed forever. The state's first rice mill was established at Stuttgart in 1907 by a group of the community's leading farmers and businessmen. Their vision helped make Stuttgart "the Rice Capital of the World," as merchants, lawyers, and other professionals flocked to the Grand Prairie to profit from providing support services to the farmers.

Today Arkansas is a national and international leader in rice production. The state devotes 1.4 million acres to the crop—43 percent of the total rice acreage in the country. Arkansas is home to the world's largest rice processing and export company, Riceland Foods, a farmer-owned cooperative located at Stuttgart, where Arkansas rice farming started over a century ago.

One

Frontier to Civil War

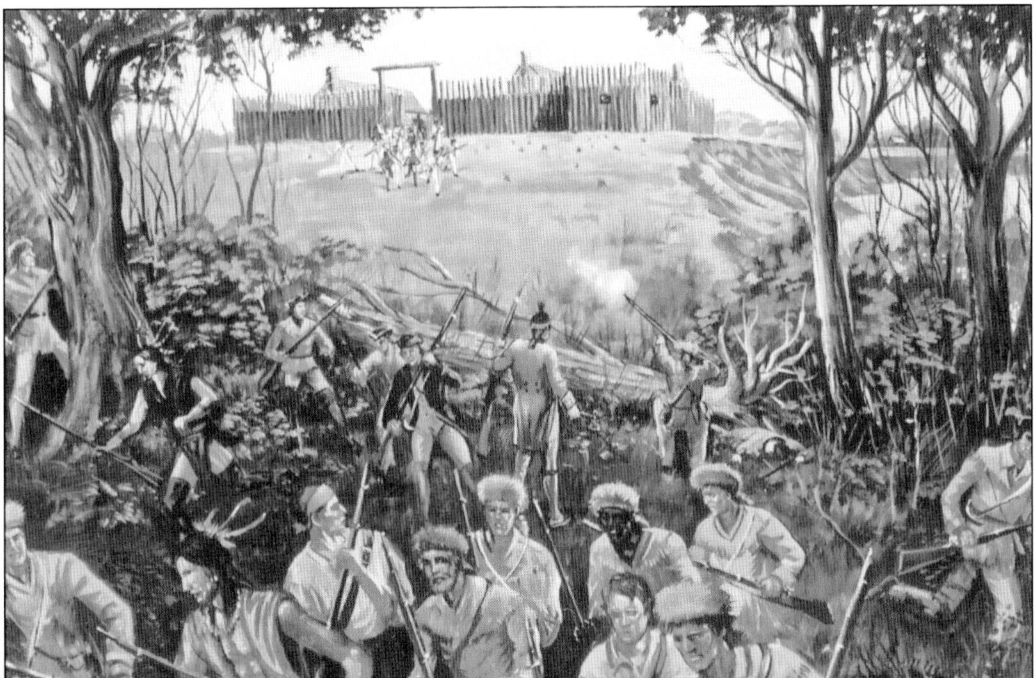

Early life was challenging and often uncertain in the newly settled regions of Arkansas. Capt. James Colbert led a band of British partisans and Chickasaw Indians in an attack on Arkansas Post during the Revolutionary War. The attackers, their oars muffled by leather, paddled up to the sleeping village before dawn and captured it easily. Their assault on the nearby stockade failed, however. The retreating raiders were pursued by the Spaniards and taken prisoner the next day. The engagement was the only battle of the Revolutionary War fought west of the Mississippi.

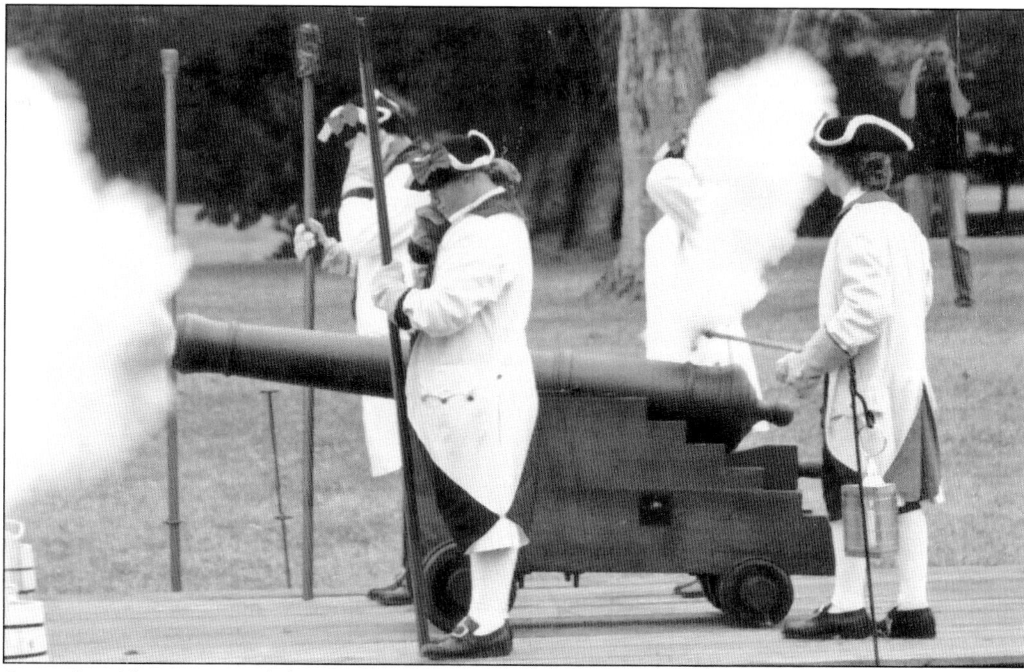

Spanish soldiers manned the ramparts of the stockade at Arkansas Post with cannons like the six-pound smooth bore, as demonstrated in 2006 by re-enactors and employees of the National Park Service. Spain later ceded the territory to France, who in turn sold it to the United States as part of the Louisiana Purchase in 1803. (Photograph by Edward Wood Jr., courtesy of the National Park Service.)

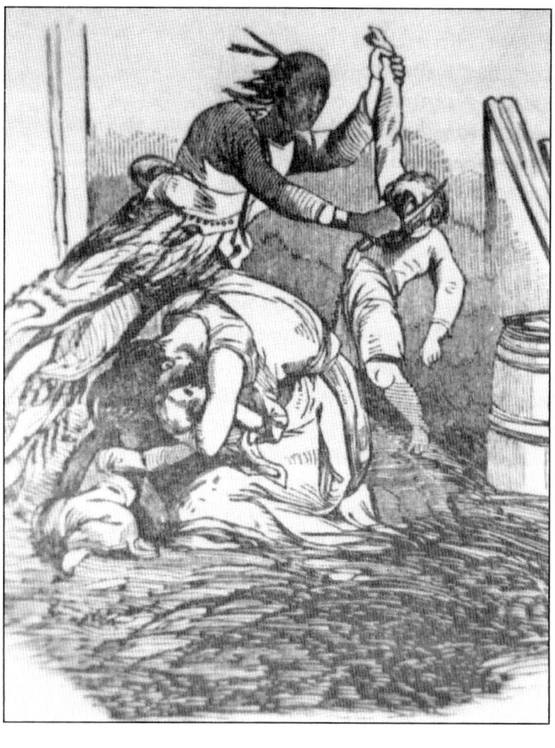

The British/Chickasaw attack during the Revolutionary War was not the first assault faced by the settlers. More than 30 years earlier, in May 1749, a force of 150 Chickasaw Indians had been urged by British allies to attack Arkansas Post. Six settlers were killed, and eight women and children were taken captive while the survivors fled to the nearby fort. After looting and burning the settlement, the raiders attempted to storm the stockade. A heavy volley from the defenders killed two of the attackers and seriously wounded their leader, forcing the Chickasaws to withdraw. (Courtesy of *Harper's Weekly*.)

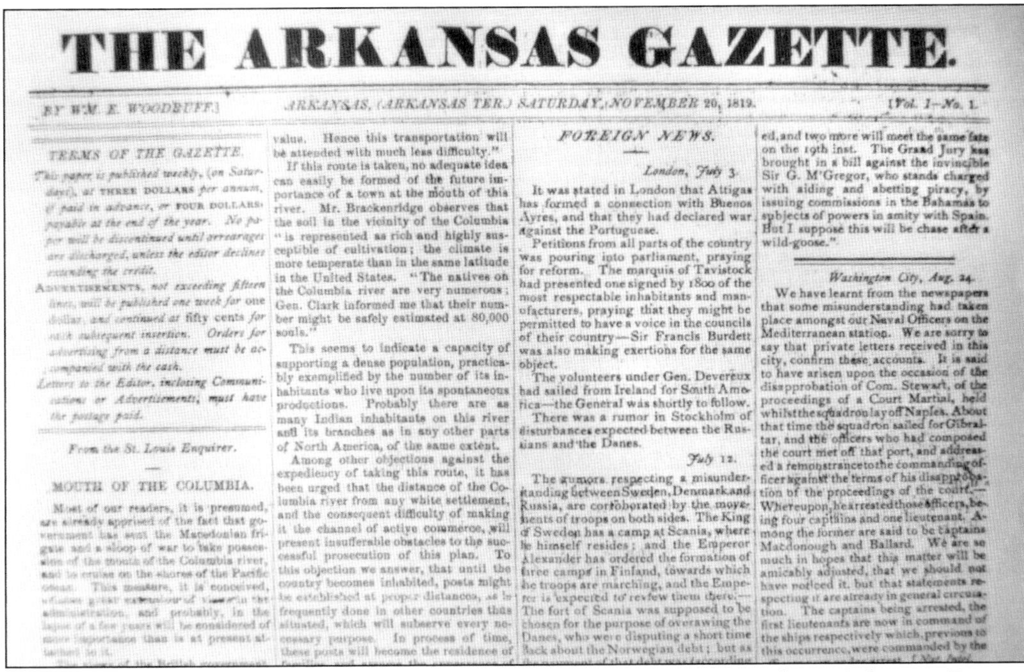

THE ARKANSAS GAZETTE.

BY WM. E. WOODRUFF] ARKANSAS, (ARKANSAS TER.) SATURDAY, NOVEMBER 20, 1819. [Vol. I—No. 1.

TERMS OF THE GAZETTE.

This paper is published weekly, (on Saturdays), at THREE DOLLARS *per annum, if paid in advance, or* FOUR DOLLARS, *payable at the end of the year. No paper will be discontinued until arrearages are discharged, unless the editor declines extending the credit.*

ADVERTISEMENTS, *not exceeding fifteen lines, will be published one week for one dollar, and continued at* fifty cents *for each subsequent insertion. Orders for advertising from a distance must be accompanied with the cash.*

Letters to the Editor, inclosing Communications or Advertisements, must have the postage paid.

From the St. Louis Enquirer.

MOUTH OF THE COLUMBIA.

Most of our readers, it is presumed, are already apprised of the fact that government has sent the Macedonian frigate and a sloop of war to take possession of the mouth of the Columbia river, and to cruise on the shores of the Pacific ocean. This measure, it is conceived, whatever great extension of views in the administration, and probably, in the lapse of a few years will be considered of more importance than is at present attached to it. [illegible]

value. Hence this transportation will be attended with much less difficulty."

If this route is taken, no adequate idea can easily be formed of the future importance of a town at the mouth of this river. Mr. Brackenridge observes that the soil in the vicinity of the Columbia "is represented as rich and highly susceptible of cultivation; the climate is more temperate than in the same latitude in the United States. "The natives on the Columbia river are very numerous; Gen. Clark informed me that their number might be safely estimated at 80,000 souls."

This seems to indicate a capacity of supporting a dense population, practicably exemplified by the number of its inhabitants who live upon its spontaneous productions. Probably there are as many Indian inhabitants on this river and its branches as in any other parts of North America, of the same extent.

Among other objections against the expediency of taking this route, it has been urged that the distance of the Columbia river from any white settlement, and the consequent difficulty of making it the channel of active commerce, will present insufferable obstacles to the successful prosecution of this plan. To this objection we answer, that until the country becomes inhabited, posts might be established at proper distances, as is frequently done in other countries thus situated, which will subserve every necessary purpose. In process of time, these posts will become the residence of [illegible]

FOREIGN NEWS.

London, July 3.

It was stated in London that Artigas has formed a connection with Buenos Ayres, and that they had declared war against the Portuguese.

Petitions from all parts of the country was pouring into parliament, praying for reform. The marquis of Tavistock had presented one signed by 1800 of the most respectable inhabitants and manufacturers, praying that they might be permitted to have a voice in the councils of their country—Sir Francis Burdett was also making exertions for the same object.

The volunteers under Gen. Devereux had sailed from Ireland for South America—the General was shortly to follow.

There was a rumor in Stockholm of disturbances expected between the Russians and the Danes.

July 12.

The rumors respecting a misunderstanding between Sweden, Denmark and Russia, are corroborated by the movements of troops on both sides. The King of Swedon has a camp at Scania, where he himself resides; and the Emperor Alexander has ordered the formation of three camps in Finland, towards which the troops are marching, and the Emperor is expected to review them there.—The fort of Scania was supposed to be chosen for the purpose of overawing the Danes, who were disputing a short time back about the Norwegian debt; but as [illegible]

ed, and two more will meet the same fate on the 19th inst. The Grand Jury has brought in a bill against the invincible Sir G. M'Gregor, who stands charged with aiding and abetting piracy, by issuing commissions in the Bahamas to subjects of powers in amity with Spain. But I suppose this will be chase after a wild-goose."

Washington City, Aug. 24.

We have learnt from the newspapers that some misunderstanding had taken place amongst our Naval Officers on the Mediterranean station. We are sorry to say that private letters received in this city, confirm these accounts. It is said to have arisen upon the occasion of the disapprobation of Com. Stewart, of the proceedings of a Court Martial, held whilst the squadron lay off Naples. About that time the squadron sailed for Gibraltar, and the officers who had composed the court met off that port, and addressed a remonstrance to the commanding officer against the terms of his disapprobation of the proceedings of the court.—Whereupon, he arrested those officers, being four captains and one lieutenant. Among the former are said to be captains Macdonough and Ballard. We are so much in hopes that this matter will be amicably adjusted, that we should not have noticed it, but that statements respecting it are already in general circulation. The captains being arrested, the first lieutenants are now in command of the ships respectively which, previous to this occurrence, were commanded by the [illegible]

William Woodruff published the first issue of the *Arkansas Gazette* from Arkansas Post on November 20, 1819. "Brigadier Gen. James Miller has accepted the appointment of Governor of this territory," reported the *Gazette*. "He is probably now on his way, and may be expected here as soon as the water rises, which is very low at present." Arkansas Post had been named capital of the recently designated U.S. territory.

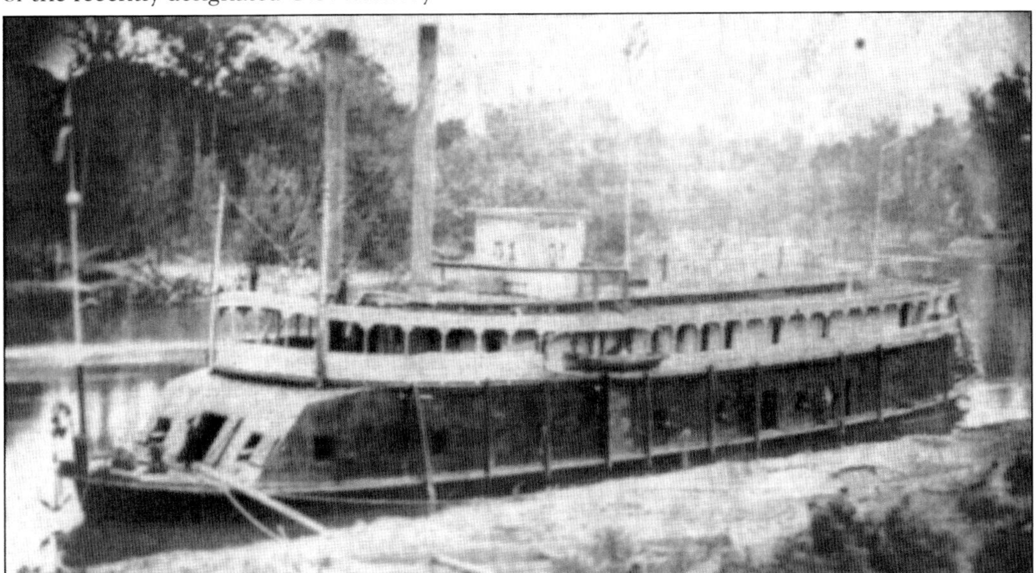

With the outbreak of the Civil War in April 1861, both sides realized the importance of controlling the western river system, including the Mississippi, the White, the Red, and the Arkansas Rivers and their many tributaries. Because the Confederacy lacked the naval resources of the North, a converted passenger steamer was converted to use as Gunboat No. 51, seen on the White River. It was armored with sheets of iron and fitted with cannons.

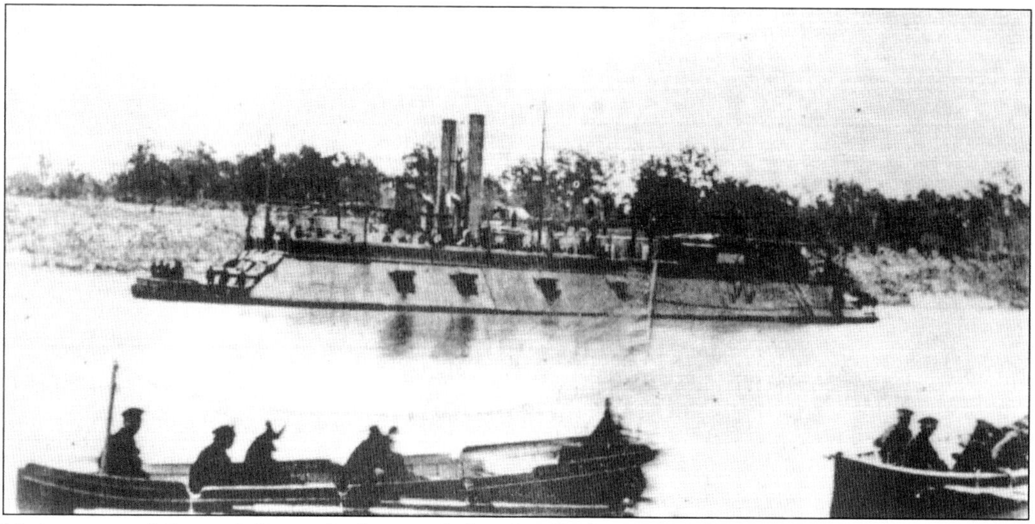

Union general Samuel Curtis had prevailed at Pea Ridge in northwest Arkansas in early 1862, crushing Confederate hopes of invading neighboring Missouri. In the wake of victory, he decided to invade Little Rock. Marching overland from Missouri, his army was slowed by bad weather and ran low on supplies. General Curtis was counting on Union forces taking control of the White River and delivering vital supplies to Jacksonport in northeast Arkansas. To do this, he brought in six new ironclad steamers such as the *Mound City*, pictured here, especially designed to navigate Southern waterways.

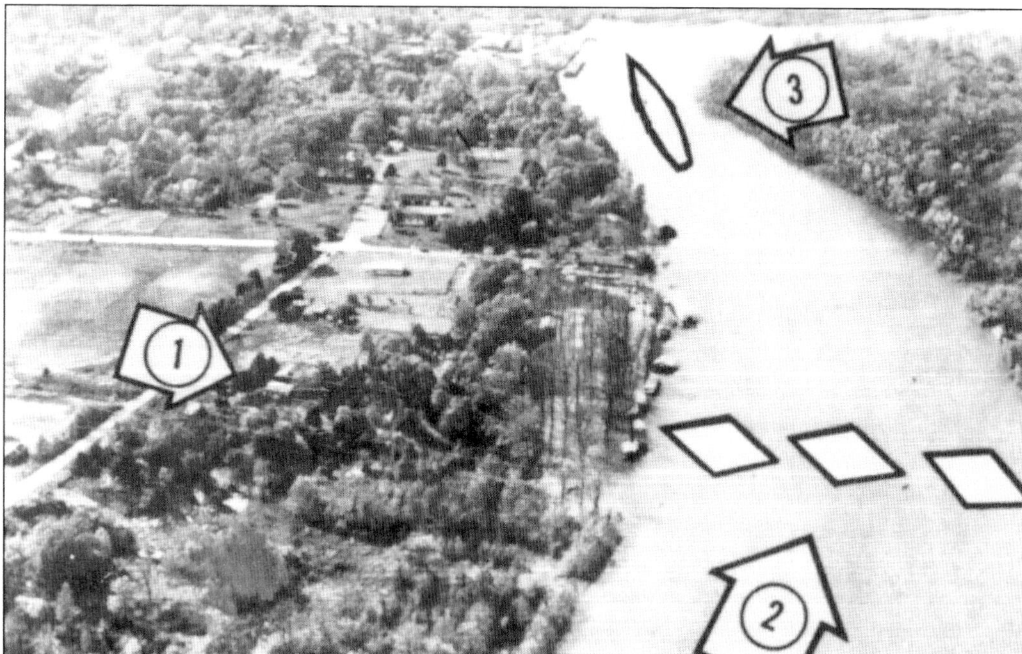

In June 1862, the Confederates attempted to halt the approaching Yankee armada at the small Arkansas County hamlet of St. Charles, on a bend in the White River, by blocking the channel with three sunken steamboats, as shown in this 1962 aerial photograph. Eight Union gunboats, led by the USS *Mound City*, steamed toward the Rebel blockade at 6:00 a.m. on June 17, 1862. (Photograph by Garner Allen, courtesy of the *Stuttgart Daily Leader*.)

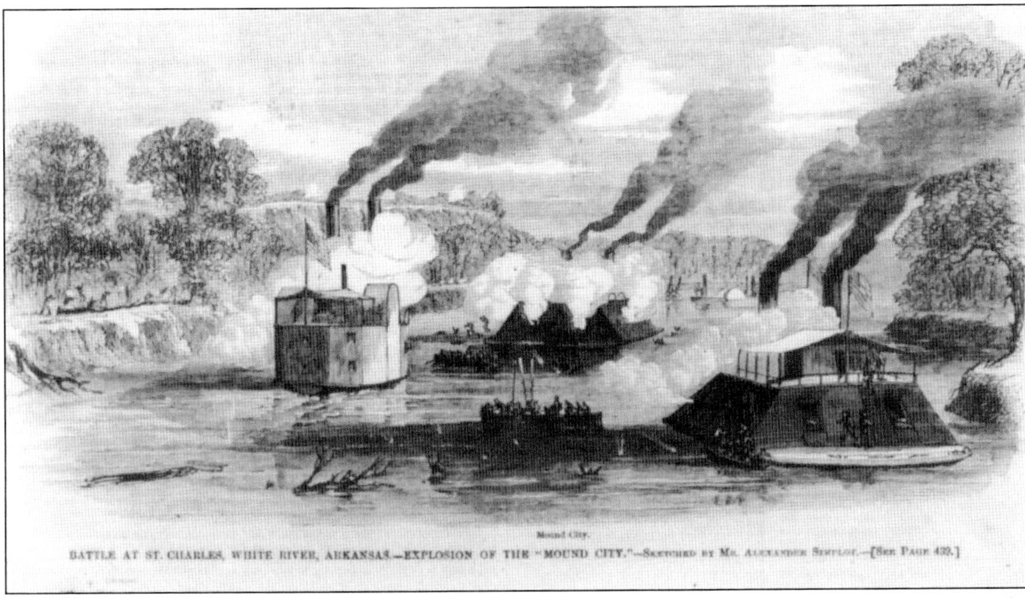

Capt. Augustus Kilty brought the *Mound City* within 600 yards of the Rebel artillery. Then the Confederates fired the deadliest single shot of the war, which struck the steam drum of the vessel, causing it to explode. All but 26 of the *Mound City*'s 175-man crew were killed or wounded. *Harper's Weekly* illustrated the encounter, reporting that some of those who dove overboard were killed by enemy sharpshooters. (Courtesy of the Butler Center for Arkansas Studies.)

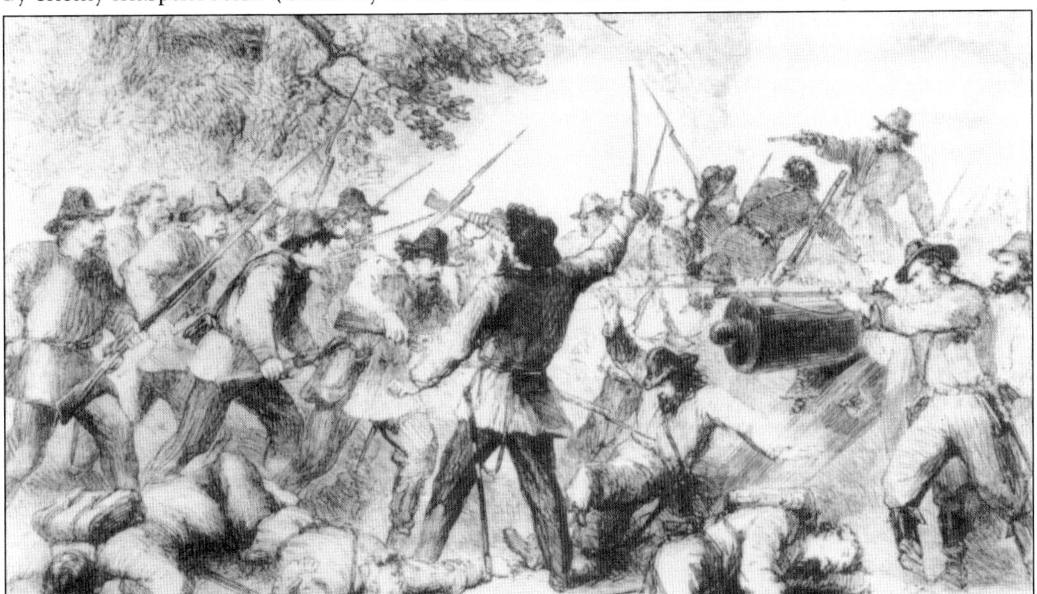

Despite the loss of the USS *Mound City*, the remaining Yankee gunboats soon silenced the Rebel artillery, enabling a regiment of Indiana volunteers to overrun the defenses. The North had won the Battle of St. Charles, but the cost had been high—150 men to the South's half-dozen casualties. Many of the initial survivors of the *Mound City* later died slow, painful deaths from scald burns. Their warship was repaired and returned to service. (Courtesy of the Butler Center for Arkansas Studies.)

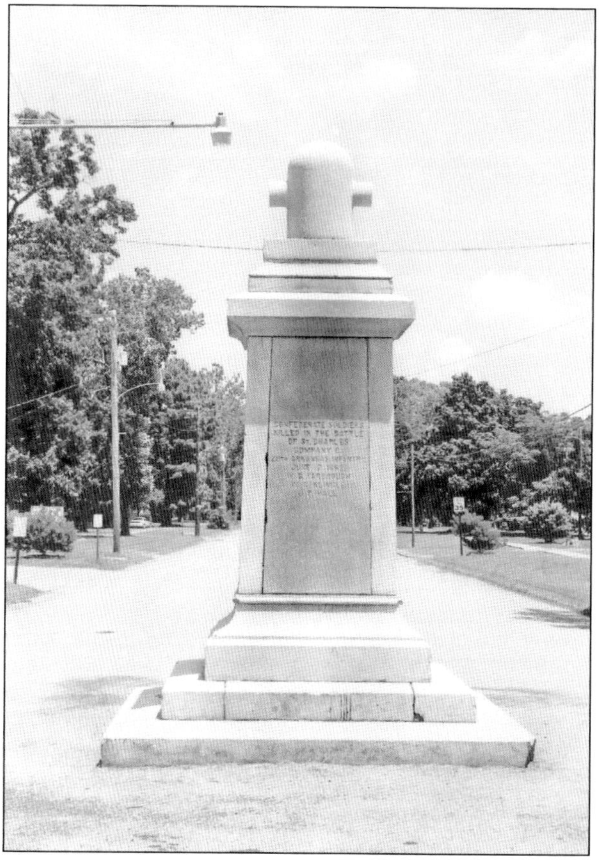

This monument was erected in St. Charles in 1919. It was paid for by a Northerner in memory of William Hickman Harte, a relative killed in the blast that destroyed the *Mound City*. The monument lists both the Union and Confederate dead. This inclusion may have been at the community's insistence, or perhaps because the benefactor was reportedly moved by meeting elderly residents who had cared for his wounded relative. U.S. Navy master William Hickman Harte, whose name (seen below) is engraved on the granite memorial standing in the middle of St. Charles's Main Street, was born in Ireland like many other soldiers who fought for both the North and the South. He was 36 years old when he suffered his fatal wounds aboard the ill-fated *Mound City*. (Photographs by Ray Hanley.)

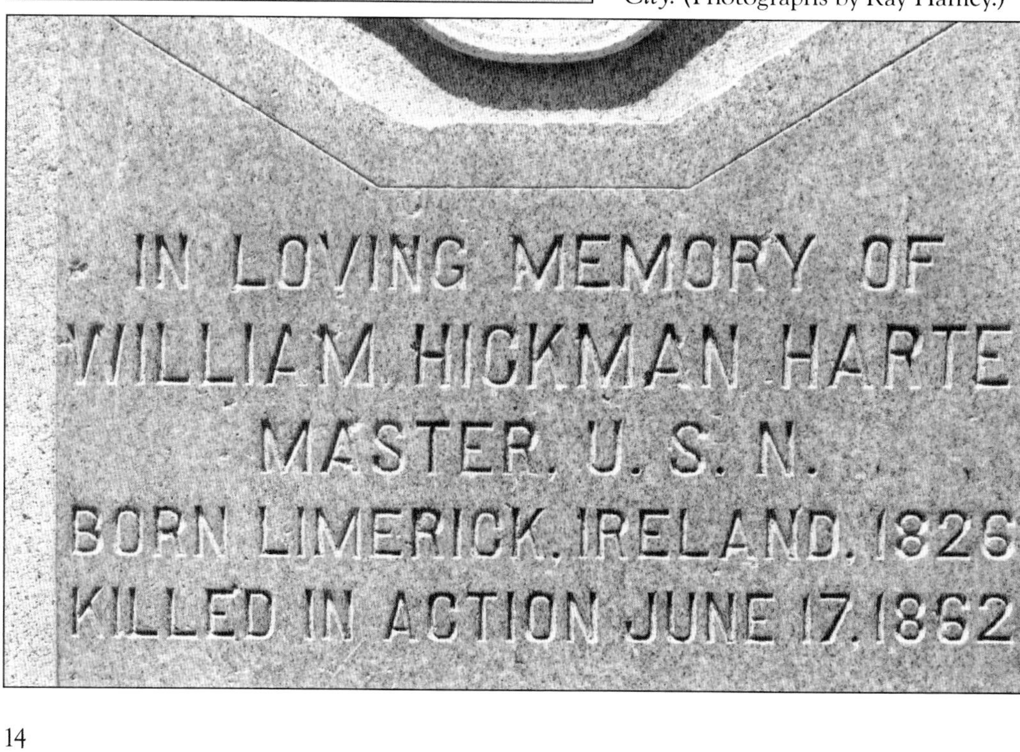

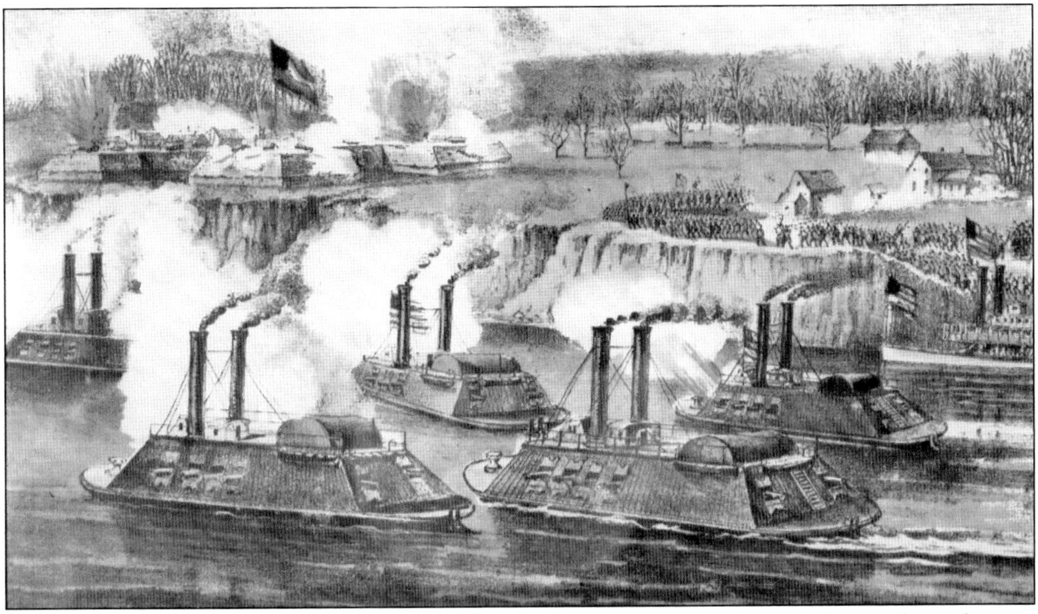

The strongest Confederate fort in the state was built at Arkansas Post, 50 miles up the Arkansas River from its juncture with the Mississippi. Fort Hindman was a huge earthen fortification intended as a base for harassing enemy efforts on the Mississippi. It also served to help guard Little Rock, 117 miles upstream. In January 1863, some 32,000 Union troops intent on taking the fortress headed upriver on transports. In the above image, Currier and Ives depict the flotilla of Yankee gunboats shelling the entrenched Rebels. The heavy bombardment soon put the defenders' artillery out of action, allowing Gen. S. G. Burbridge to lead an infantry charge into the fort's earthworks. Below, the planting of the Union Stars and Stripes and the waving of the Confederate white flag of surrender have been dramatized by an artist who apparently accompanied the victorious Northern army. (Courtesy of the Butler Center for Arkansas Studies.)

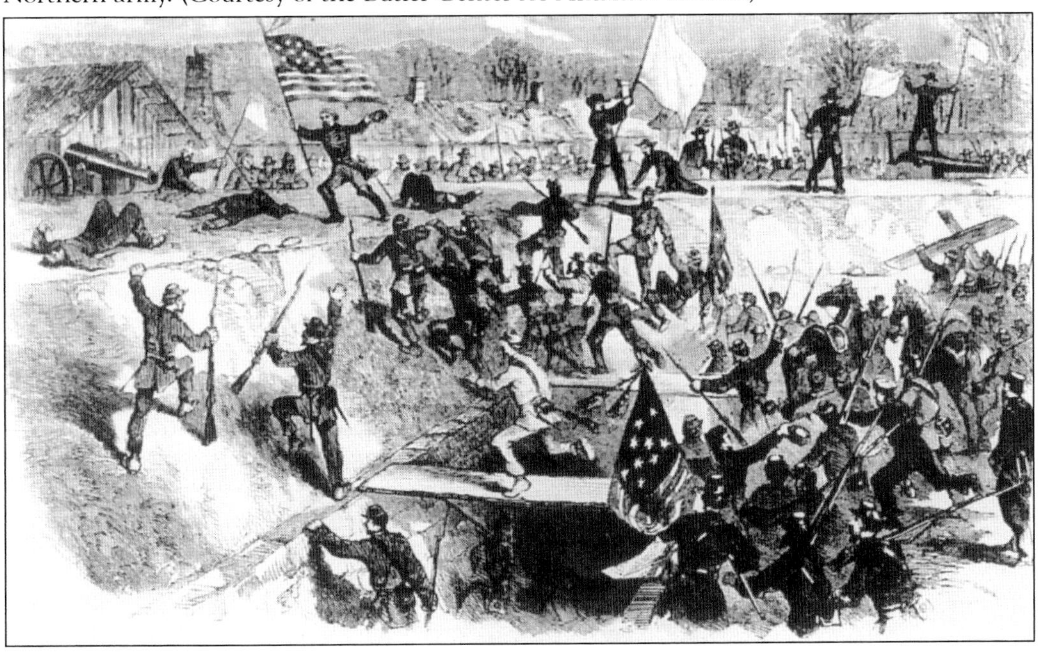

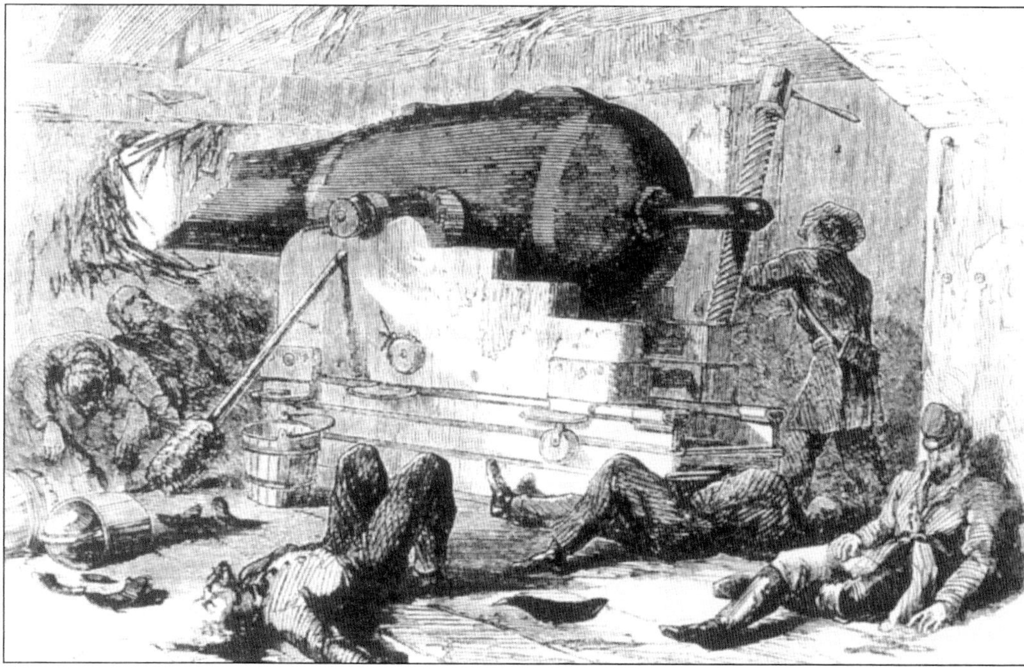

The devastating impact of the Union gunboats' pounding of Fort Hindman is illustrated here by *Harper's* Weekly; the sketch shows the fort's casement and nine-inch gun wrecked and its crew decimated. Southern casualties in the battle approached 150, while the North lost (killed or wounded) over 1,000 infantrymen, due primarily to the blistering small-arms fire mounted by the well-fortified Rebels. (Courtesy of the Butler Center for Arkansas History.)

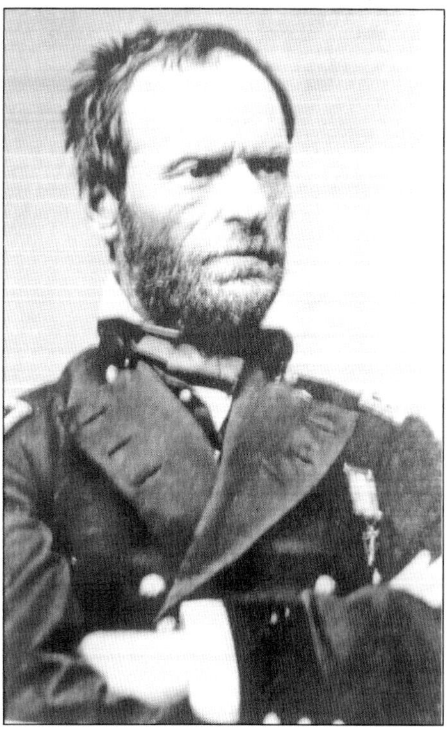

Gen. William Tecumseh Sherman helped lead the assault on Fort Hindman. Recalling his walk through the ruins after the battle, he wrote, "The fresh made parapet had been knocked down in many places, and dead and wounded men lay around very thick. . . . It was as fierce an engagement of six hours as has occurred during the war." General Sherman, who famously declared, "War is hell," would later be called both hero and tyrant for his scorched-earth march through Georgia. The town of Arkansas Post was destroyed in the fighting and never reconstructed. The site is now a national monument on the Arkansas River, which has looped in to reclaim the earthworks of Fort Hindman.

Fort Hindman's 4,900 "Johnny Reb" defenders were commanded by Gen. Thomas J. Churchill of Little Rock. General Churchill had fought at Pea Ridge and at Richmond, Kentucky, the previous year. Taken prisoner along with many of his troops, he was later exchanged for Union prisoners and returned to the war. Churchill served as governor of Arkansas from 1881 to 1883. In 1905, he died in Little Rock at age 81 and was buried at Mount Holly Cemetery.

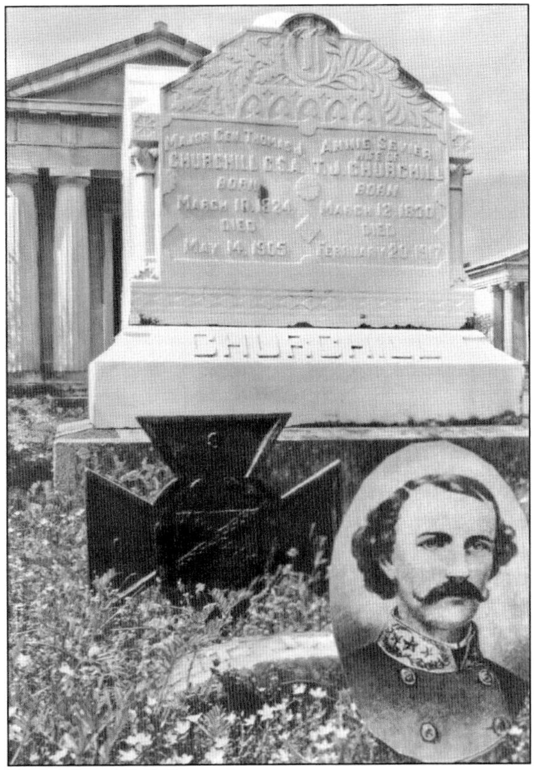

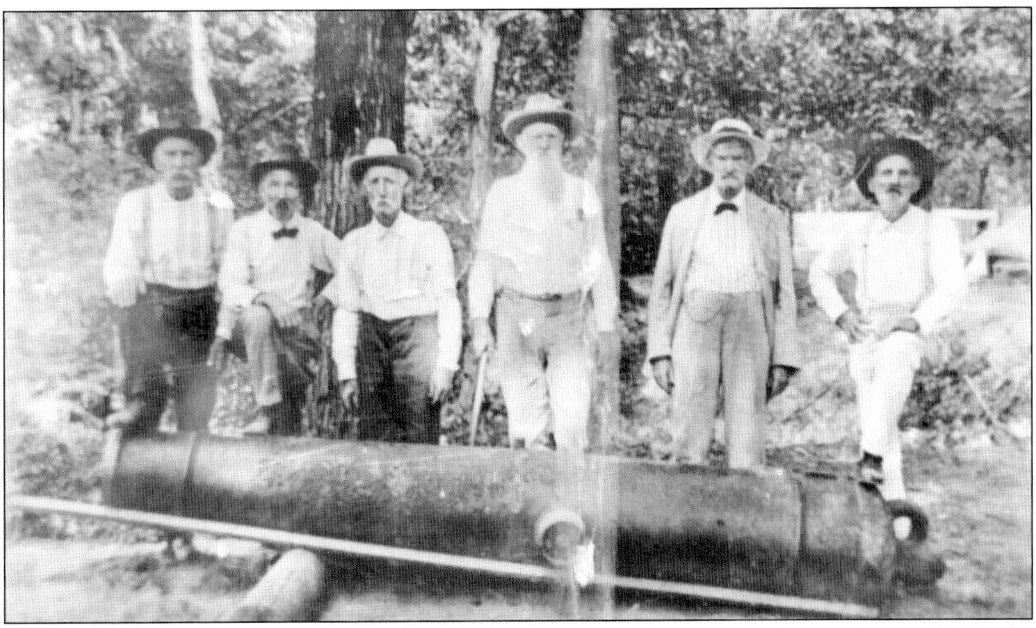

The Camp Fagan group of the United Confederate Veterans poses at Arkansas Post in 1920—57 years after the Battle of Arkansas Post—with one of the cannon from the 1863 engagement. The men were attending a reunion encampment at the time. Felix Allen (far left) was from the nearby town of Casscoe and would be the last of the six to die. (Courtesy of Arkansas Post State Park.)

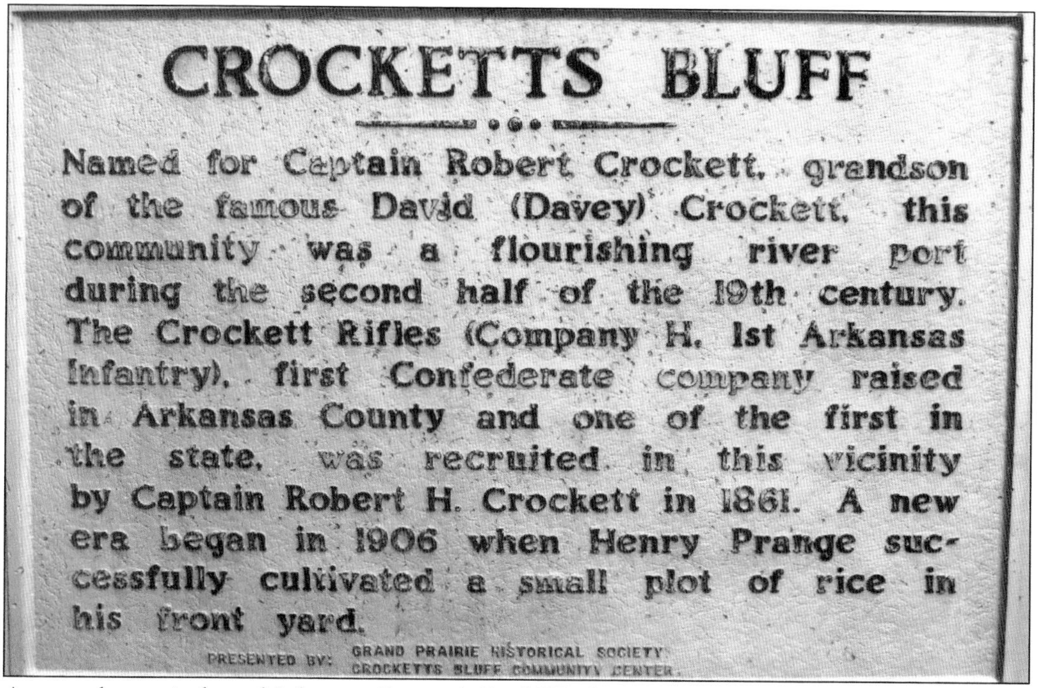

Among the reminders of Arkansas County's Civil War heritage is this plaque, erected during the state's centennial year of 1936 at historic Crockett's Bluff. The grandson of frontiersman Davey Crockett recruited the first Confederate company in Arkansas County.

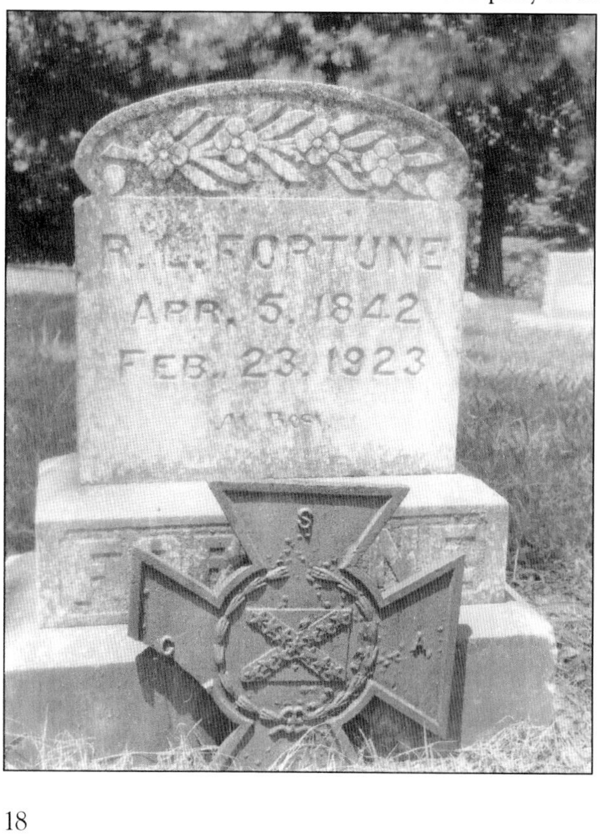

More than 60,000 Arkansans served in the Confederate army, and a number of them rest today in cemeteries across Arkansas County. The grave of R. L. Fortune, in the Shiloh Baptist Church Cemetery, bears the Confederate Cross of Honor. The front of the cast-iron Maltese cross is inscribed, "1861–*Deo Vindice*–1865," the Latin phrase meaning "God is our vindicator" or "vindicated by God." The reverse side, seen here, bears the Confederate flag and the letters CSA, for Confederate States of America.

Two

STUTTGART
QUEEN CITY OF THE GRAND PRAIRIE

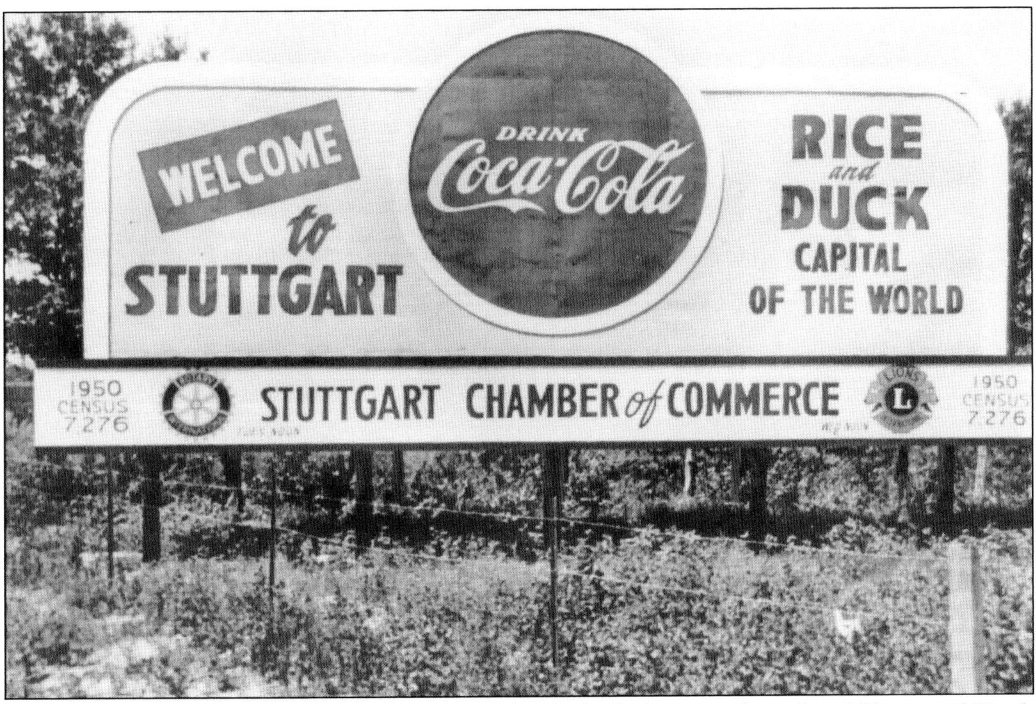

By 1950, Stuttgart and its 7,276 citizens had firmly laid claim to the title of "Rice and Duck Capital of the World." At the time, the town had only been incorporated for some 60 years. Since its founding, the city has been an island of prosperity upon the rich prairie of Arkansas and carries an equally rich history well worth the telling. (Courtesy of the Museum of the Arkansas Grand Prairie.)

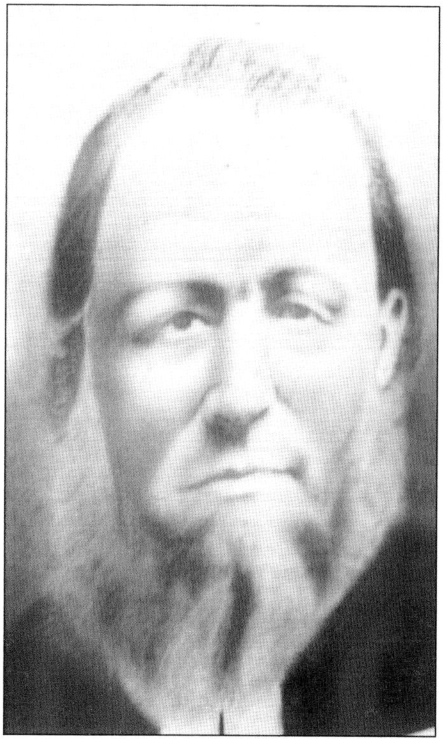

The father of Stuttgart was Rev. Adam Buerkle, a Lutheran minister born in Germany in 1825. After serving in several Northern states, Reverend Buerkle arrived in Arkansas County; he bought 11,000 acres of farmland and prepared to bring a large group of German immigrants to settle the area. A master businessman, Buerkle continually bought and sold land to develop the area. A post office he founded in 1880 was named Stuttgart for his former home in Germany. Buerkle lived to age 71, when, too ill to stand, he preached his last sermon while seated; he died a few days later in 1896. During his life, he fathered 15 children, 12 of whom survived to mourn his passing.

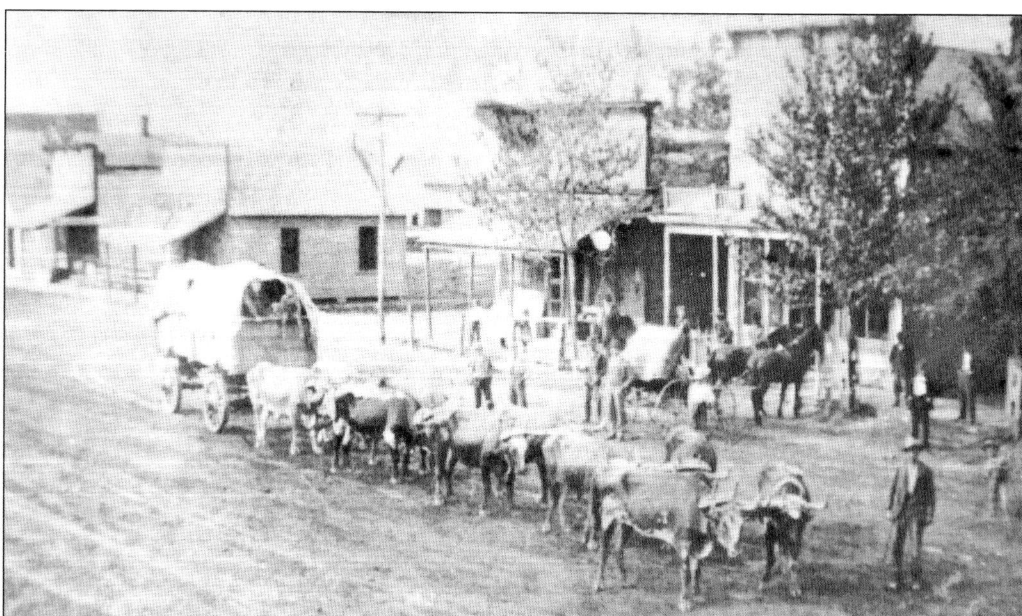

After Reverend Buerkle's founding of Stuttgart, the immigrants arrived in a steady stream, by rail and even by wagon. The first 65 settlers he welcomed included among their numbers 17 Lutheran ministers. Many more were families of German immigrants looking for better opportunity than they had found in the Northern United States. (Courtesy of the Museum of the Arkansas Grand Prairie.)

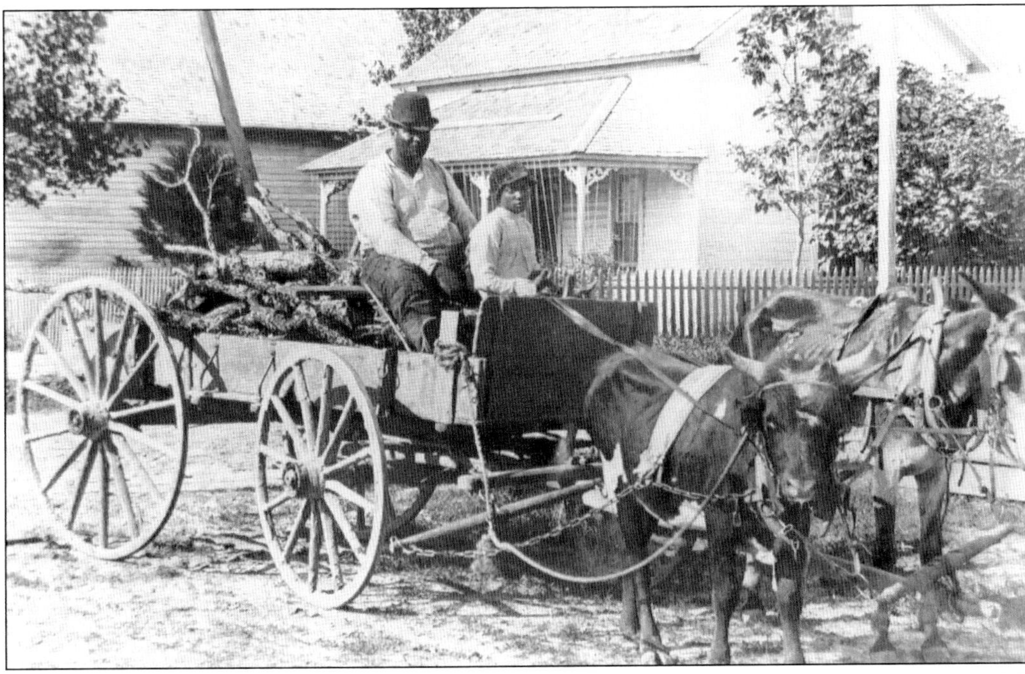

Though founded by German immigrants, the town of Stuttgart created a prosperity that grew the colony into a bustling city for many, including black Arkansans from the Mississippi Delta region. The townspeople worked hard, including this man and his son, who are apparently gathering firewood in their wagon, drawn by an oddly matched skinny mule and an equally thin ox. Perhaps they have collected limbs from the yards of the large homes being built in the town by the 1890s. (Courtesy of the Museum of the Arkansas Grand Prairie.)

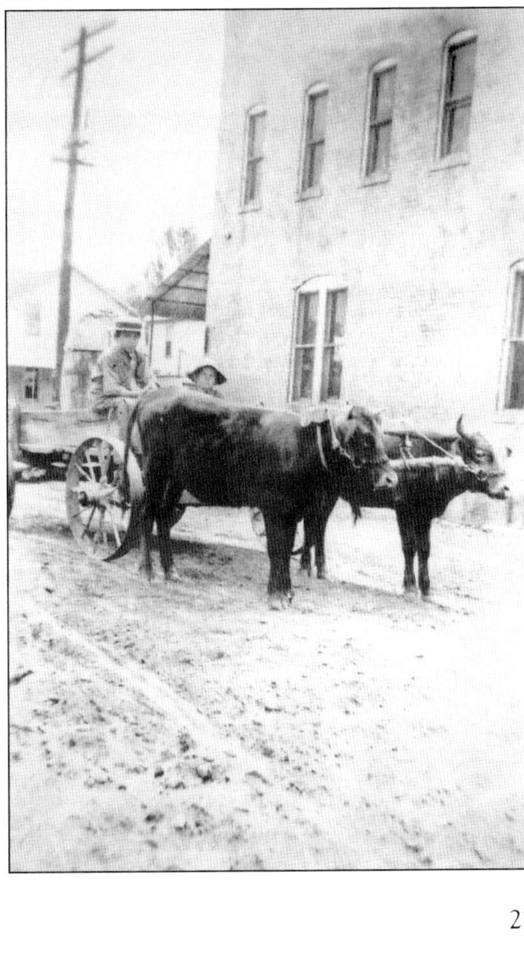

The agricultural wealth that made Stuttgart bloom was possible because of the rich Grand Prairie soil that was deposited over a layer of clay. In wet weather, however, it sometimes took oxen to pull the wagons on the roads, as in the case of these young boys, who have driven their team into town around 1900. (Courtesy of the Museum of the Arkansas Grand Prairie.)

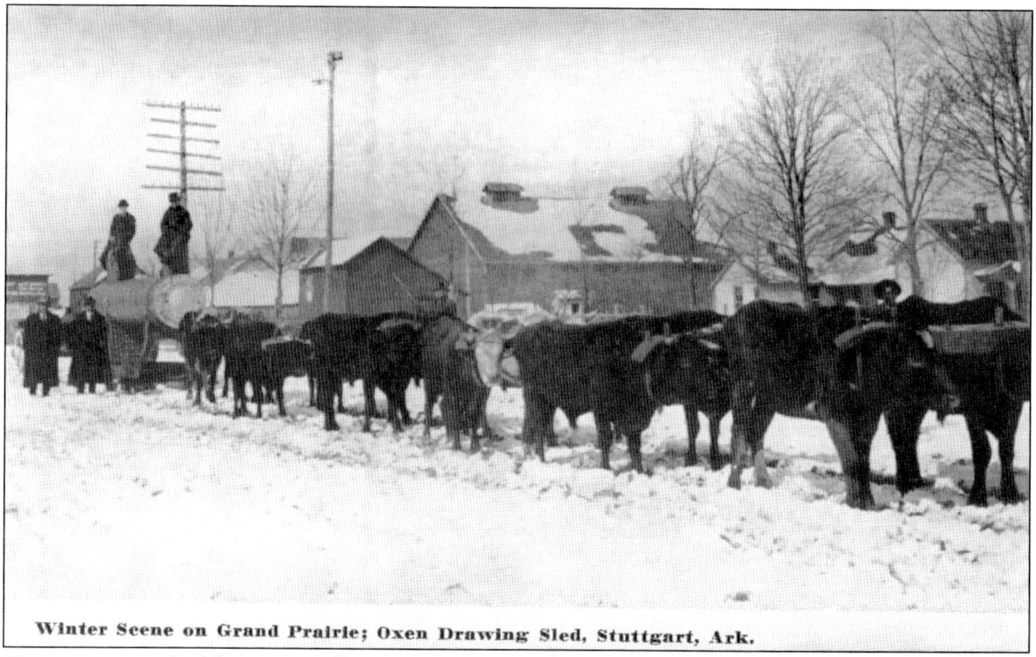

Oxen were invaluable—especially on a rare snowy day—in moving heavy loads such as this large steam boiler needed for a water well drilling operation conducted by the Layne-Arkansas crew. The company began service on the Grand Prairie in 1907 and still does business today, with trucks and tractors having long ago replaced the oxen.

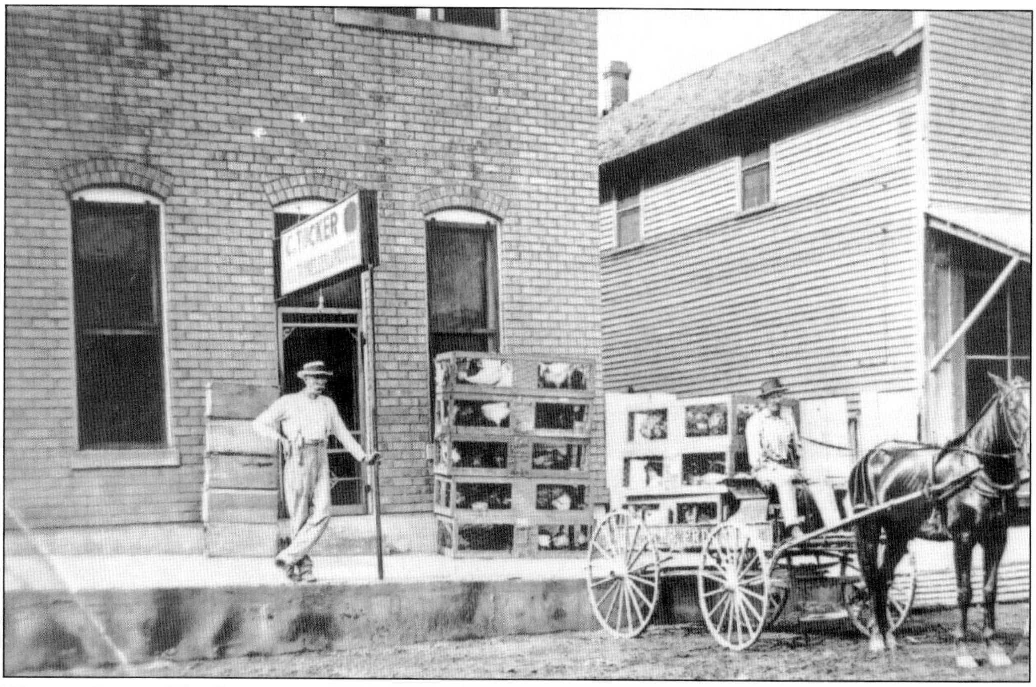

The products of the farms sprouting across the Grand Prairie made their way into Stuttgart, either for shipment to other markets or, like these chickens, for the city folks' Sunday dinner. (Courtesy of the Museum of the Arkansas Grand Prairie.)

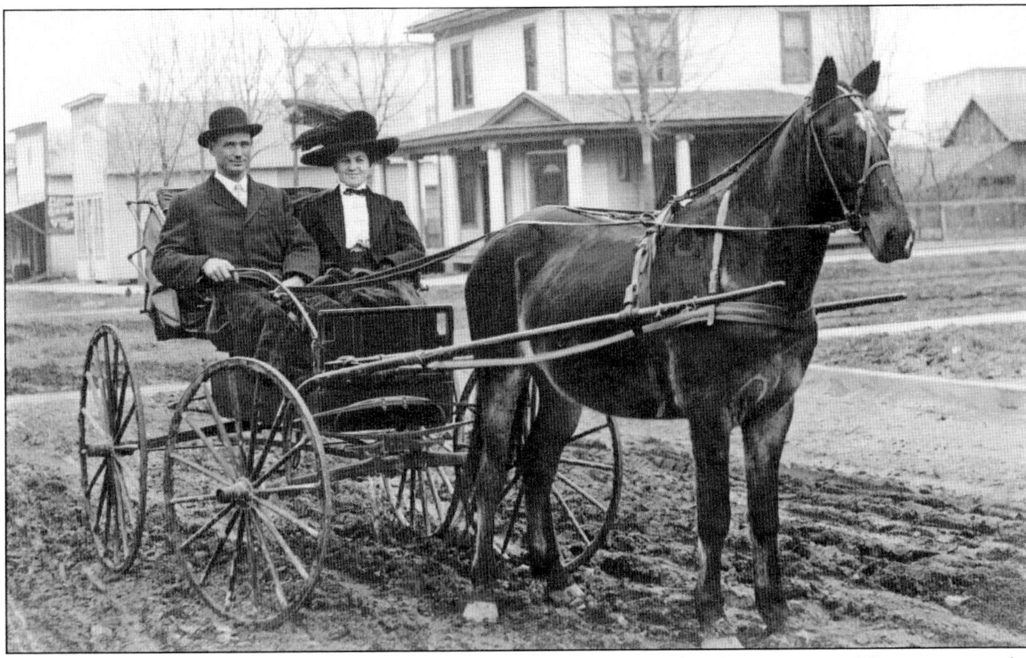

Intermingled among mule- and oxen-drawn farm wagons on the dirt streets of Stuttgart in the early 1900s were buggies driven by the well-dressed residents who had prospered and built fine homes, thanks to successful business ventures in the young, growing city. This couple, as noted on the back of the postcard, is preparing to drive to the tiny Prairie County town of Ulm in 1911.

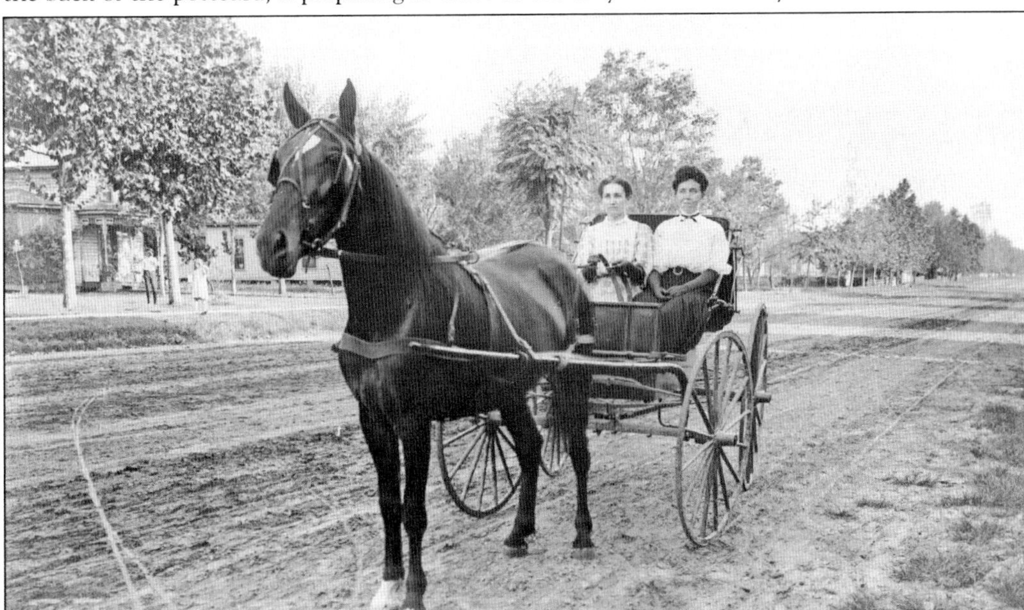

The horse-and-buggy was a prized possession in the first decade of the 20th century, as reflected in a series of postcards made in Stuttgart. Maude Brierton, the young woman driving this rig, noted on the card that her friend Stella "was about to laugh & it was the day I took sick. The fellow was cutting all sorts of figures to get May to put her ears up and Stella forgot about her own mug. We laugh and laugh about our faces but don't care as it was the horse's picture we wanted."

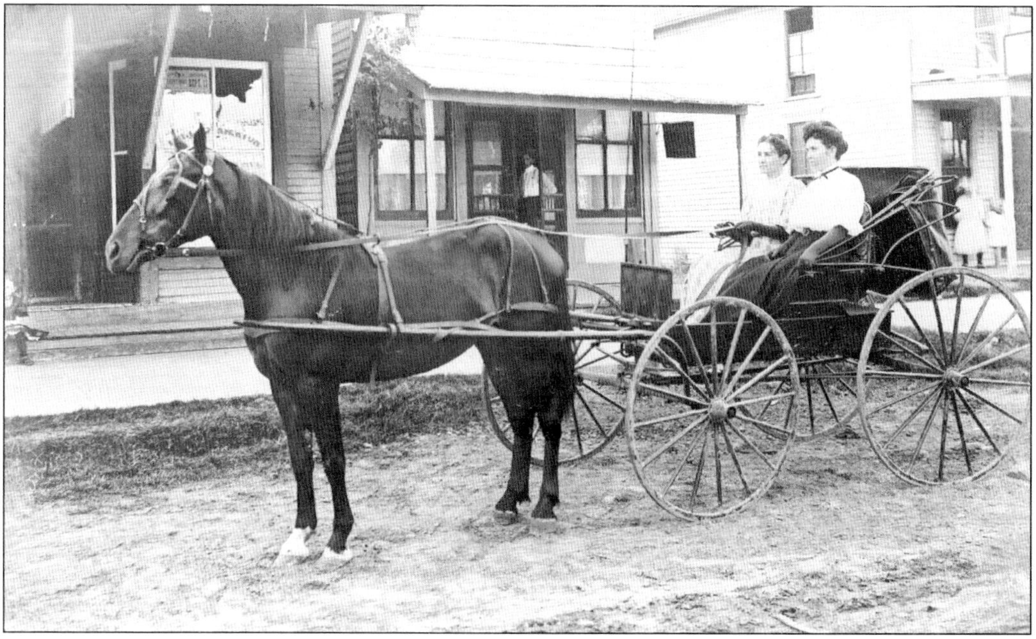

Maude Brierton, driving with friend Stella, later stopped their buggy before the Brierton Real Estate office to get another photograph of the horse, May. Their pose has apparently drawn the attention of a man peeking from a partially opened screen door.

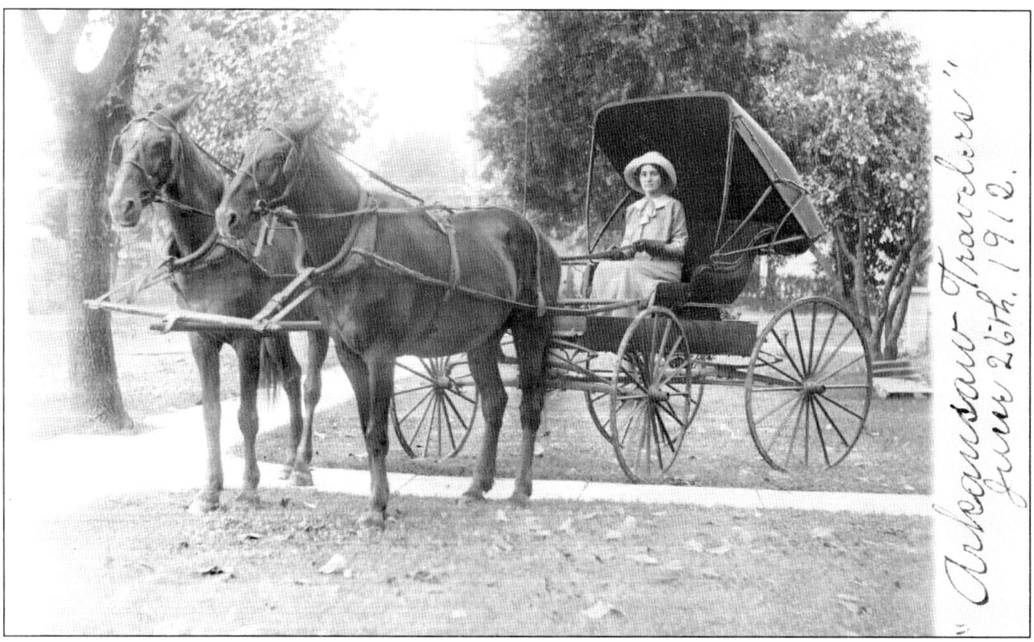

On a June day in 1912, the "Arkansas Travelers" were Maude Brierton and her horses Gypsy and Garnet, shown on a card mailed to her sister Daisy in Illinois. Maude wrote, "Come and take a ride with me behind old steadies. I am wearing my linen hat and tan serge dress. You can see the blooms on the tree like Grandpa got here."

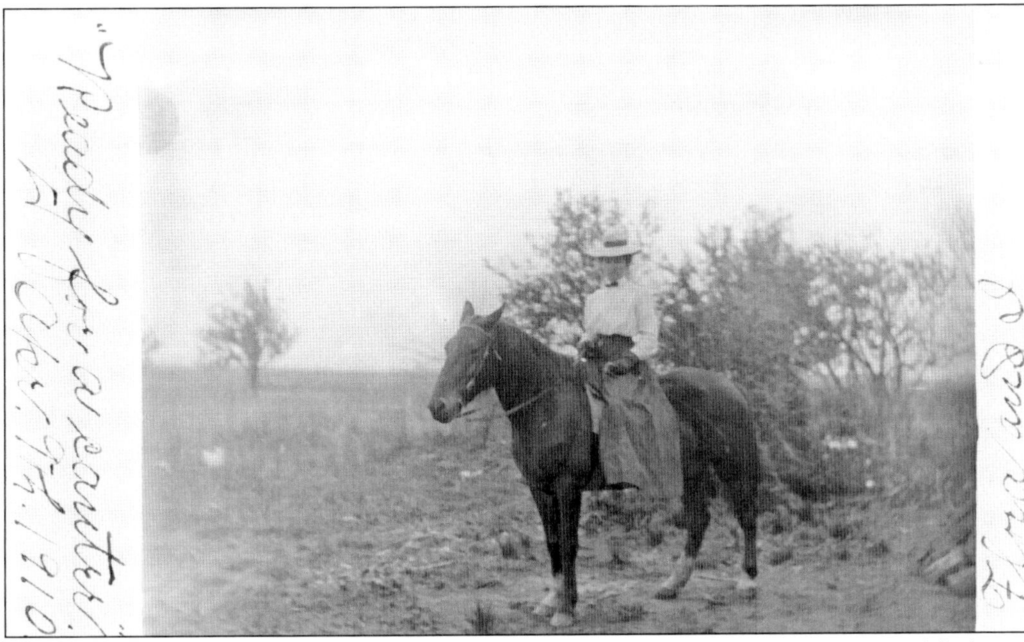

Maude and the other ladies who settled Stuttgart not only rode in buggies, but atop saddle horses as well. This note to her sister hints at life in 1910: "We got 23 little Chickens and 6 more hens sitting. The children are studying their lessons, Alice has just sent us a big loaf of fresh bread by Blossom & Birdie. They did not come in, afraid of the measles but I don't think there is any danger now as they did not have much fever."

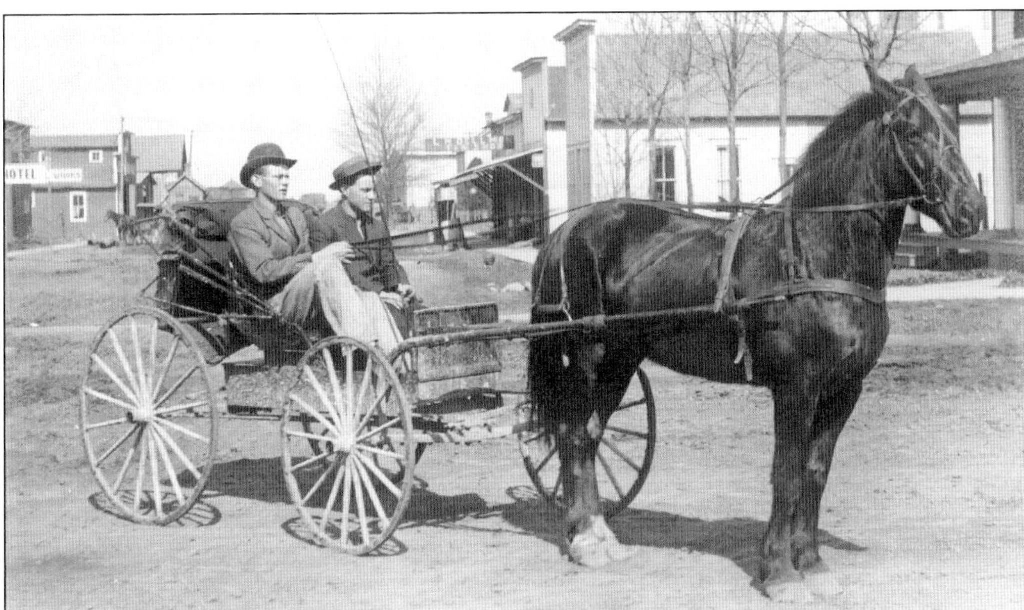

Herman Martin (left) and Bill Cobb, their buggy splattered with mud, pose on Stuttgart's Main Street around 1900. The town's wooden store buildings were the dominant features at the time.

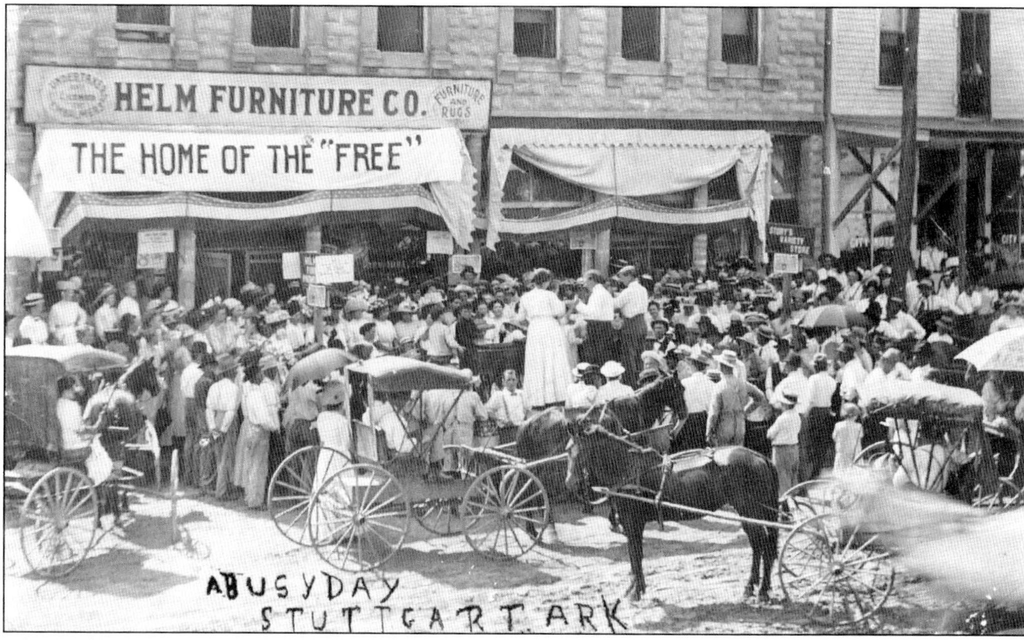

The Helm Furniture Company is noted on its sign as also providing an undertaker and licensed embalmer, a combination common in that era. On this Saturday in 1911, the store has drawn a large crowd with a promotion called the Home of the "Free." The men and women on the platform are demonstrating newly arrived Singer sewing machines. It seems the writer of the card was not interested in sewing, as he wrote, "I was out the other morning & killed 35 squrriles [*sic*] before noon."

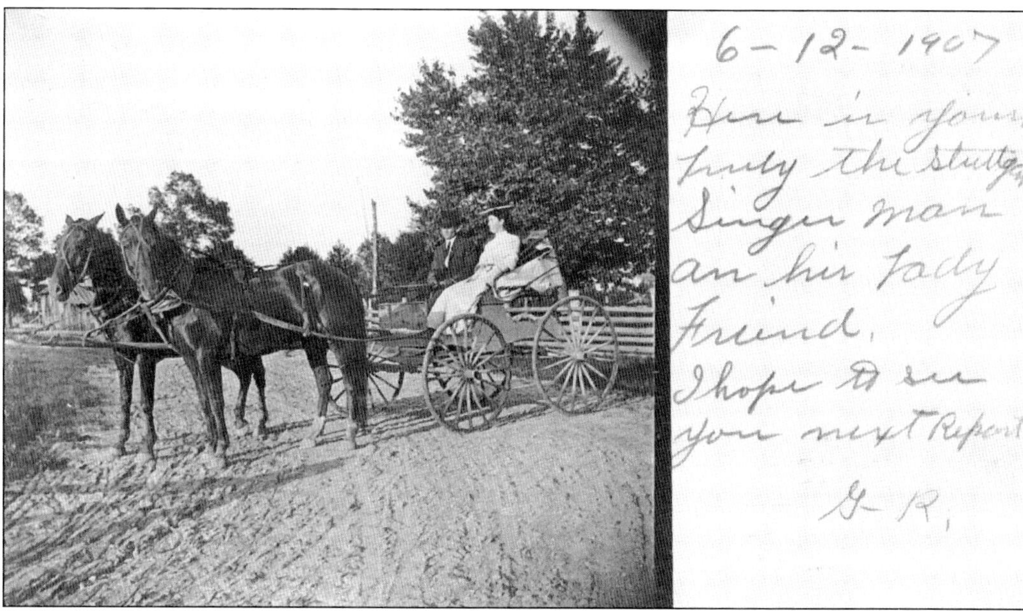

"Here is yours truly the Stuttgart Singer Man and his lady friend. I hope to see you next report." The puzzle remains as to whether this 1907 message identifies the driver as merely vocally talented, or perhaps as a vendor of the Singer sewing machines promoted by stores like the Helm Furniture Company.

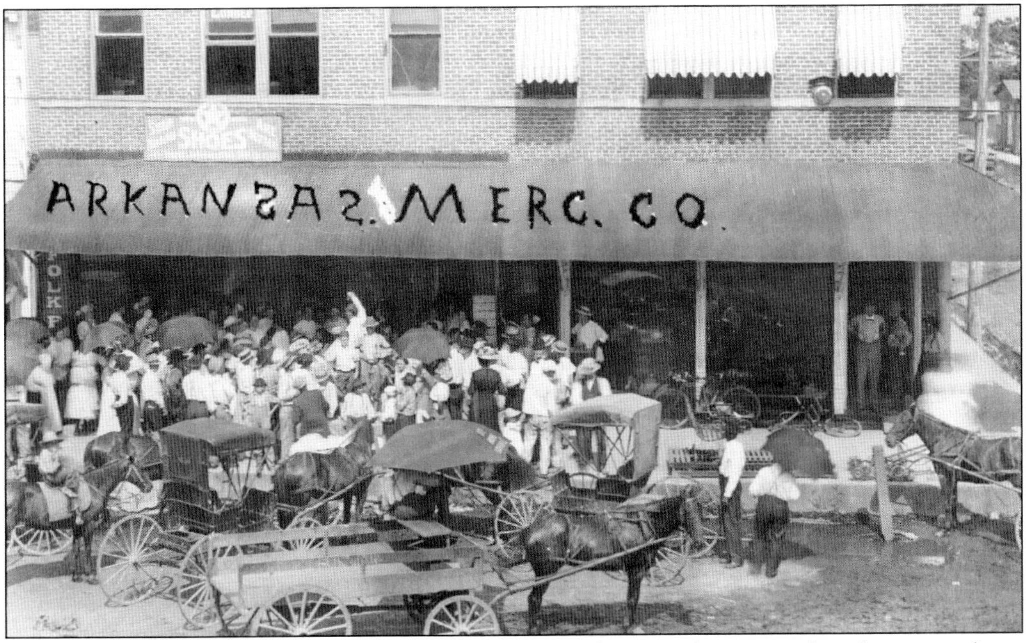

New products, whether sewing machines or the latest farm implements, often drew crowds on Saturdays when promoted in advance by enterprising merchants like the owners of the Arkansas Mercantile Company on Stuttgart's Main Street in 1911. Umbrellas provide shade on what was likely a hot day, made muggy after a recent rainfall.

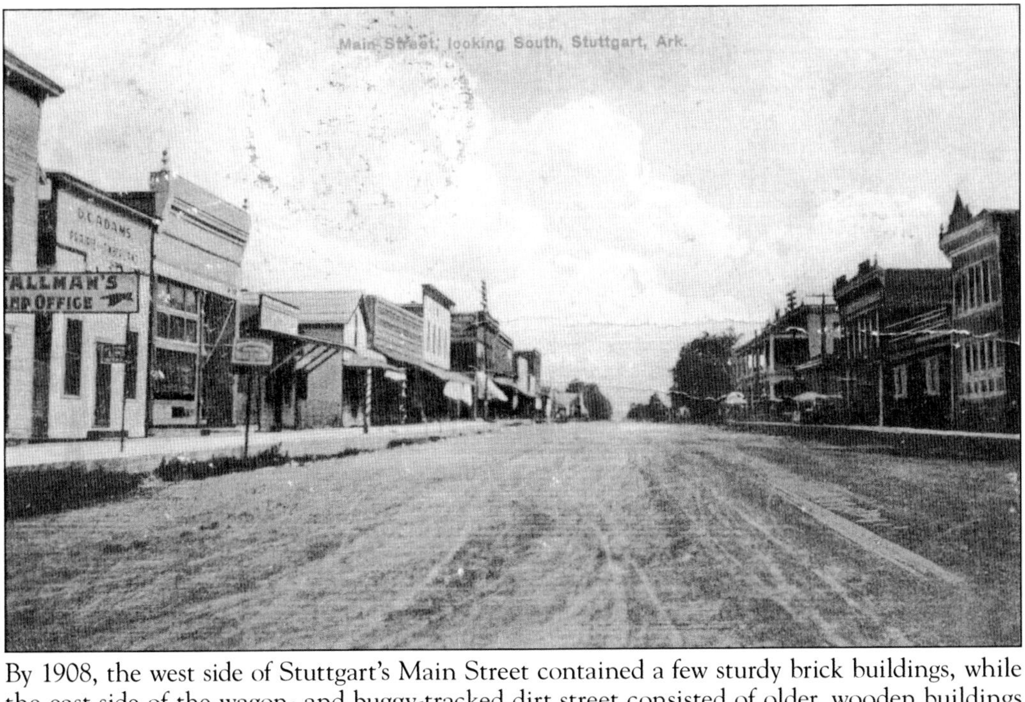

By 1908, the west side of Stuttgart's Main Street contained a few sturdy brick buildings, while the east side of the wagon- and buggy-tracked dirt street consisted of older, wooden buildings fronted by a concrete sidewalk. The D. C. Adams Prairie and Timberland office was promoting sales in the surrounding countryside.

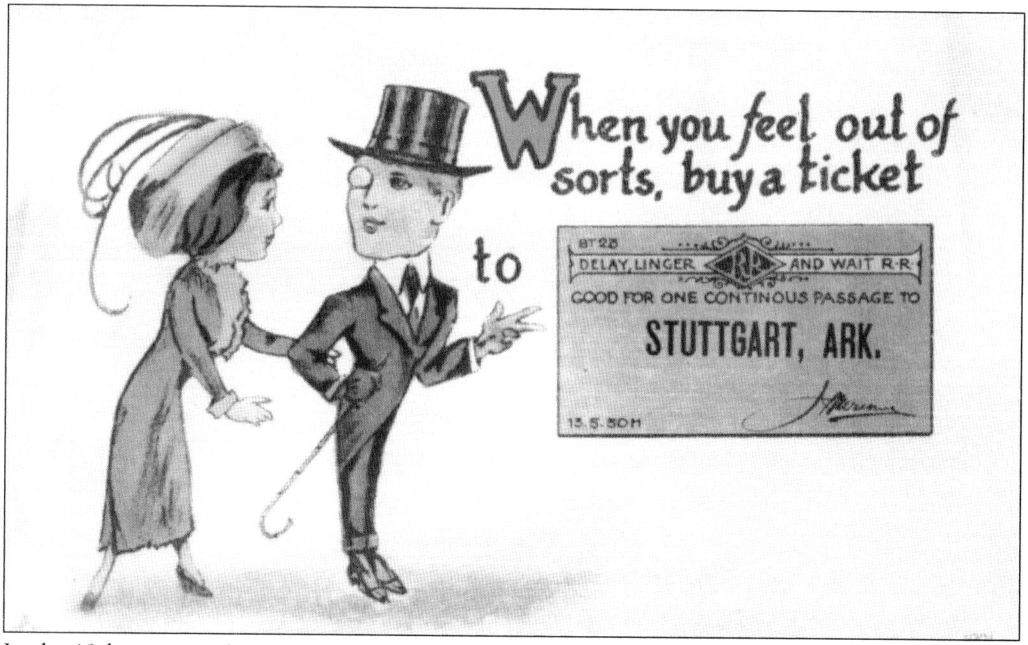

In the 19th century, American towns lived or died depending on their ability to attract a railroad connection. Reverend Buerkle, Stuttgart's founder, had made the town a success in this regard by securing a stop on Jay Gould's narrow-gauge Paramore Railroad in 1882. The full-size Cotton Belt Railroad came later, making the town's growth possible. The above postcard promoted rail travel to Stuttgart. "New Station will be a dandy," read the 1910 headlines regarding the Cotton Belt's plan to build a new station. The 326-foot-long depot and platform, seen below, cost $50,000. The postcard's message notes the crowd is "waiting for the excursion train, fall of 1910." Prospective settlers and businessmen were likely coming to assess the potential to relocate to Arkansas County.

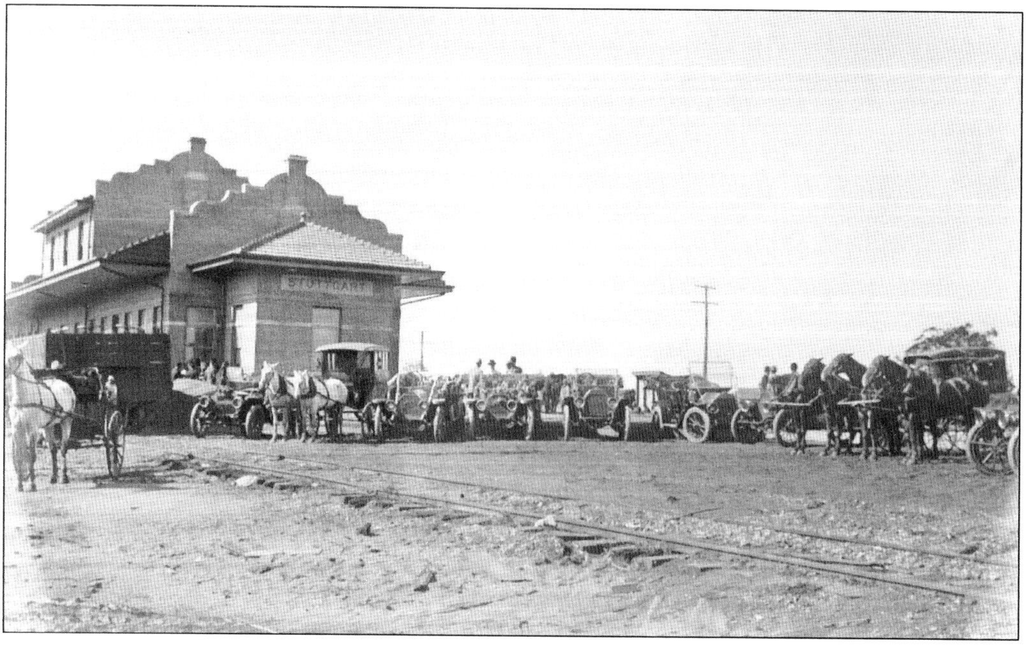

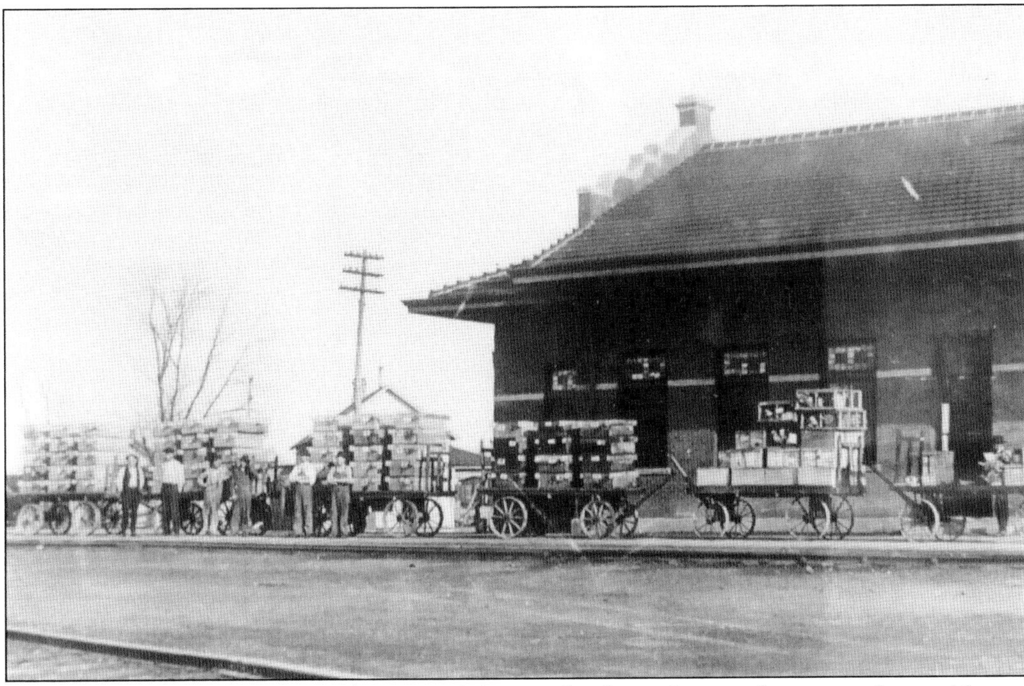

The depot saw the comings and goings of thousands of people over the years, along with tons of freight and crops. In this *c.* 1910 photograph, the carts are filled with crates of chickens and other goods likely offloaded from a departed freight train, perhaps bound for the local stores. Sadly, passenger service ended in 1959, and the depot was razed a few years ago. (Courtesy of the Museum of the Arkansas Grand Prairie.)

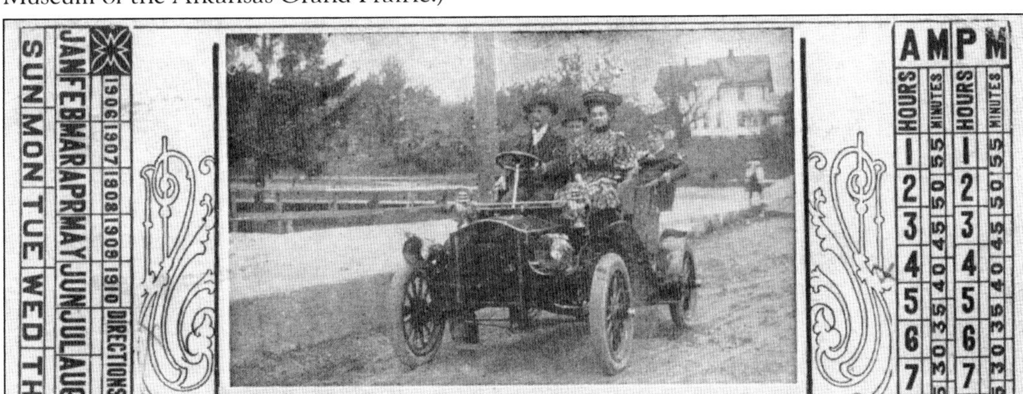

A visitor to Stuttgart in 1907 mailed this card home to Michigan stating that she had arrived. The marks on the card's coded boxes indicate that "Linna" arrived at 4:00 a.m. on a July morning, an unlikely schedule whether traveling by automobile or train.

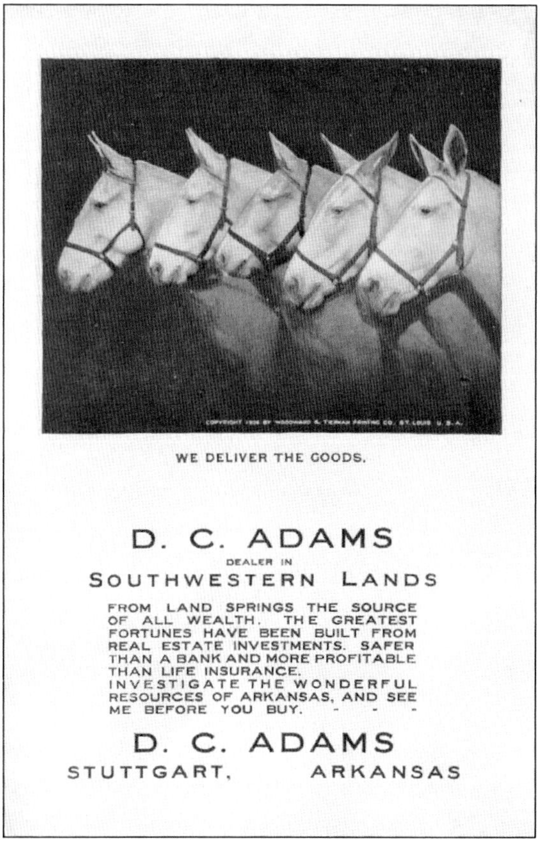

"We deliver the goods," boasts land speculator D. C. Adams. "Investigate the wonderful resources of Arkansas and see me before you buy." Adams's office on Stuttgart's Main Street, seen on page 27, advertised by mailing postcards like this nationwide in the years before World War I, seeking to sell Arkansas farm and timberland.

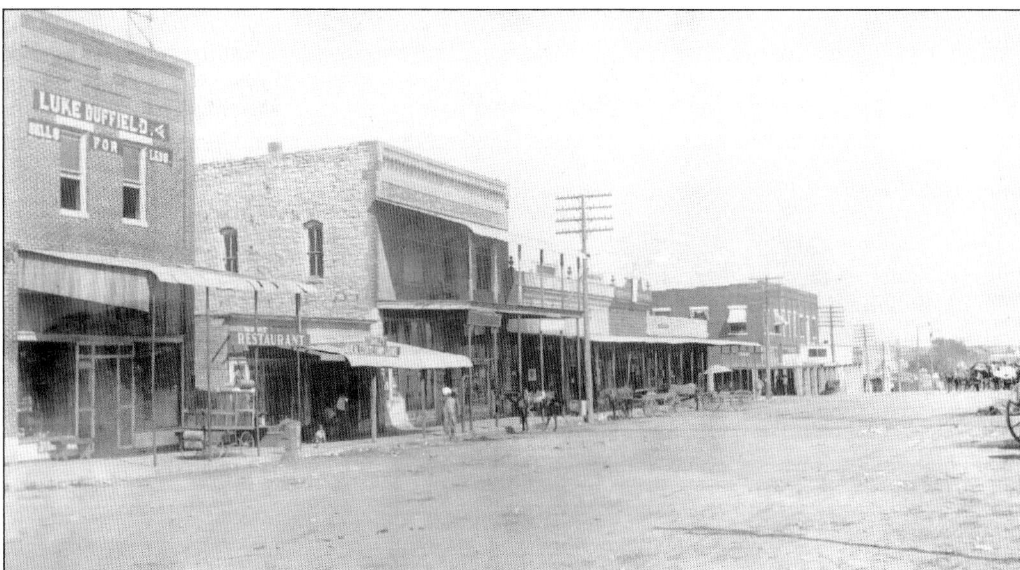

Though this card is postmarked 1917, the photograph most likely dates from around 1910. Among the businesses on Main Street are Luke Duffield's "Sells For Less," a restaurant, and Oakley's Real Estate and Farm Loans. "Rice is fine but still pumping," records the sender.

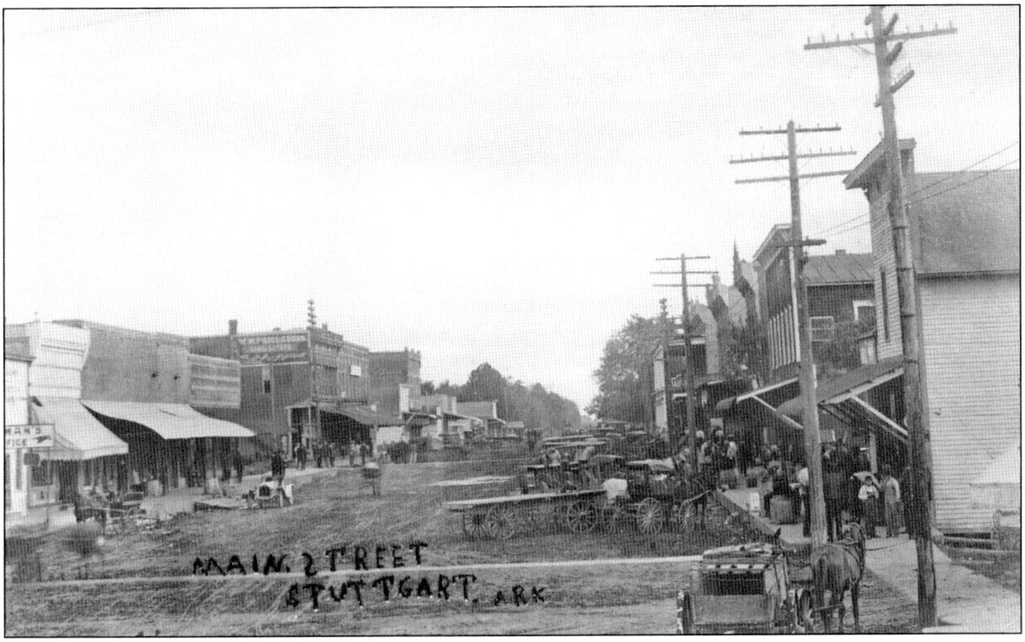

By 1909, an early automobile was seen on the dirt Main Street to the left, while wagons otherwise lined the street to load and unload goods. In another note to Daisy Dixon of Versailles, Illinois, her sister Maude Brierton wrote, "Dear Sister, many thanks for papers, your dress & waist are pretty. My little horse May died last night with congestion, she suffered so much so I feel bad. Had a telegram from Mrs. McKinney saying Mr. McK passed away at 6 o'clock."

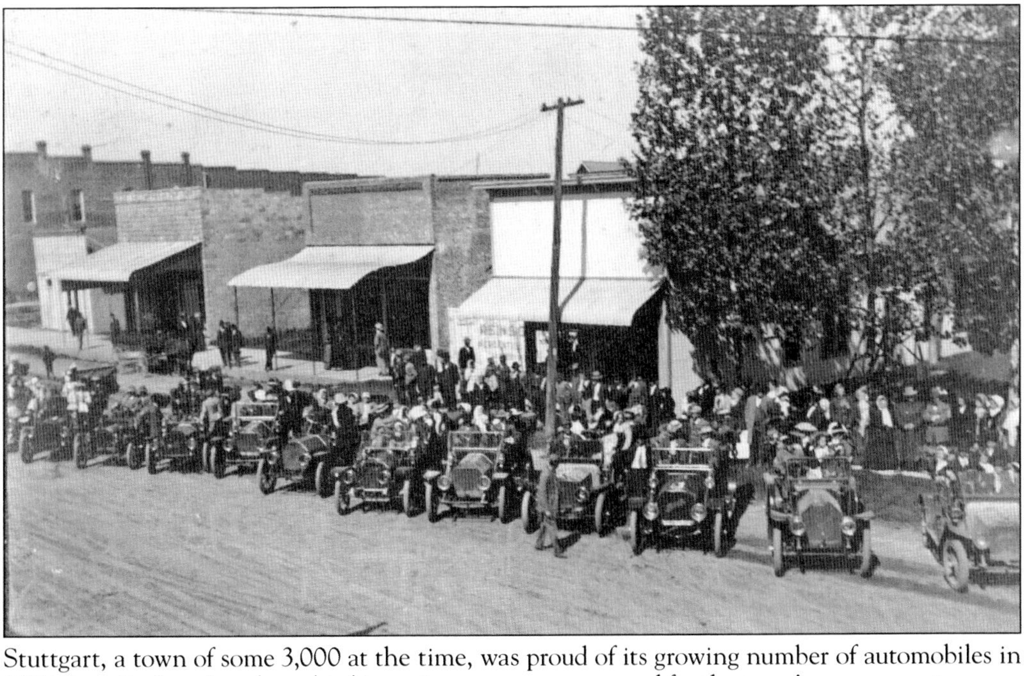

Stuttgart, a town of some 3,000 at the time, was proud of its growing number of automobiles in 1909. In a display of modern thinking, city promoters arranged for the town's car owners to group the vehicles on Main Street. Here a crowd of well-dressed townspeople looks on as a photographer captures the scene from atop a building across the street.

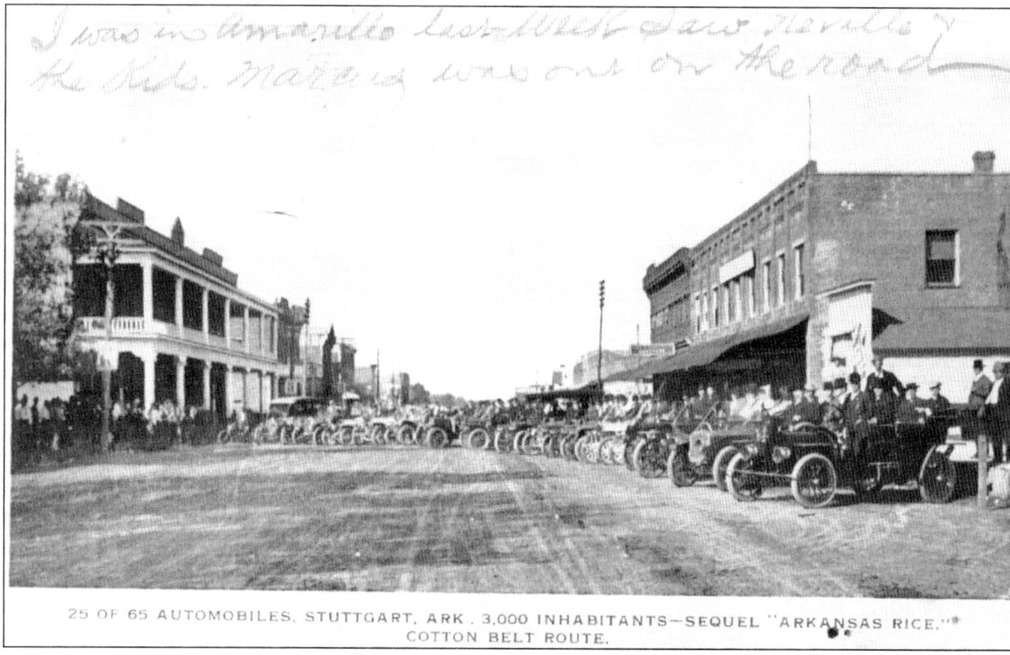

Postmarked 1909 and with a view likely taken on the same day as the previous photograph, this postcard notes the presence of 25 of the total 65 automobiles in Stuttgart. The town's premier lodging at the time was the columned Hotel Price, seen on the left.

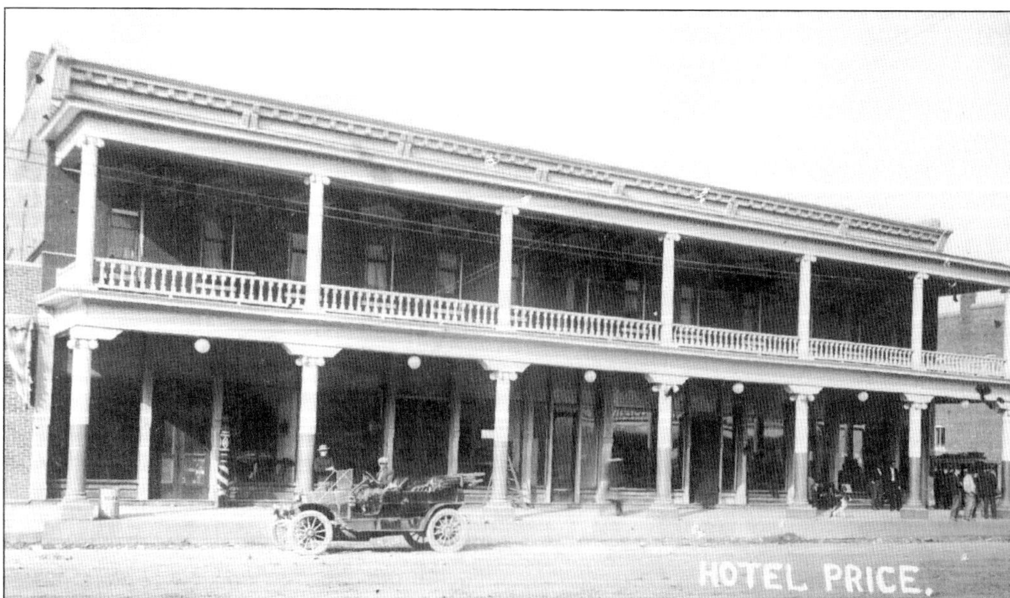

The Hotel Price opened in the early 1900s as the finest lodging in Arkansas County. Guests could sit on the upper balcony and watch the busy commerce of Main Street below. Pictured around 1915, the hotel burned in the 1920s. On the reverse of this postcard, a young boy wrote to his brother in Illinois, "I beat in picking strawberries so sen[d] me my five dollars."

Established in 1923 at a cost of $215,000, the five-story Hotel Riceland quickly became Stuttgart's premier lodging choice, offering 68 guest rooms. The advertisement to the right appeared in a promotional magazine around 1930, showing the hotel's affiliation with businesses in Conway and Little Rock, "For a Greater Arkansas."

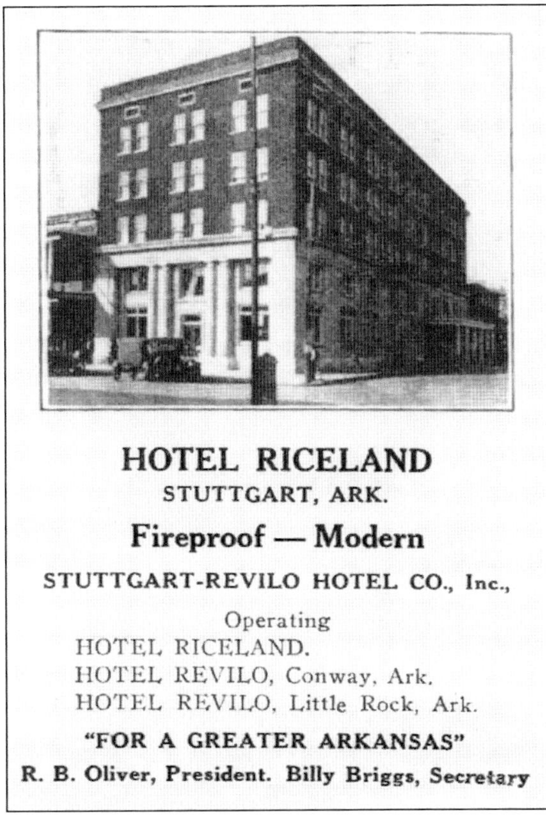

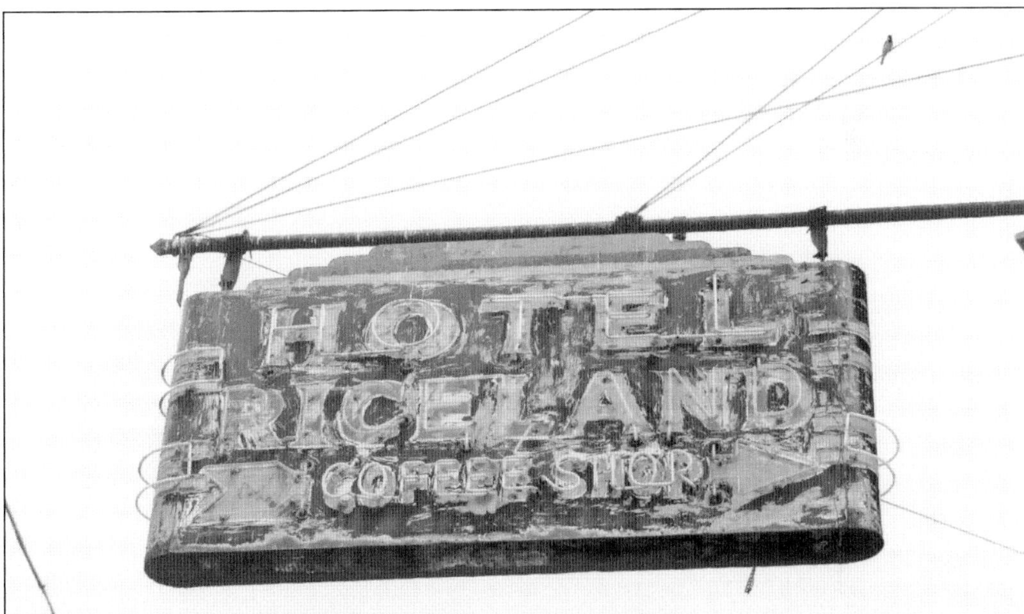

Falling victim to the motoring public's preference for motels, the venerable Hotel Riceland closed in 1970. Today it stands vacant but hopeful, its faded sign still swaying over the sidewalk on Main Street. (Photograph by Ray Hanley.)

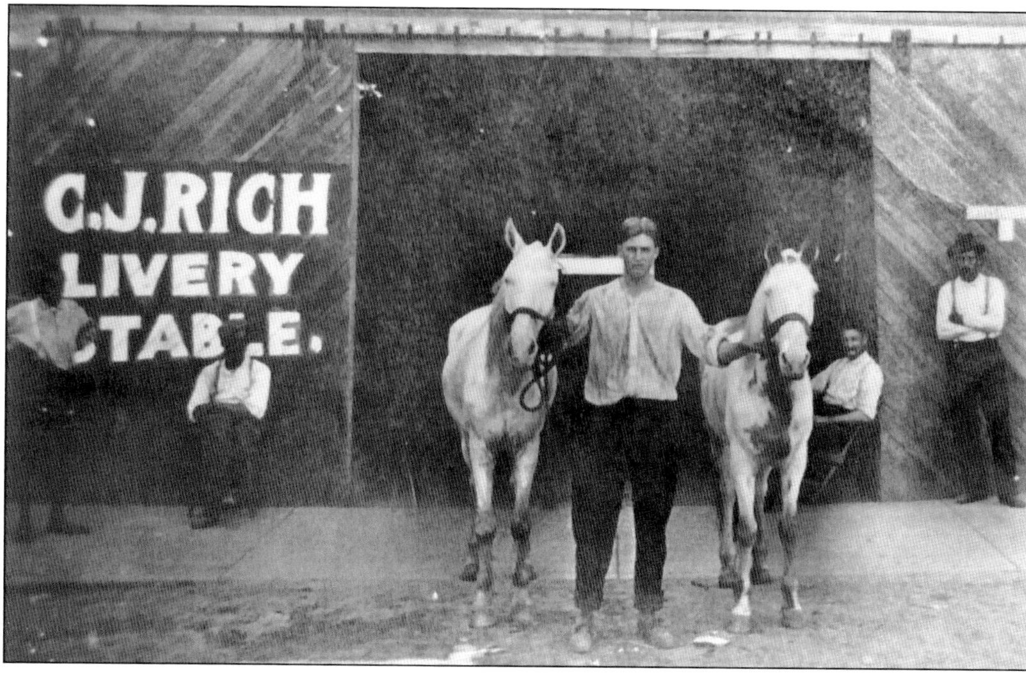

Prospective investors, perhaps having arrived on the excursion train of 1910, would have wished to survey the surrounding lands and may have rented a horse and buggy from the C. J. Rich Livery Stable, seen above. Selling their nearby farm, Charles J. Rich and his brother Harry moved to Stuttgart in 1904 and opened a livery and feed business on Main Street. With the coming of the automobile, the brothers then started the city's first taxi service in conjunction with their livery stable in the same building, as seen in the photograph below, taken about 1911. (Courtesy of the Museum of the Arkansas Grand Prairie.)

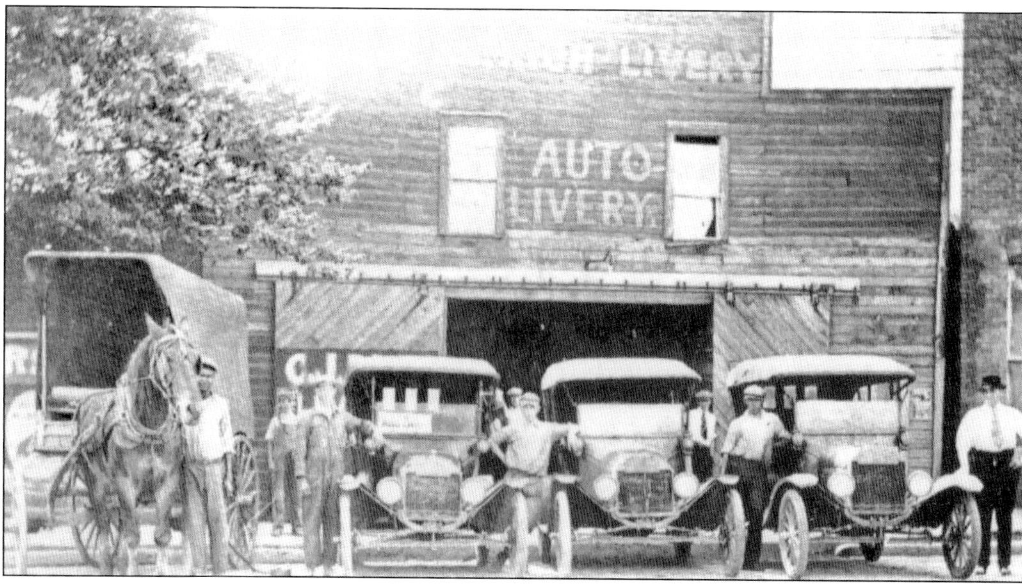

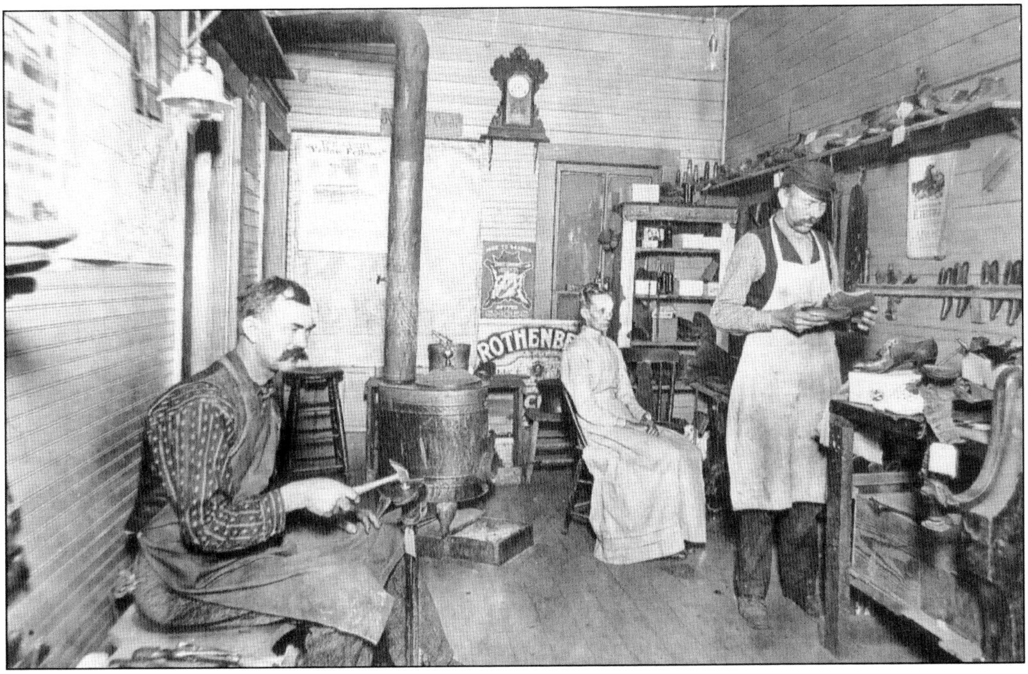

While Rich's Livery Stable could shoe the community's horses, town residents and visitors in need of their own shoe repair visited Jake Simmimaker's shoe shop, located on Fourth Street between Main and Maple Streets. In this photograph, Jake is to the left, putting a sole onto a child's shoe. Seated beside the stove is his wife, Isabell, while his brother is inspecting a new shoe. The cobbler's trade is now a dying craft. (Courtesy of the Museum of the Arkansas Grand Prairie.)

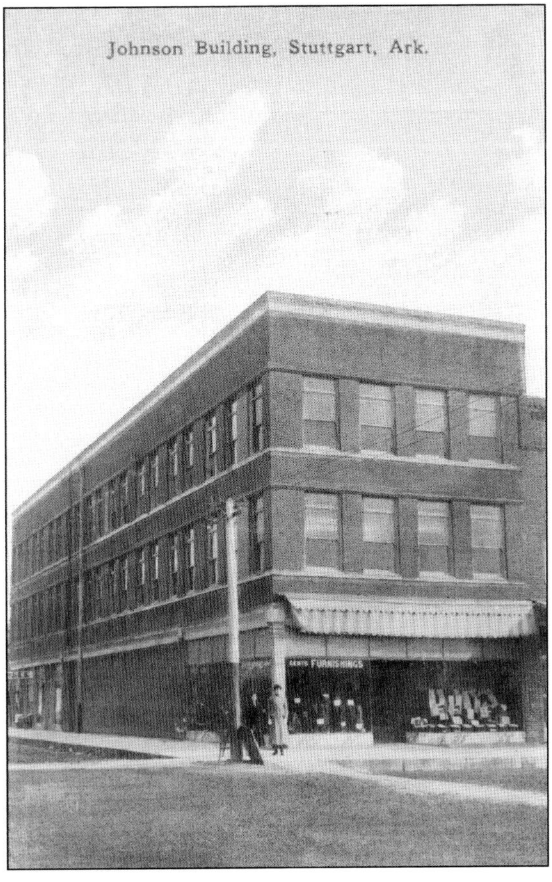

Among the most substantial buildings in Stuttgart by 1910 was the Johnson Building on Main Street, built on a lot sold by Adam Buerkle, Stuttgart's founder. It housed a "Gent's Furnishings" clothing store on the ground floor and offices on the upper floors. In subsequent years, the building housed several banks, including First National. It remains the only three-story building on today's Main Street.

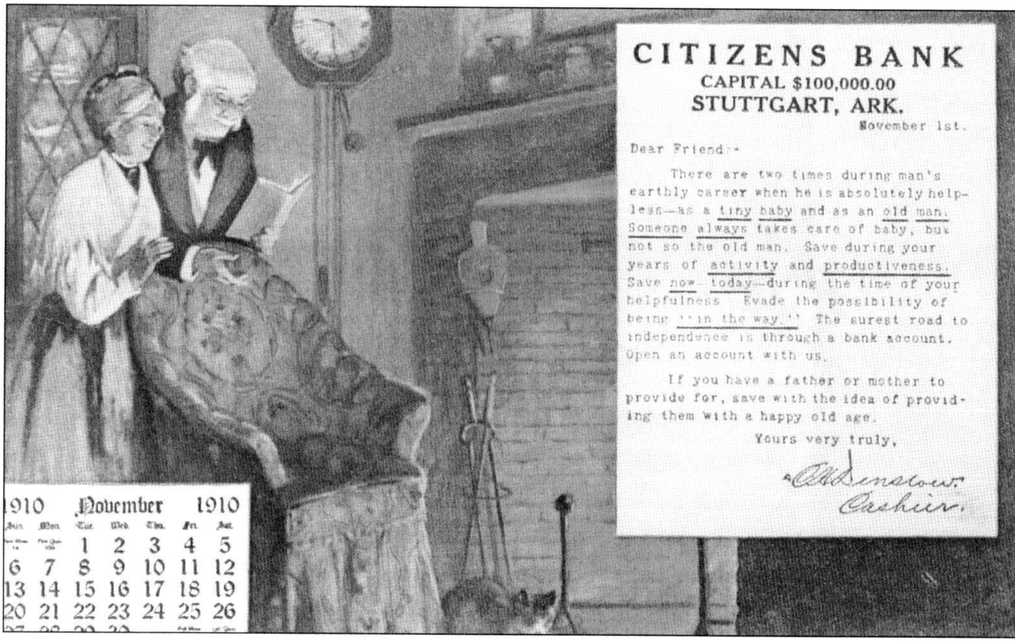

Like any prosperous town, Stuttgart had several banks, including the Citizens Bank, which boasts of a $100,000 capital on the above 1910 postcard. A supposedly personal note from the bank's cashier made the case for saving money: "There are two times during men's earthly career when he is absolutely helpless—as a tiny baby and as an old man." In an era before serious federal regulation, many banks opened and then quickly closed if bad business decisions were made. The two tellers' cages below were located at the Farmers and Merchants Bank, which opened in 1910 and closed not long afterward; another bank soon opened in the same building. (Courtesy Museum of Arkansas Grand Prairie.)

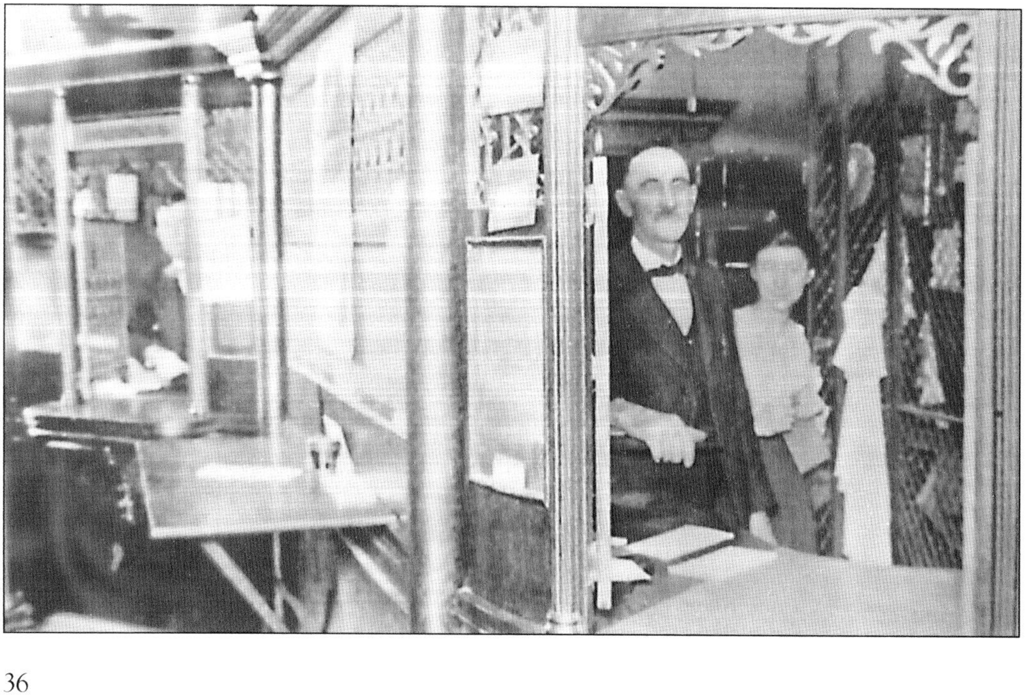

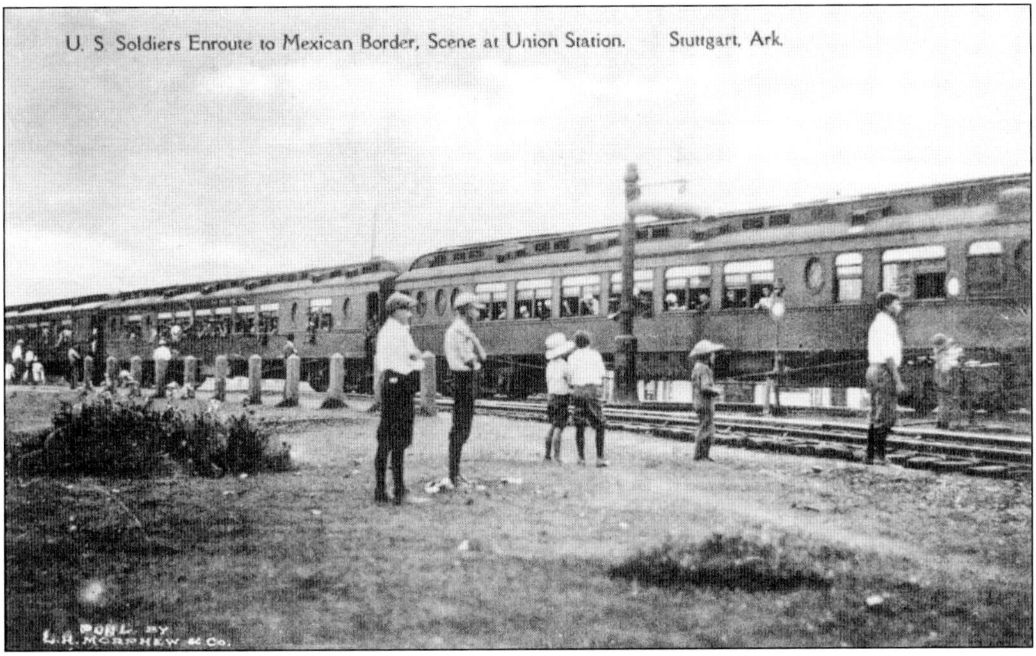

In 1916, Stuttgart served as a rest stop for a train carrying U.S. Army troops to Texas to join the command of Gen. "Blackjack" Pershing, whom President Wilson had ordered into Mexico in pursuit of Pancho Villa and his rebel soldiers after their attack on the town of Columbus, New Mexico.

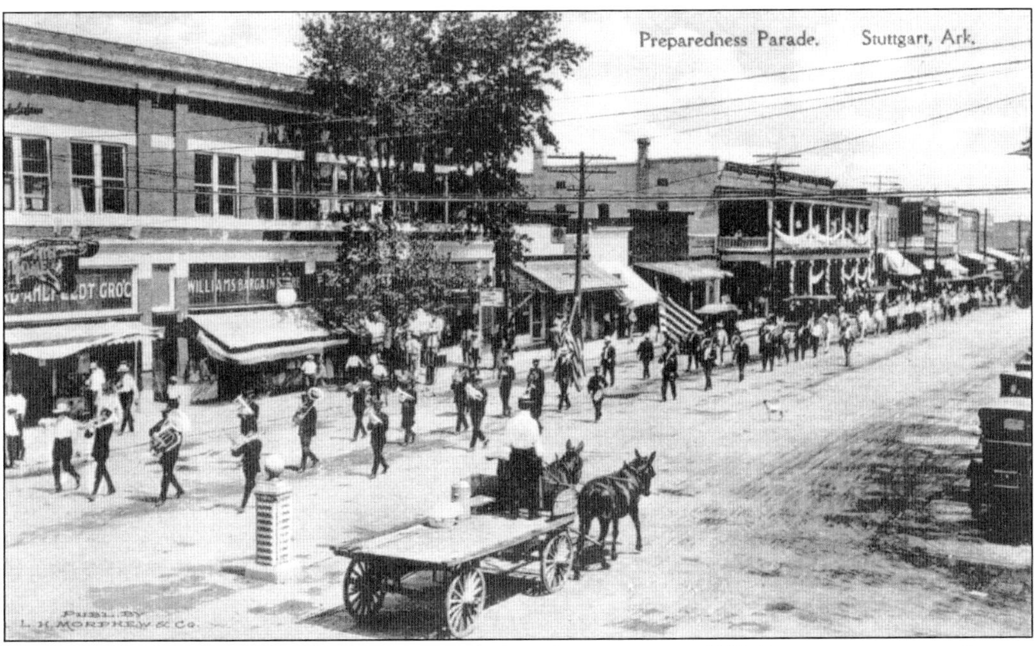

As the clouds of World War I began to spread over the country in 1917, Stuttgart was one of many small towns that put on Preparedness Parades for the young men who might soon be called to service. Stuttgart formed a company of troops that was temporarily housed in barracks on the edge of town.

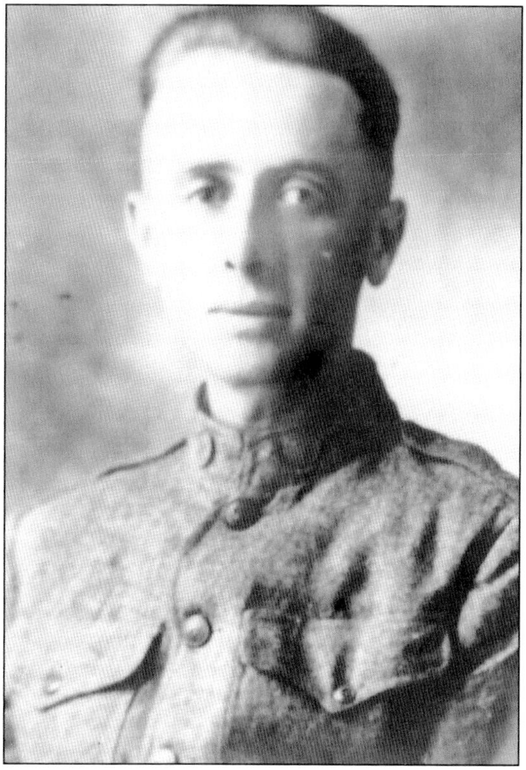

Rice farmer Lee W. Miller had arrived in the community of Sunshine in 1904 and, by 1909, had brought in his first rice crop. With the coming of World War I, Miller laid down his plow and "took up the sword" to help his country defeat the Germans. He hired someone to tend his farm while at war. Upon his return from Europe, Miller raised a crop of rice every year until his retirement in 1972. (Courtesy Museum of Arkansas Grand Prairie.)

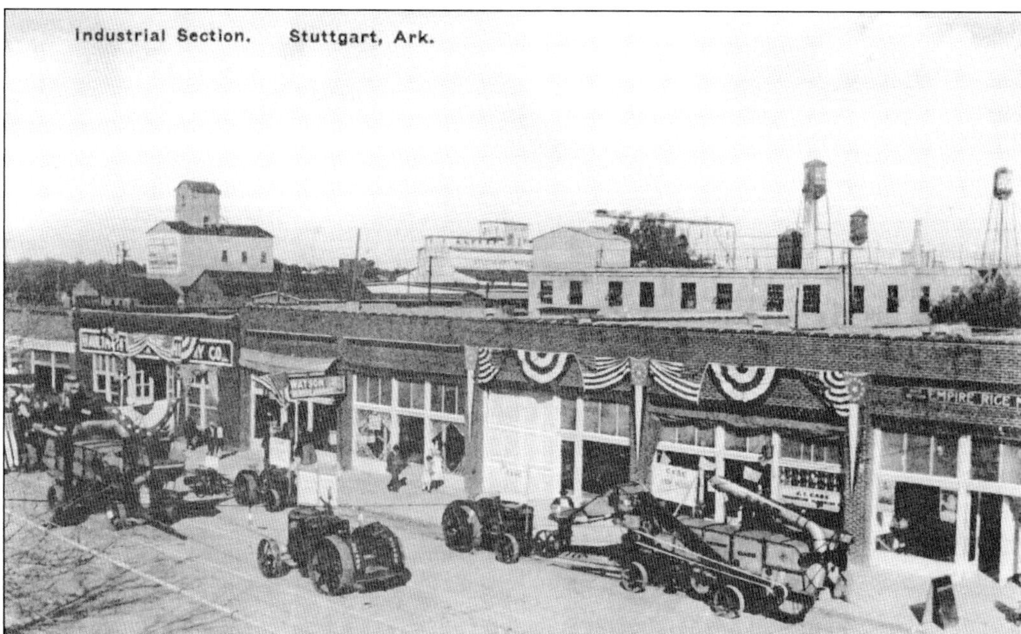

This farm machinery, pictured a few blocks off Main Street, served in Stuttgart's Preparedness Parade as a symbol of the area's agricultural richness and its contribution to the war effort. American flags and bunting are prominent in front of the J. L. Case implements dealership and the Watson Meat Market. The Stuttgart rice mill rises in the center distance.

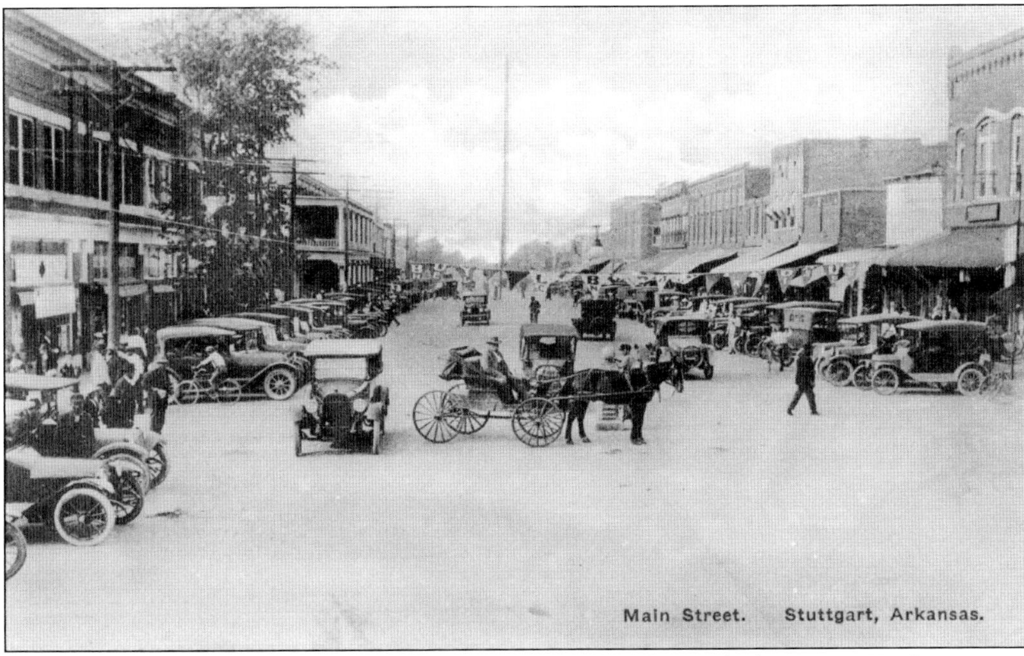

By 1918, Stuttgart's Main Street was filled with Model T Fords—with the exception of prominent citizen Joseph I. Porter sitting in his buggy. Upon the death of Porter's father, a Confederate general, he and his mother moved to Arkansas County. He became wealthy through the lumber business and real estate transactions and as an organizer of the town's first rice mill. Porter died in 1919.

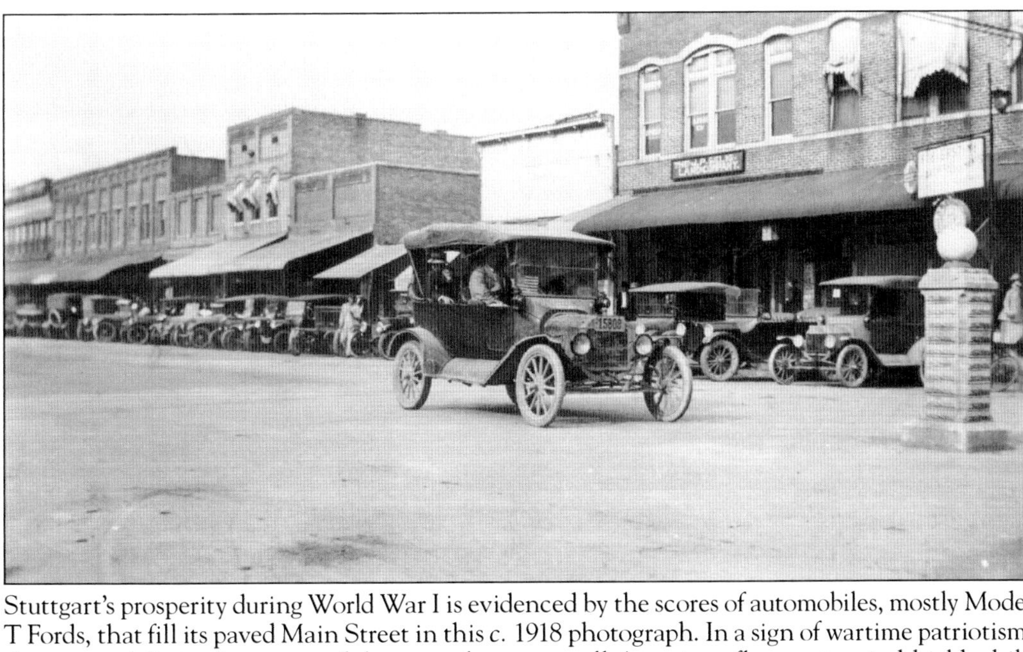

Stuttgart's prosperity during World War I is evidenced by the scores of automobiles, mostly Model T Fords, that fill its paved Main Street in this c. 1918 photograph. In a sign of wartime patriotism, the automobile in the center of the street bears a small American flag on its windshield while passing the J. P. Selig Land Company and the F. E. Erstine Hardware store.

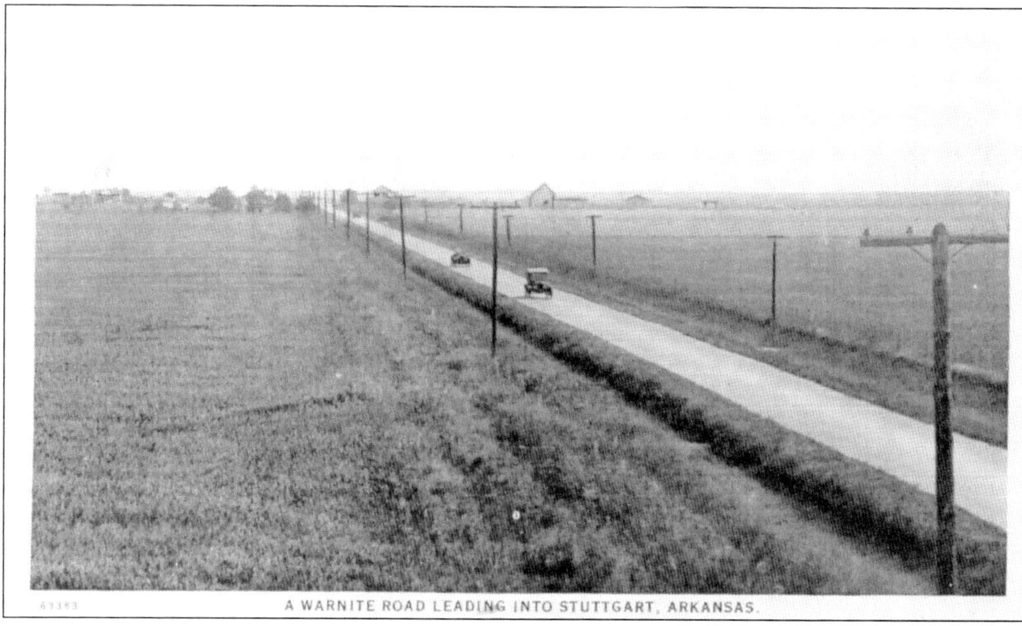

By the 1920s, the highways leading into Stuttgart were beginning to be paved, at least for the first few miles outside of town. This postcard promotes a "Warnite" road leading into town, apparently a reference to the brand or type of paving material.

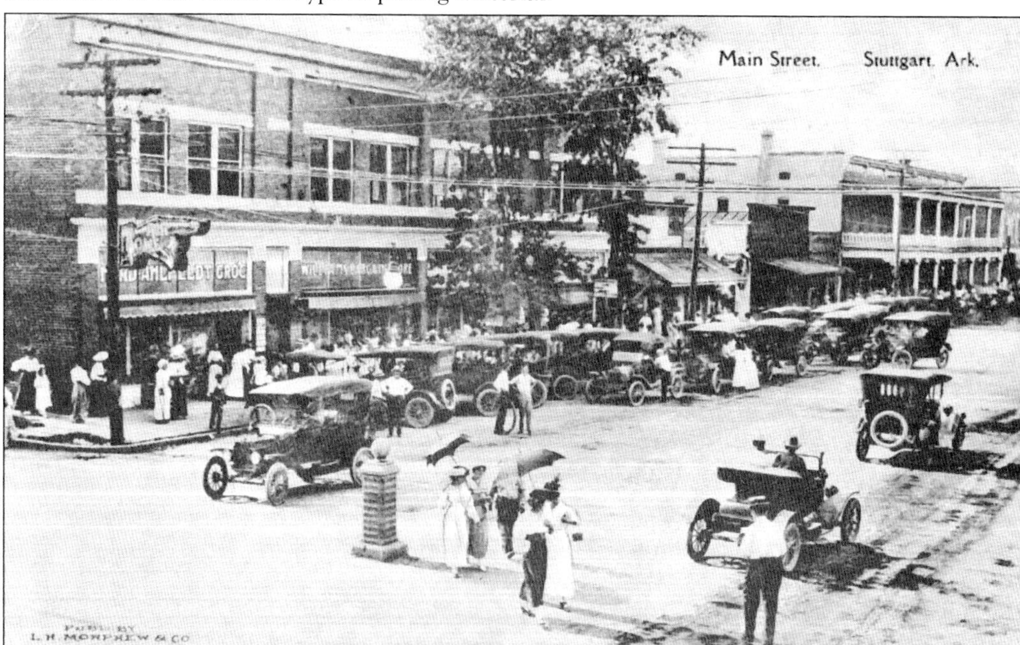

Visitors from Indiana wrote home in 1920 to say, "We are spending a few days here." Perhaps the early-day tourists took in a show at the Air Dome Theater, indicated by the pointing-hand sign on the electrical pole to the left. Down the street, the columned Price Hotel might have offered the visitors a shady second-story veranda from which to look upon Stuttgart's busy Main Street. The stone column in the middle of Main Street, seen on these pages, seems to have been an early attempt to organize the flow of traffic before the advent of road striping.

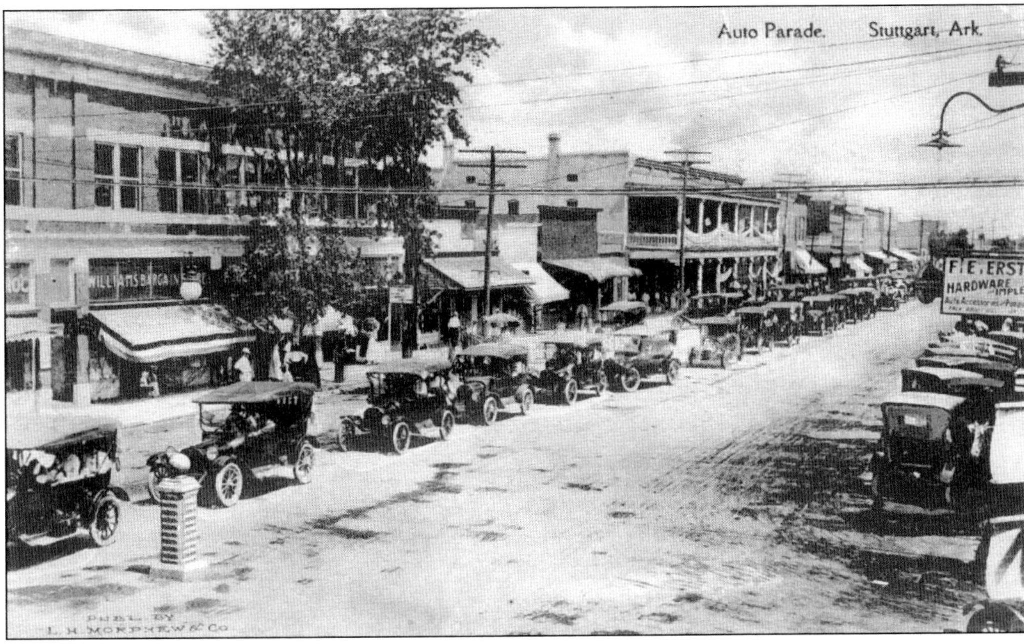

Like most communities, Stuttgart liked parades; the one seen above gave an excuse for the town's automobile owners to show off their vehicles in a long line down Main Street in 1920. "I'm in town today, we had a rain yesterday, the road man has been grading our roads as they can't be drove over with a car." By the mid-1920s, the number of automobiles had expanded to crowd Main Street, seen below, assuring that Stuttgart had laid claim to its share of the country's Roaring Twenties prosperity.

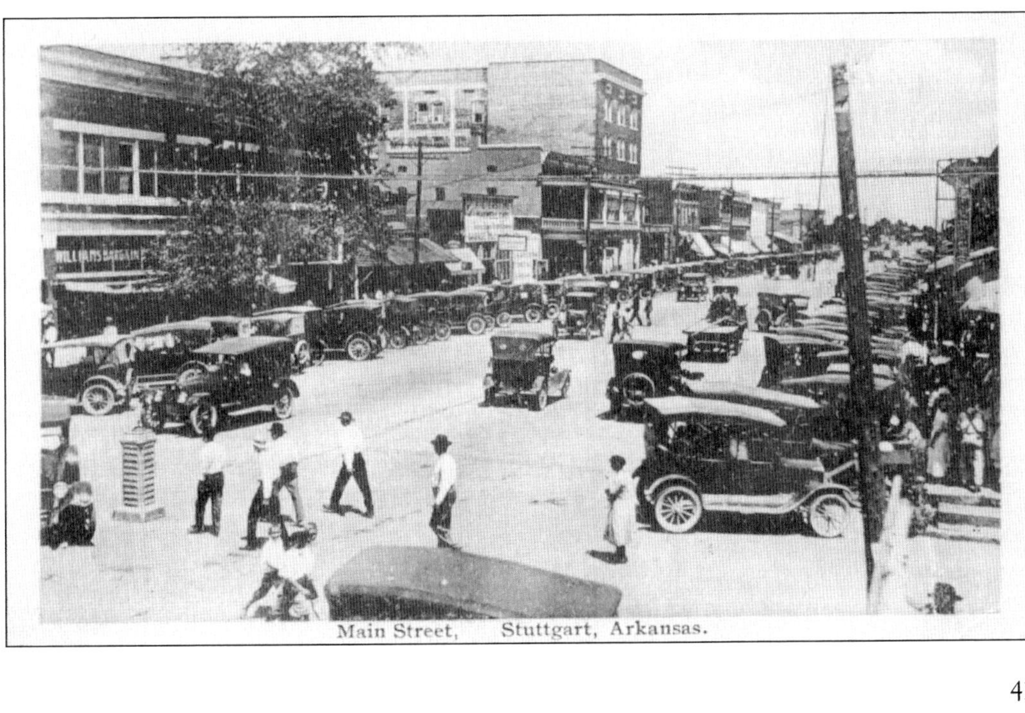

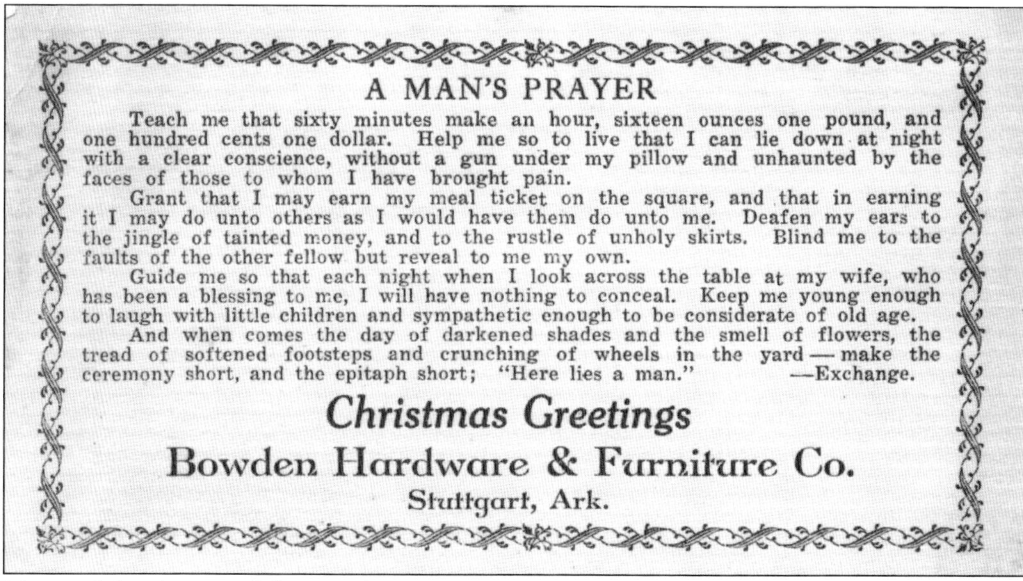

A MAN'S PRAYER

Teach me that sixty minutes make an hour, sixteen ounces one pound, and one hundred cents one dollar. Help me so to live that I can lie down at night with a clear conscience, without a gun under my pillow and unhaunted by the faces of those to whom I have brought pain.

Grant that I may earn my meal ticket on the square, and that in earning it I may do unto others as I would have them do unto me. Deafen my ears to the jingle of tainted money, and to the rustle of unholy skirts. Blind me to the faults of the other fellow but reveal to me my own.

Guide me so that each night when I look across the table at my wife, who has been a blessing to me, I will have nothing to conceal. Keep me young enough to laugh with little children and sympathetic enough to be considerate of old age.

And when comes the day of darkened shades and the smell of flowers, the tread of softened footsteps and crunching of wheels in the yard — make the ceremony short, and the epitaph short; "Here lies a man." —Exchange.

Christmas Greetings

Bowden Hardware & Furniture Co.

Stuttgart, Ark.

Many of the drivers of the cars lining Main Street probably shopped at Bowden Hardware and Furniture Company. For a Christmas around 1920, the store mailed this card carrying a remarkably timeless essay on the value of living an honorable life.

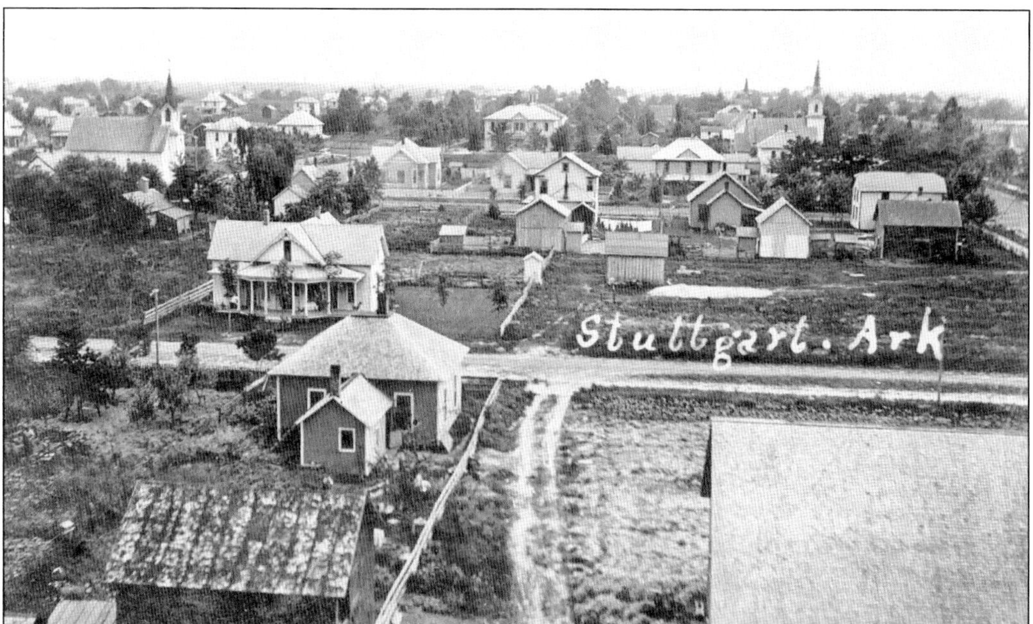

By the time of this c. 1908 postcard, Stuttgart was filling in vacant spaces to become a prosperous small city. Likely taken from atop a water tower, the view captures at least three church steeples, several backyard gardens, and an outhouse at the center.

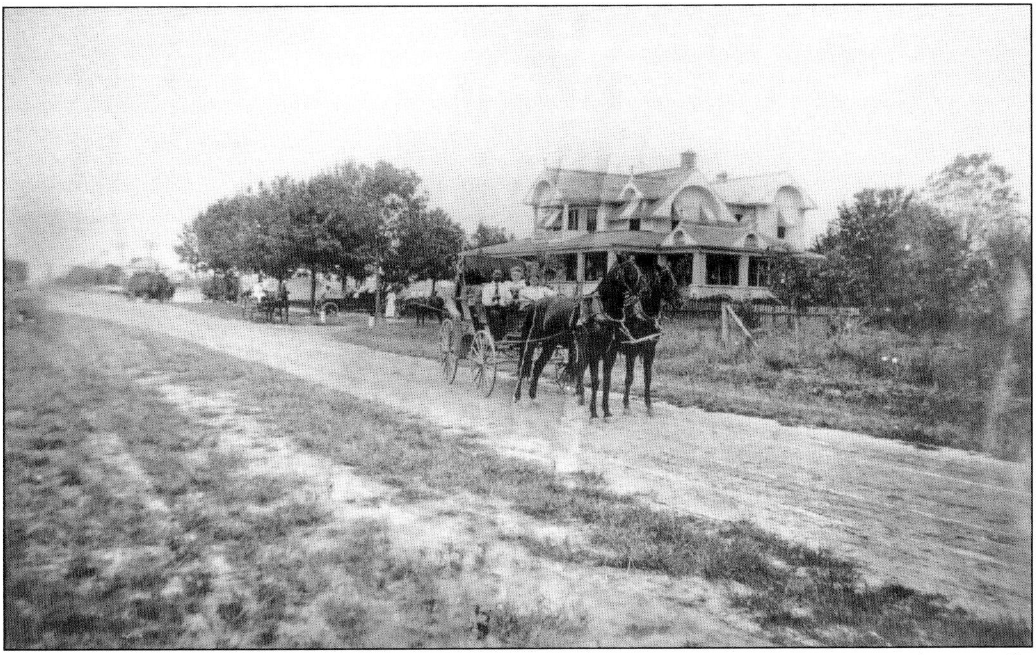

The prosperity of the area's farms gave a number of families in Arkansas County—and especially in Stuttgart—the means to build fine homes. Perhaps the finest was the home erected by William M. Price on East Second Street. Seen above when it was first built around 1900, the house fronted a dirt street used by buggies and wagons, and it would endure as the city grew around it. Price was a prosperous real estate agent, livestock breeder, and farmer with 7,000 acres. By the World War I era, when the postcard below was made, the Price family had a large, shiny automobile parked on the concrete drive. In subsequent years, the home became the center of the Stuttgart Country Club but was razed in the late 1980s.

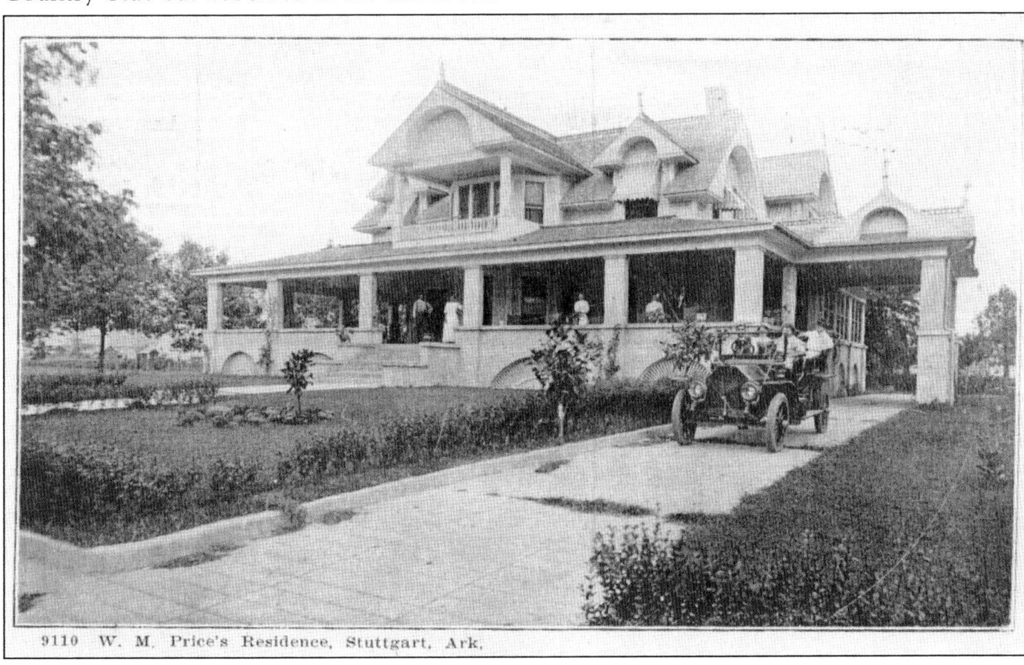

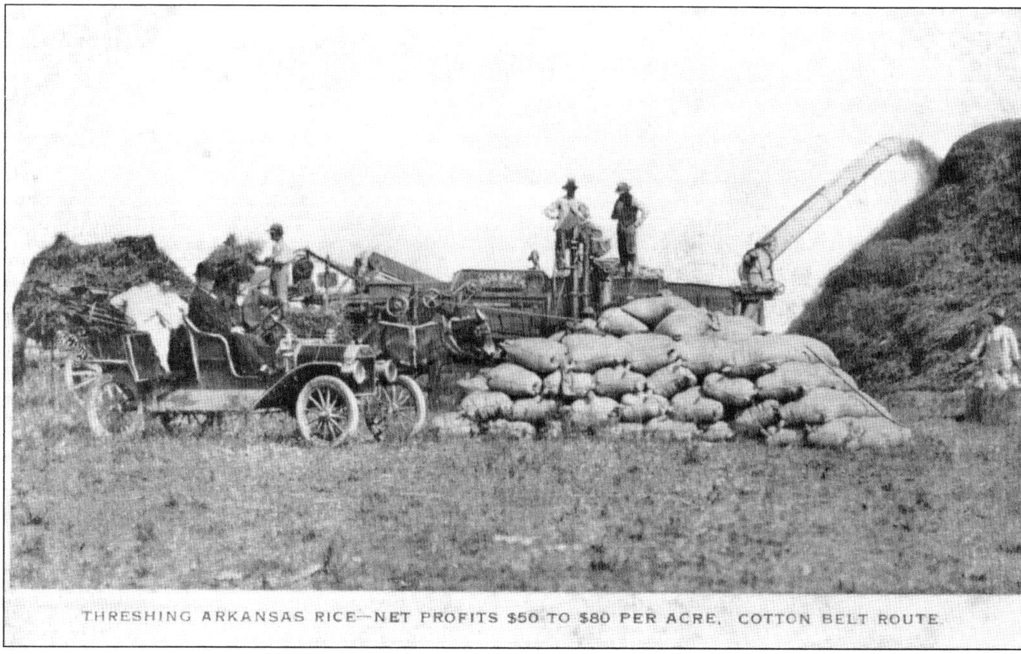

William M. Price observes his rice harvest from the comfort of the open-topped luxury automobile seen parked in his Stuttgart driveway on the previous page. According to the caption on this c. 1915 postcard, the rice fields netted Price $50 to $80 an acre.

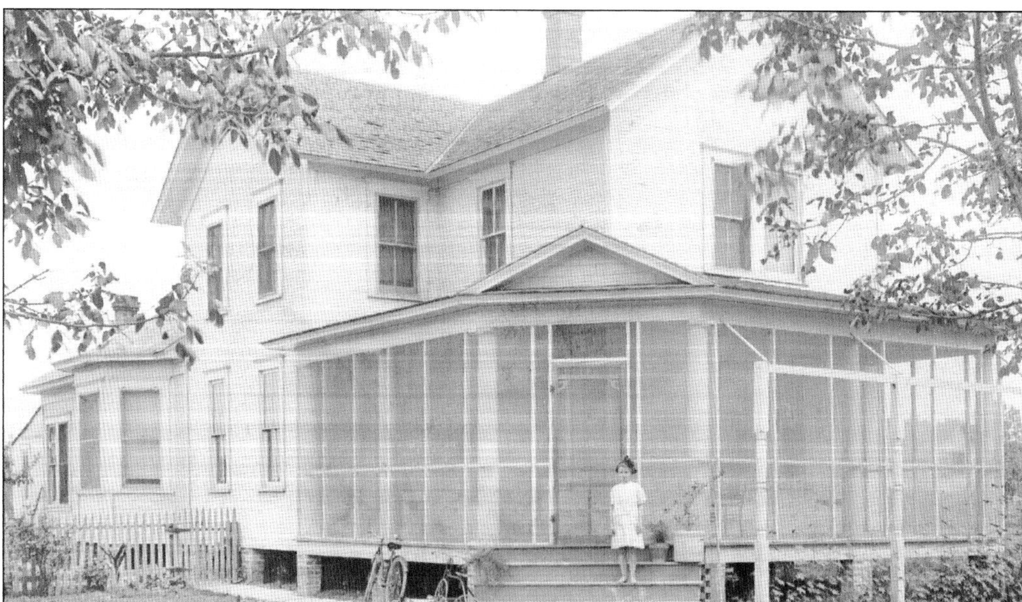

In contrast to the residence of the prosperous Price family, many homes in Stuttgart offered more basic amenities but were still large to accommodate the sizable families of the era. This postcard was mailed to Pine Bluff in 1914, though the home's exact location is lost to history. On the steps of the screened wraparound porch is young Louise John, who probably enjoyed the bicycle, tricycle, and doll carriage found nearby.

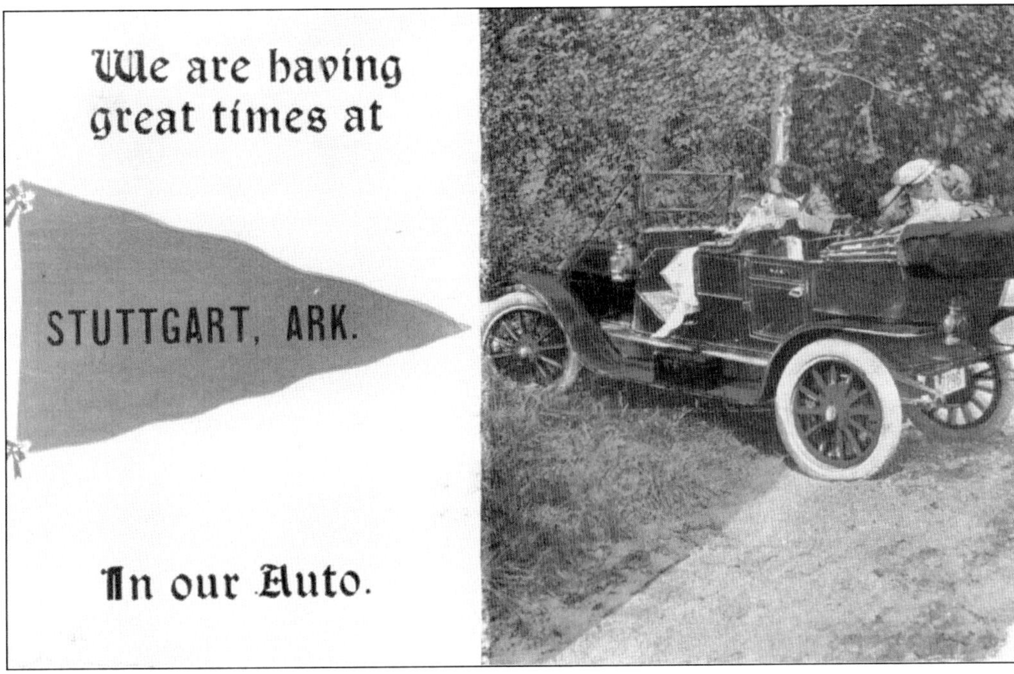

These two comic cards spoofing automobile romance were sent to Daisy Dixon in Illinois in 1914 and 1918. Her sister Maude Brierton's comments describe plans for Christmas visits and dinner parties, including a trip "to the country for holly and mistletoe." She notes that, even in winter, "the roads are dusty again," a nuisance of the time.

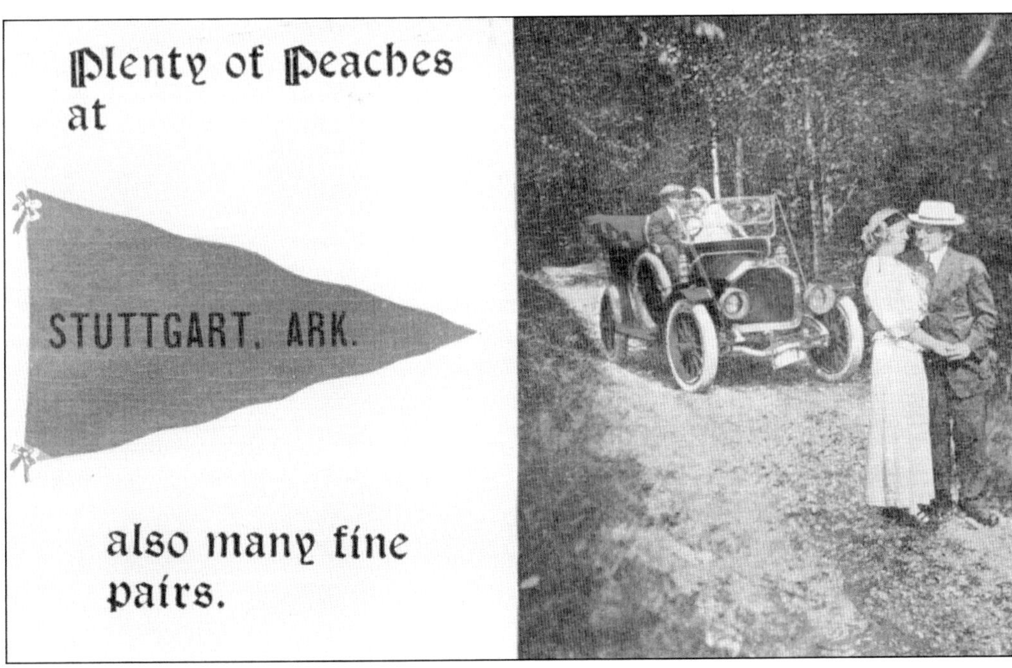

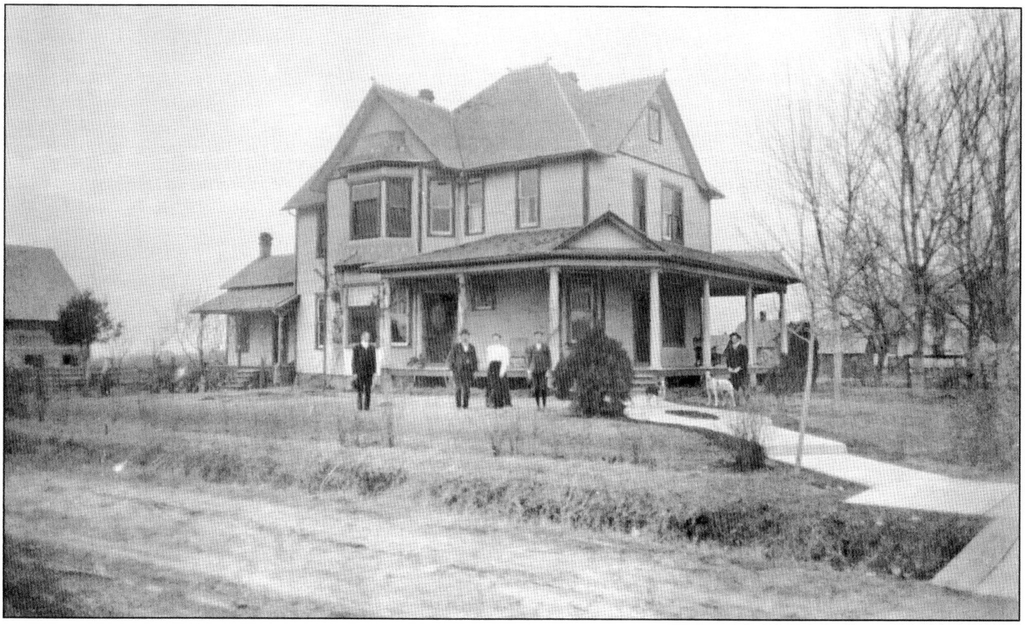

Dr. W. H. Moorehead moved first to DeWitt, Arkansas, in 1890 and then to Stuttgart in 1899, building a large home on College Street. Dr. Moorehead addressed the above card to a cousin in 1908. His son Robert is standing with the dogs, to the right of the walk, while Dr. Moorehead and his wife are flanked by sons Lloyd (left) and Earle. Robert would later serve in World War I. On a research trip to Stuttgart, the authors were pleased to find the grand home restored, surrounded today by large trees not present on Dr. Moorehead's 1908 postcard.

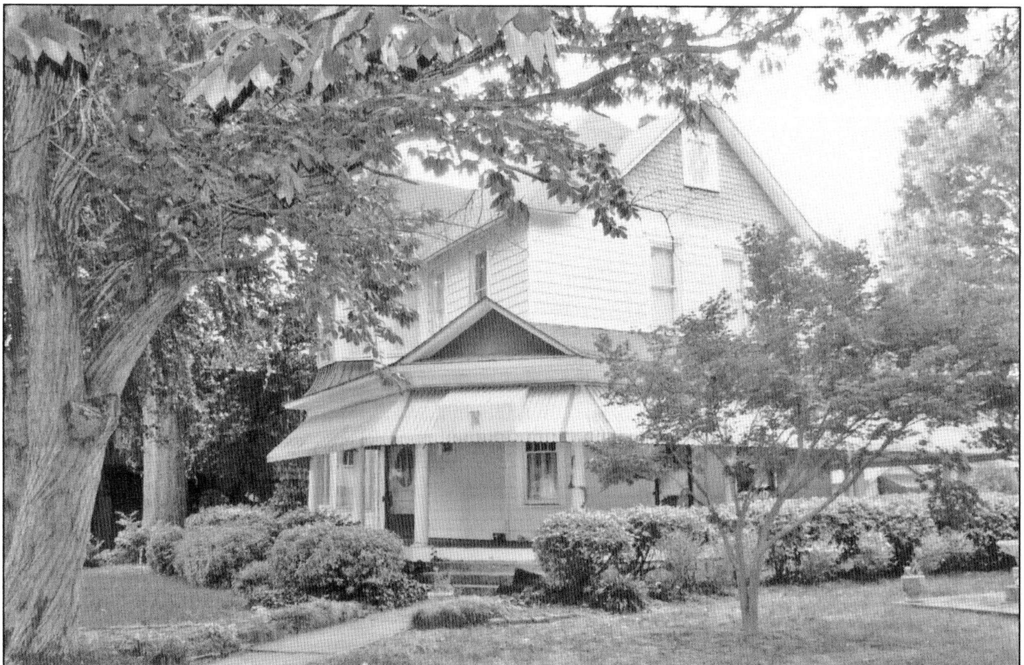

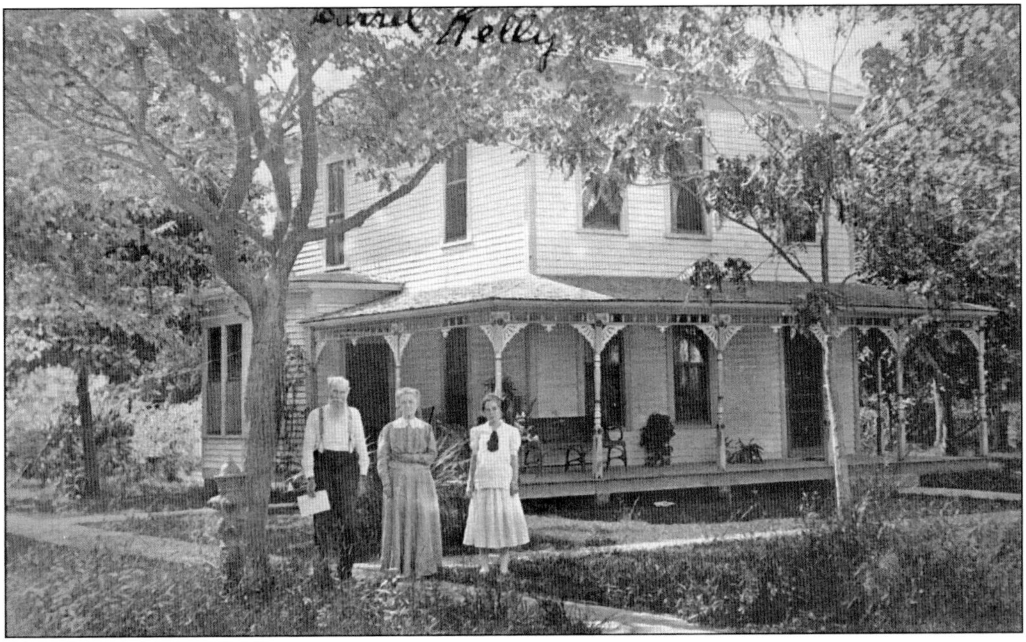

Darrel and Mary Kelly's home in Stuttgart was captured on a postcard mailed to Missouri in 1912. To the left of the man, presumably Mr. Kelly, can be seen a tall fire hydrant—a mark of pride symbolizing a first-class city of the era. Also indicative of Stuttgart's prosperity were the sidewalks that laced through the better residential areas of the rapidly growing city.

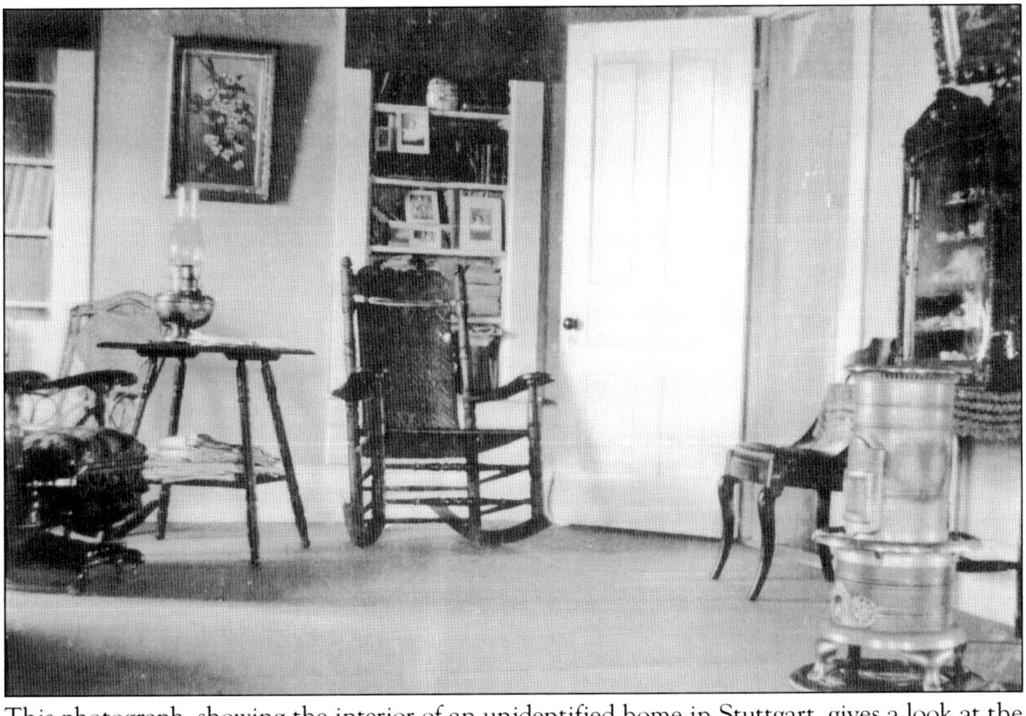

This photograph, showing the interior of an unidentified home in Stuttgart, gives a look at the furnishings of the "front parlor," including its kerosene lamp, rocking chairs, heating stove, and family portraits on the shelf. (Courtesy of the Museum of the Arkansas Grand Prairie.)

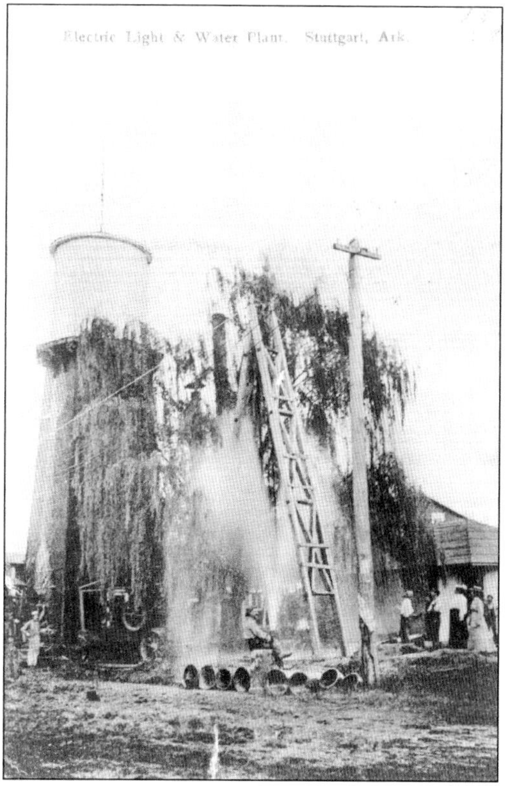

Another sign of Stuttgart's status as a first-class city was its Electric Light and Water Plant, seen on this 1908 postcard. The privately owned plant stood at what is today Sixth and Main Streets. Sent to Iowa, the postcard notes, "This is not very far from our place. We have had Typhoid fever, all but Papa. Early and Gerald are sick yet, but are better."

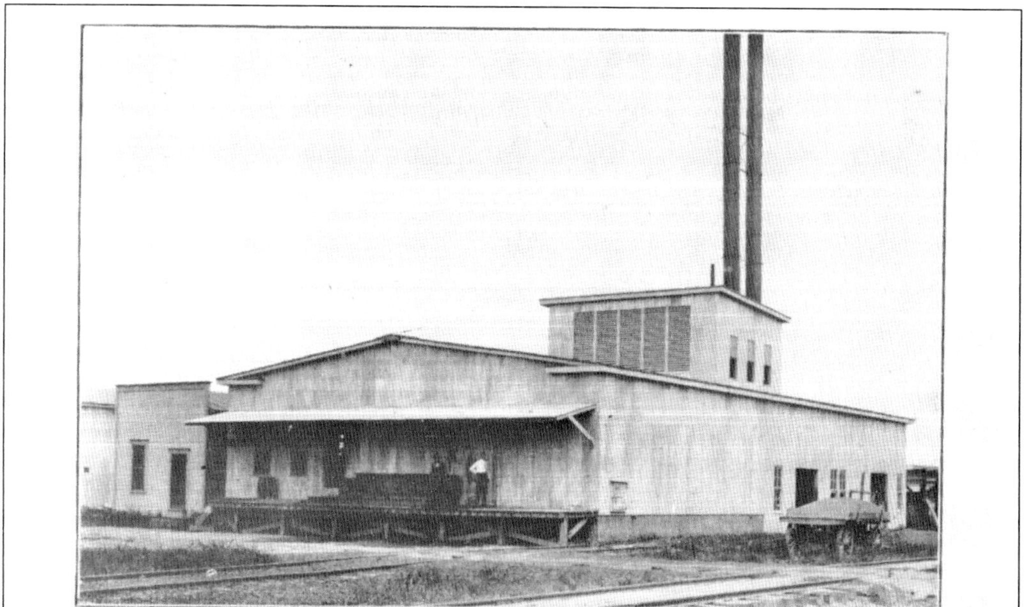

The homes of Stuttgart lacked modern refrigeration to keep food safe and drinks cool. Their needs were met in the manner of the day—by home-delivered blocks of ice from the Crystal Ice Company, its First Street location pictured here around 1915. The card's sender states that he is "busy sowing rice, got 30 acres done, and 75 more to put in. H. Boyle."

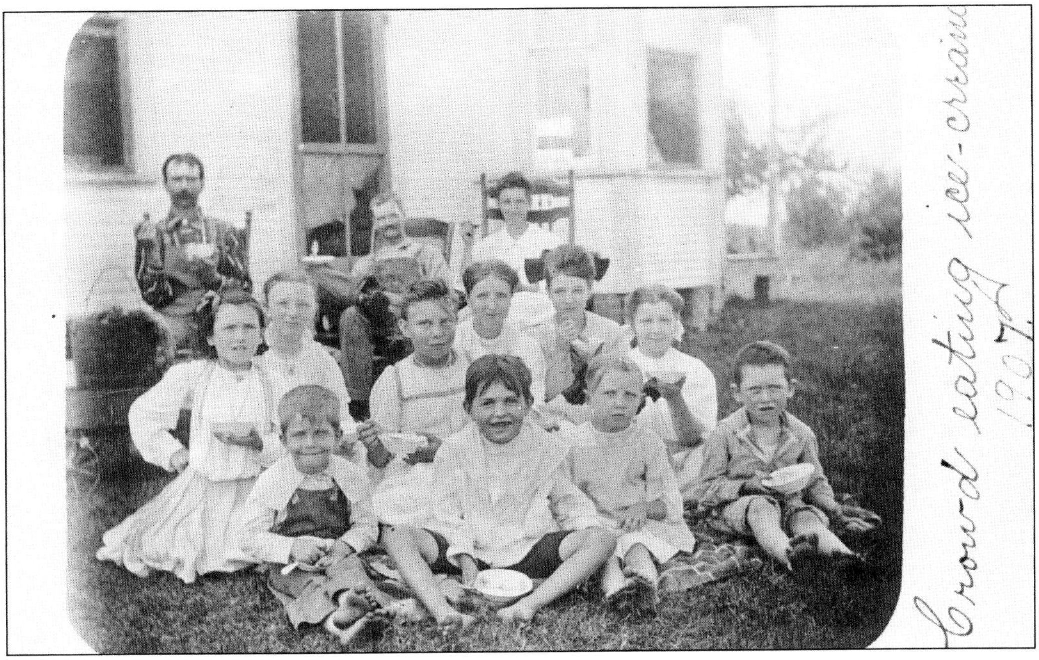

Some backyard photographs are timeless, especially when they include children and dogs. The Brierton family, seen above with neighborhood children, enjoys homemade ice cream in 1907. Though wearing their Sunday best, the children are barefoot, while the adults rest in chairs brought out from inside the house. Below, Jack Menges proudly poses with a matched pair of dogs around 1910.

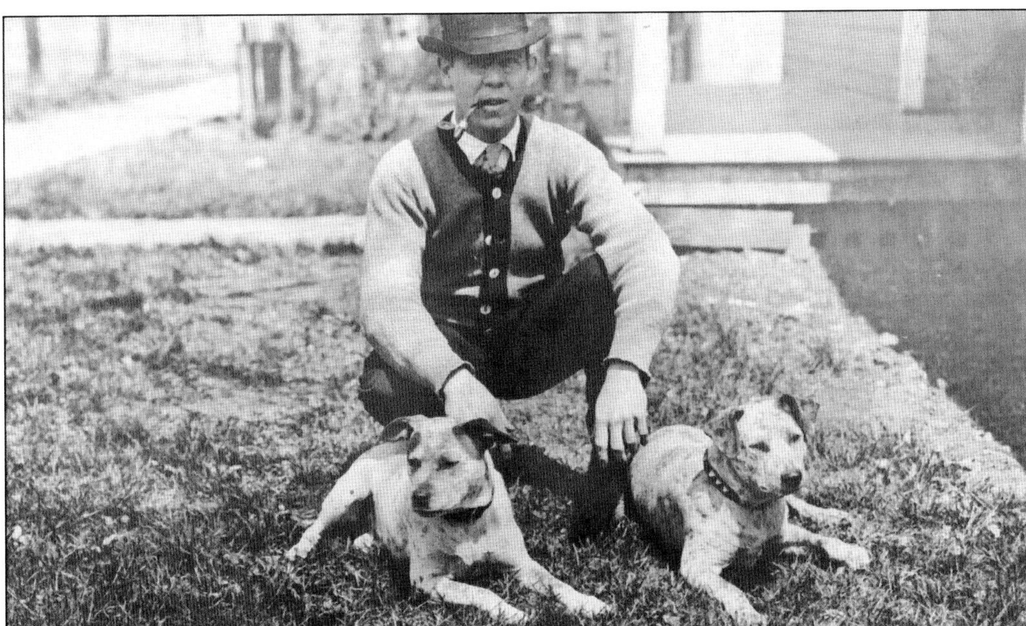

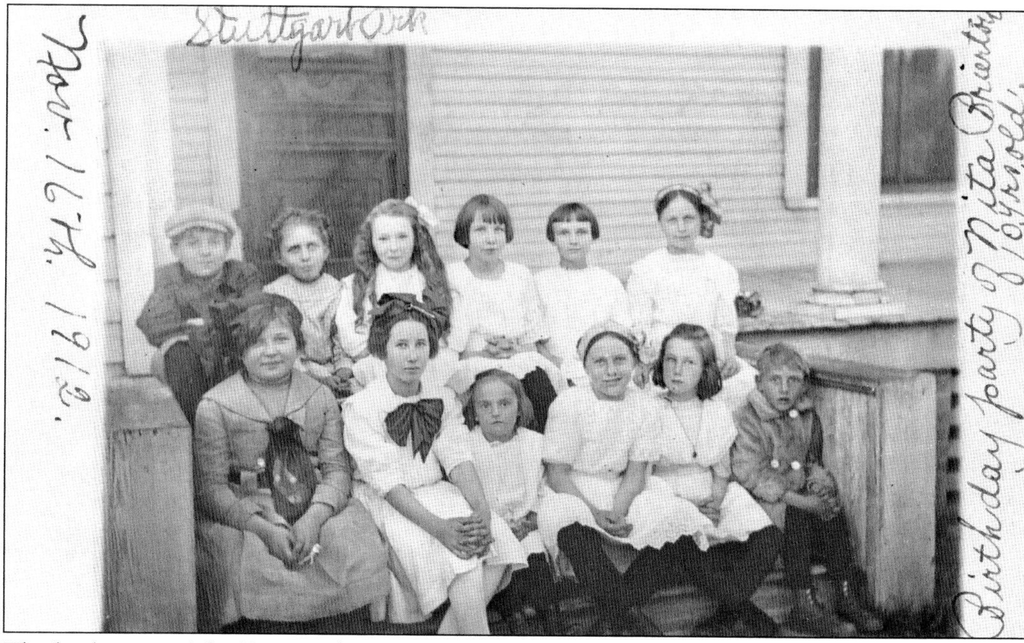

The back steps of the Brierton home in 1912 could have held no more children. The small boy to the right appears squeezed into the corner by a row of girls at the 10th birthday party of Nita Brierton, who sits fourth from the left in the second row. That unlucky boy is Teddy Barnhart, presumably a friend of Nita's brother Bennie, who wears a cap in the second row.

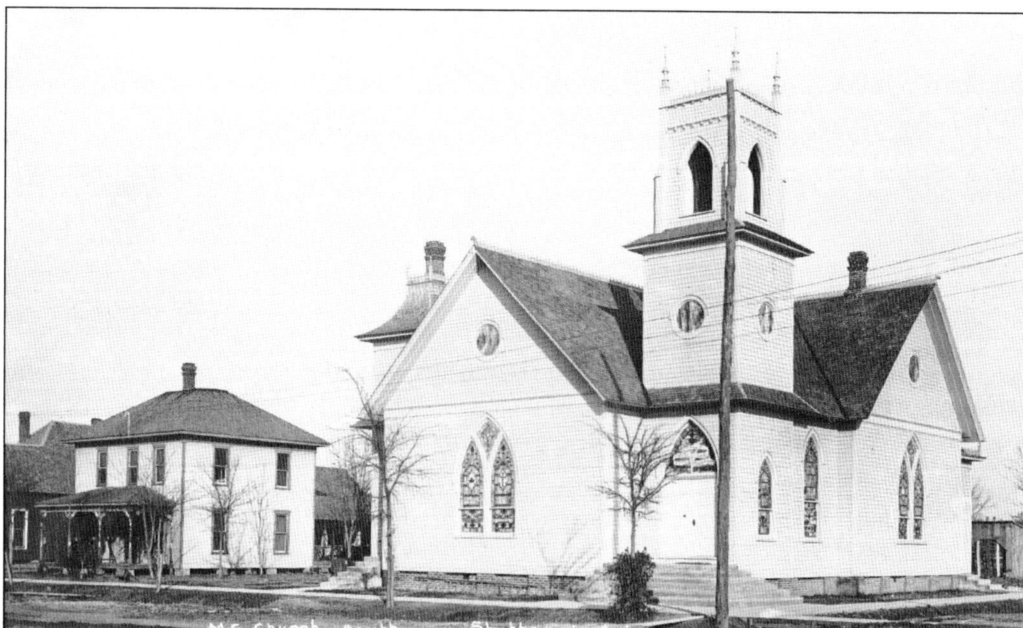

Some of the children above might have been found on Sundays in Stuttgart's Grand Avenue Methodist Church South, seen here in the early 1900s at the corner of Seventh and Grand. The congregation has since relocated, and the original church building no longer stands.

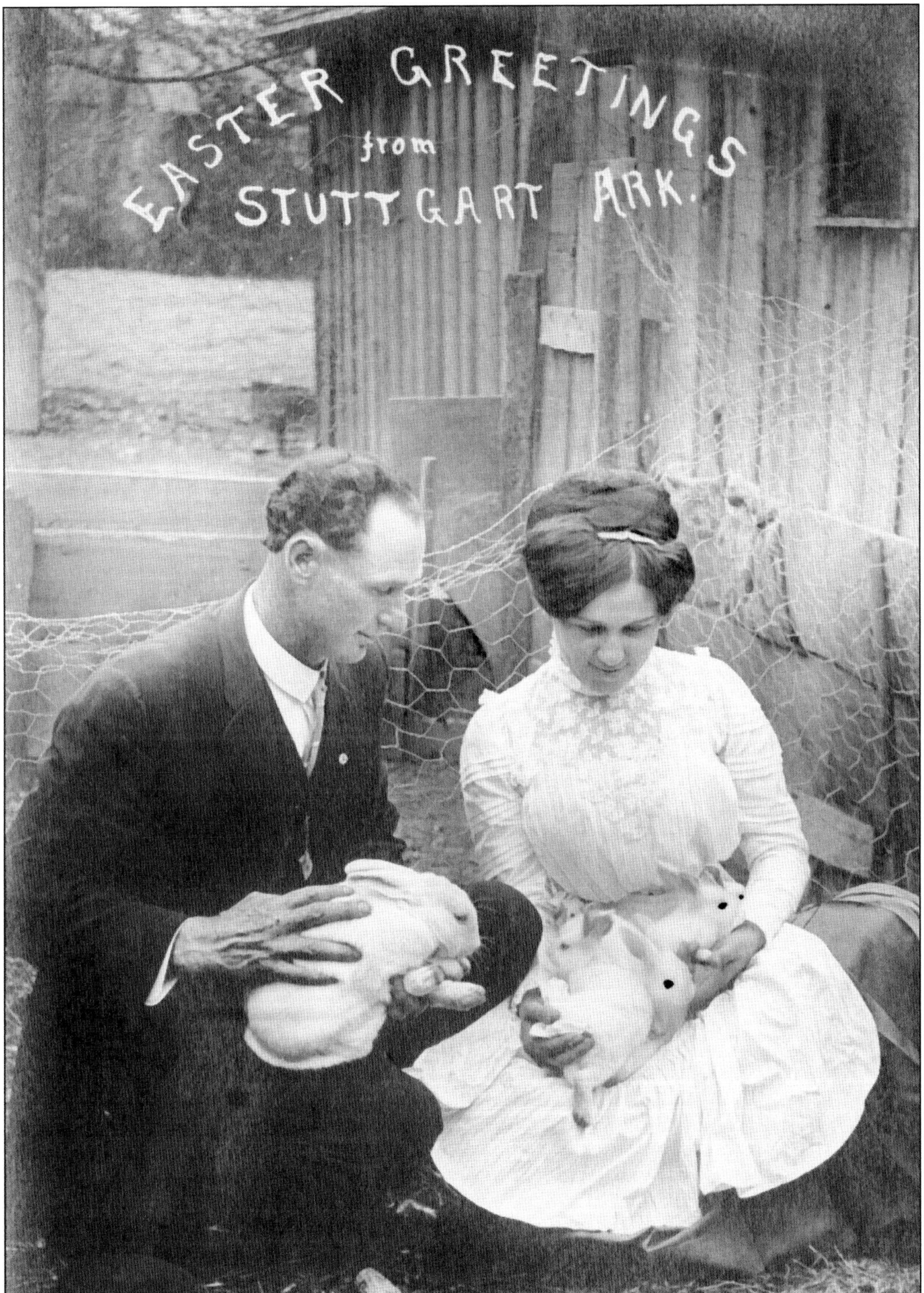

On Easter Sunday in 1911, a couple poses with rabbits, perhaps after attending church. The man's large, rough hands suggest that he only dressed up on Sundays and most likely worked in the fields or at other manual labor during the week.

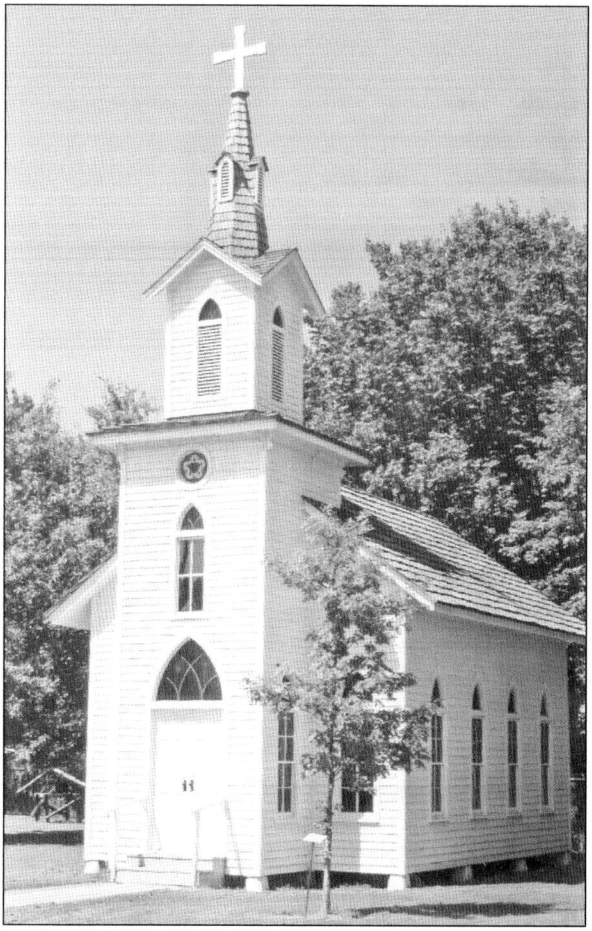

The church with the most direct ties to Stuttgart's origins is the Emanuel Evangelical Lutheran Church, organized by the town's founder, Rev. Adam Buerkle, in 1879. For the 18 years he served as pastor, the congregation's services were held in the Buerkle home. The first church building, a white frame structure with a bell tower, was not finished until 1900. It was replaced by a new building in 1951, though a three-quarter-size replica can be found today at the Museum of the Grand Prairie. (Photograph by Ray Hanley.)

Over some early disagreement, eight families left the church of Reverend Buerkle in 1882 and founded St. John's Lutheran Church, initially on a 10-acre site at the Lone Tree Cemetery. Realizing Stuttgart was going to be the area's population center, the congregation moved its church building into town by ox team, settling it at Fourth and College. This sturdy brick church replaced the pioneers' white frame building at the same site in 1914. Modern Stuttgart continues to support two vibrant Lutheran churches.

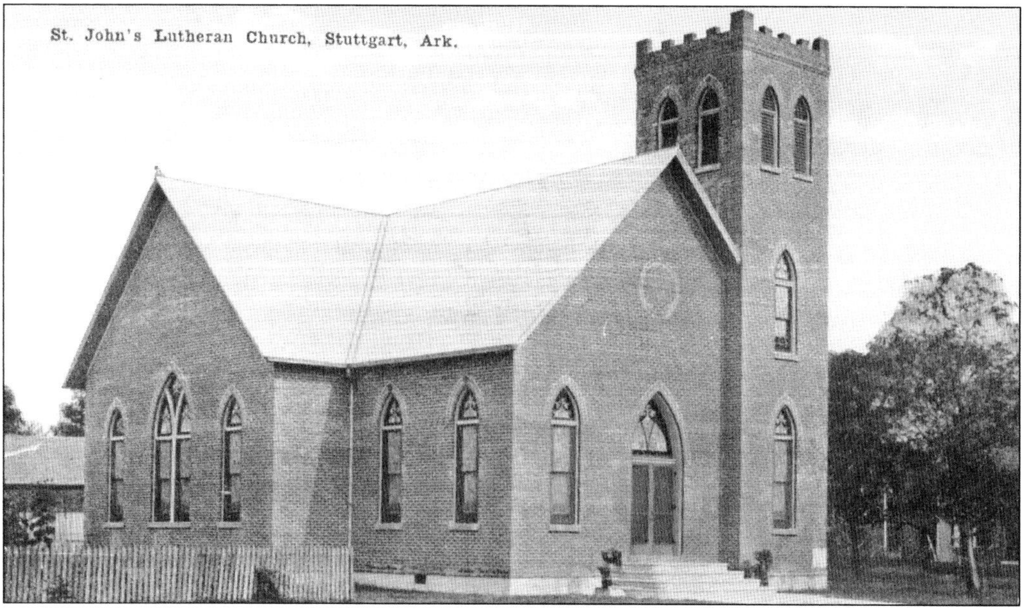

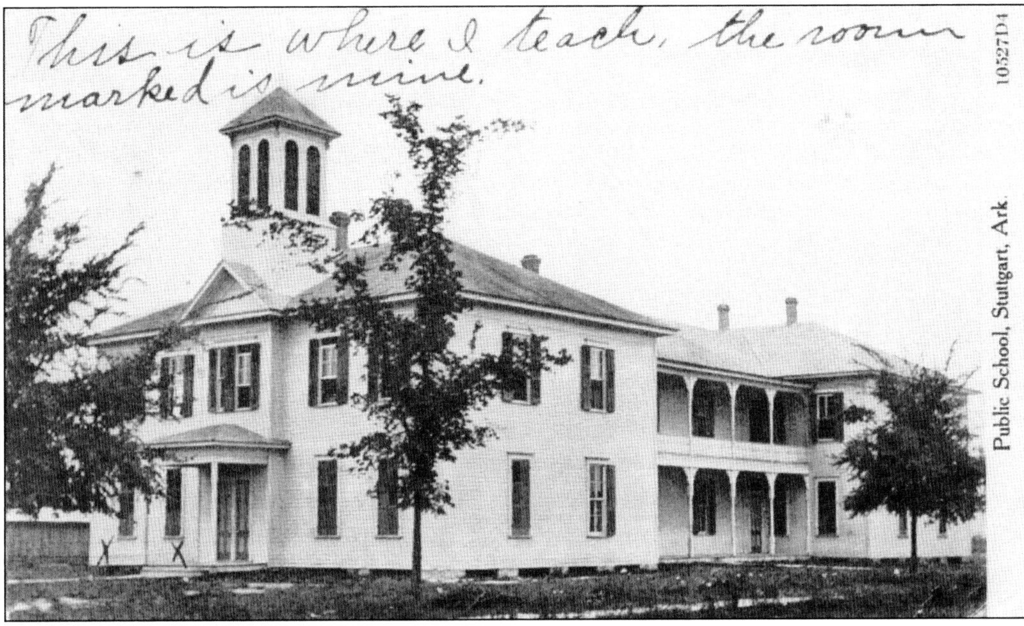

The families who settled Stuttgart opened the first school for their children in 1882, in a rough frame building costing $200. The new school, erected in 1889, is seen above in a 1907 photograph revealing an addition on the back. "This is where I teach," wrote Belle Coulter of the front classroom indicated. Below is the primary school class of 1909, which included seven-year-old Nita Brierton (seventh from the left in the third row), along with several barefoot boys. At the time, the average annual salary for Arkansas schoolteachers was $273 for a 107-day year. The wooden school building was replaced with a new brick one in 1912; the old structure served as a courthouse for a time and was then razed.

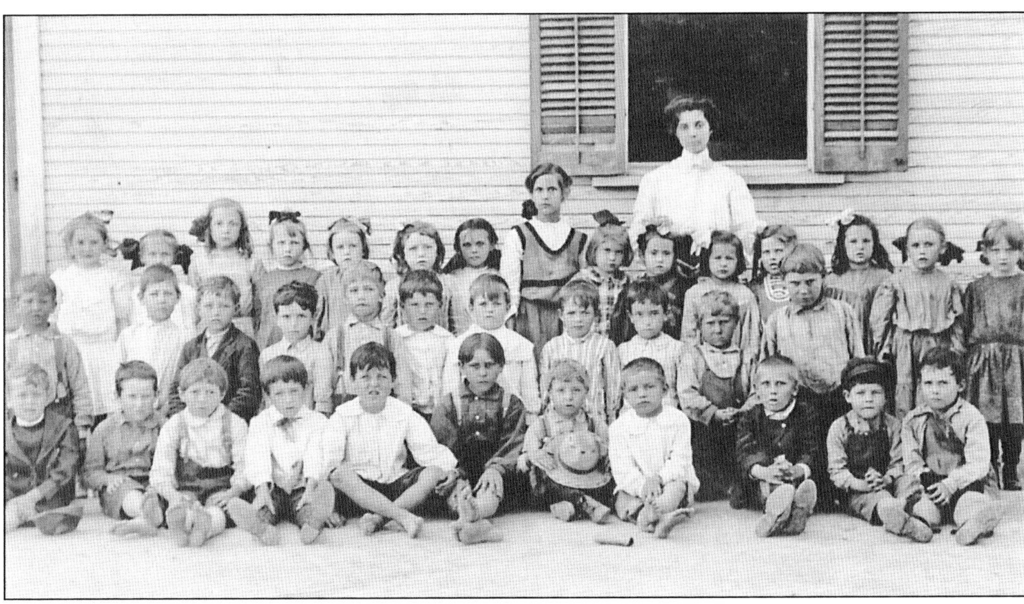

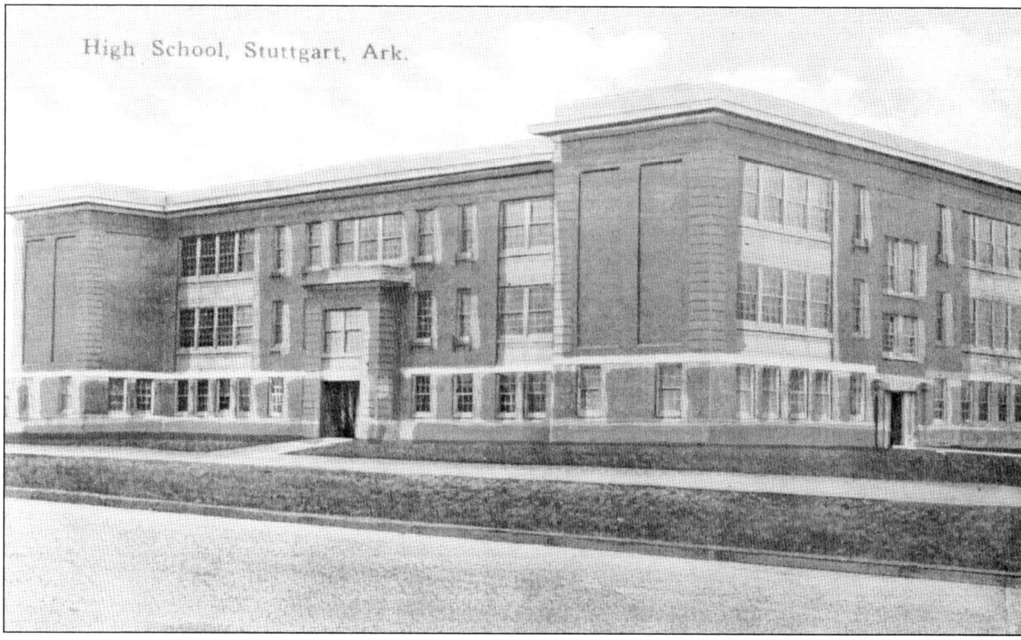

In 1912, Stuttgart opened its new high school at Ninth and Lowe Streets, pictured on the above card. The sender noted in 1913, "It sure is pleasant in the land of the Sunny South. Dust is flying on the country roads." Below, the seventh-grade students of the new school pose in 1914 with their teacher, listed as "Miss Giddeon." The school building served until 1967 before finally being replaced.

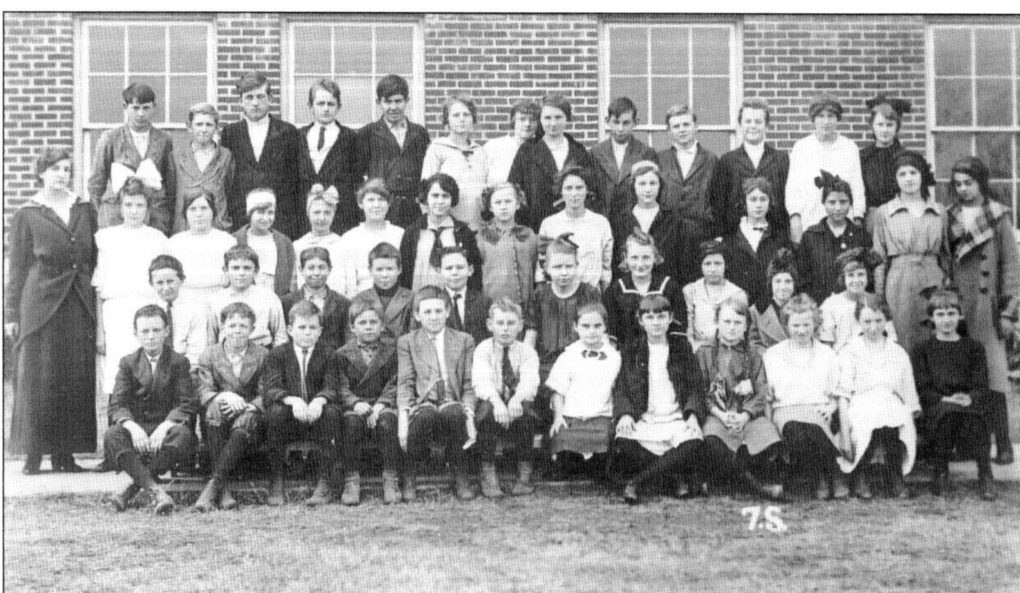

Homecoming and parades have long been a part of high school tradition. This postcard shows an Overland four-cylinder car in the Stuttgart homecoming parade of October 1909, with students Bessie Thielman, Edna Goodrich, Clara White, Minnie Oberly, and Dorothy Williamson. Notice the driver's position on the right side, in an era before such issues were settled.

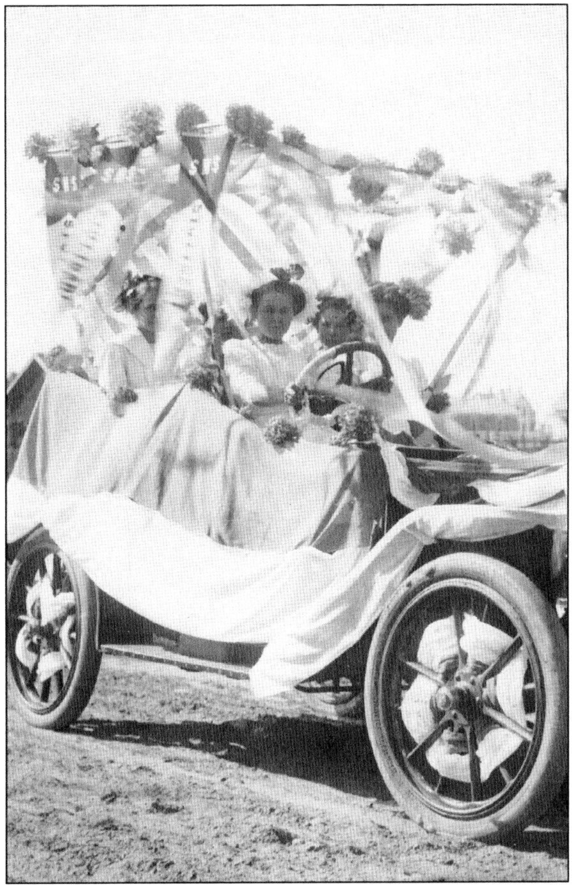

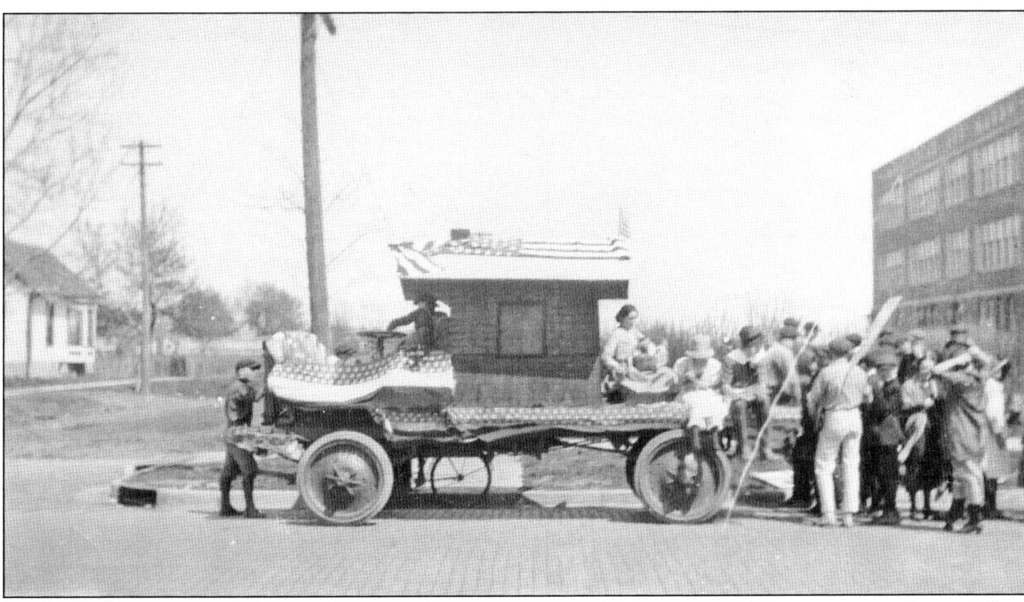

The 1912 school building can be seen to the right as students prepare their patriotic-themed float on a windy day around 1915.

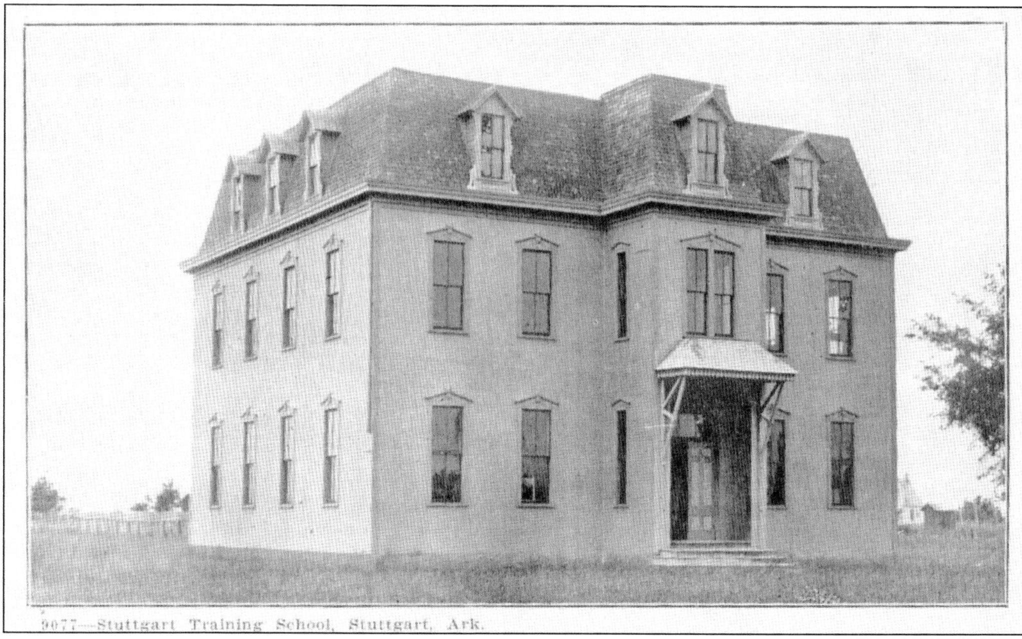

Stuttgart College, a private school, opened in this sturdy building in the 1890s but lost its status as a college shortly after 1900. The institution thereafter became the Stuttgart Training School, as noted in the caption of this 1909 postcard. That program offered foreign language instruction and vocational trade training for the few years it operated.

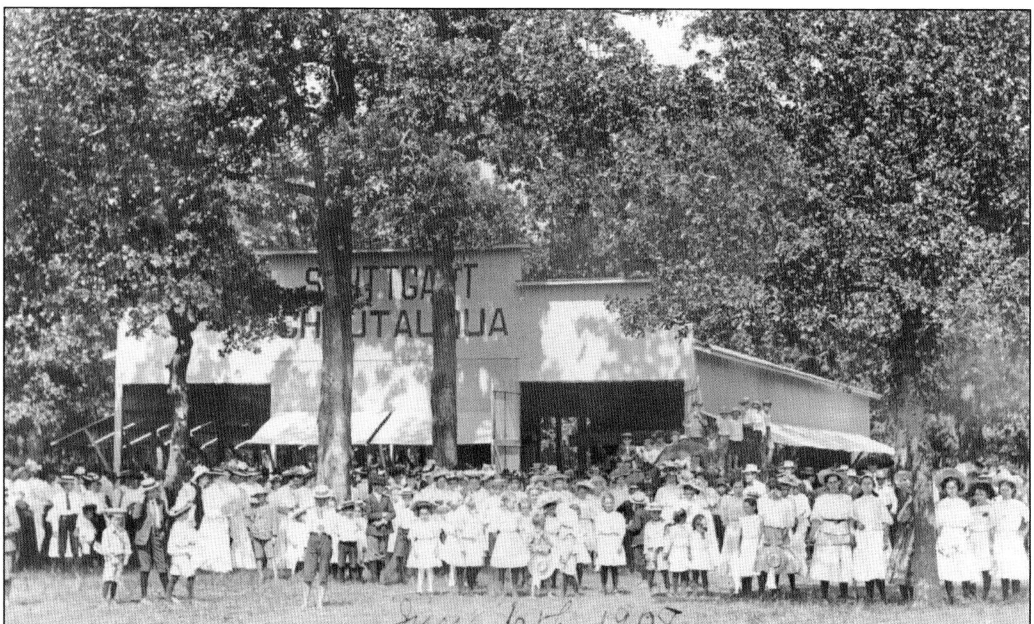

The Chautauqua movement began in upstate New York in the 1800s, initially with the goal of training Sunday school teachers. It evolved into a series of traveling lectures on cultural topics of the day, bringing speakers to small towns across the country. Stuttgart hosted the Chautauqua lectures in this open-sided building in 1908.

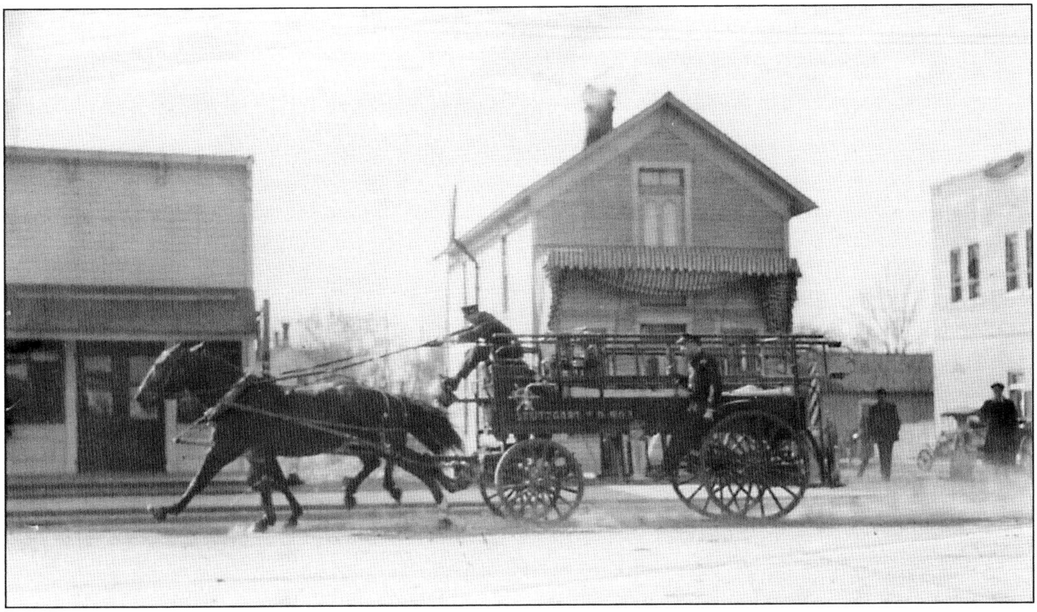

The homeowners and merchants of Stuttgart expected fire protection, and within the limits of available technology, they got it. In the above photograph, a horse-drawn ladder truck rushes down Main Street to a fire in 1915. The driver of the fire wagon, S. E. Lauhon, earned $55 a month, while his assistant in the photograph, Roy Bishop, earned $40. In 1916, Stuttgart got its first motor-powered fire truck, seen below after being freshly unloaded at the Rock Island depot. The truck is being driven by Lee J. McDonald, seated next to fire chief Doug Mahel. (Courtesy of the Museum of the Arkansas Grand Prairie.)

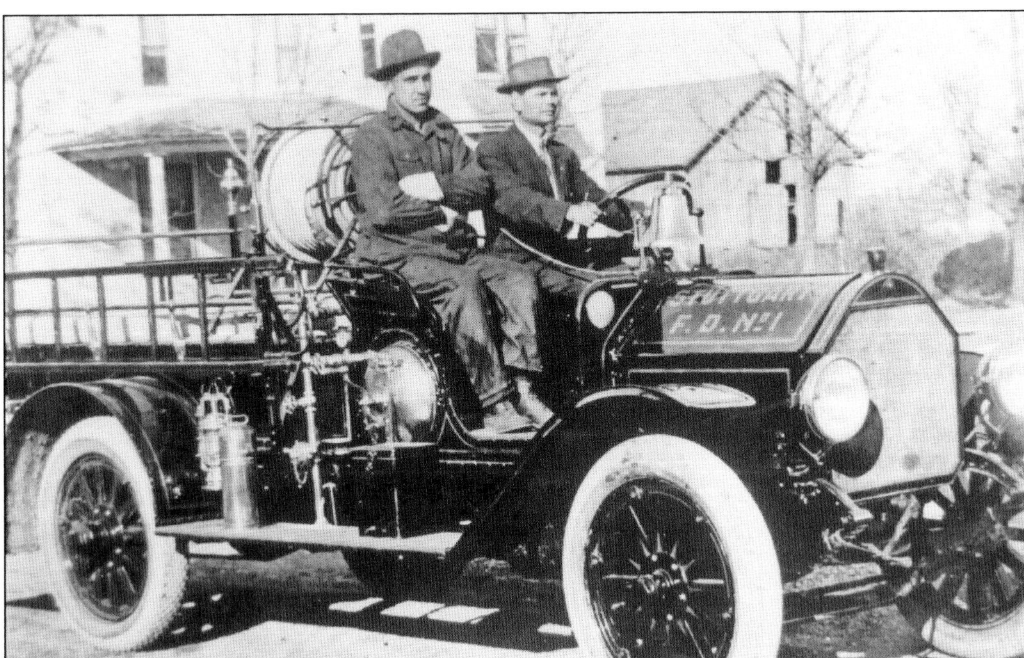

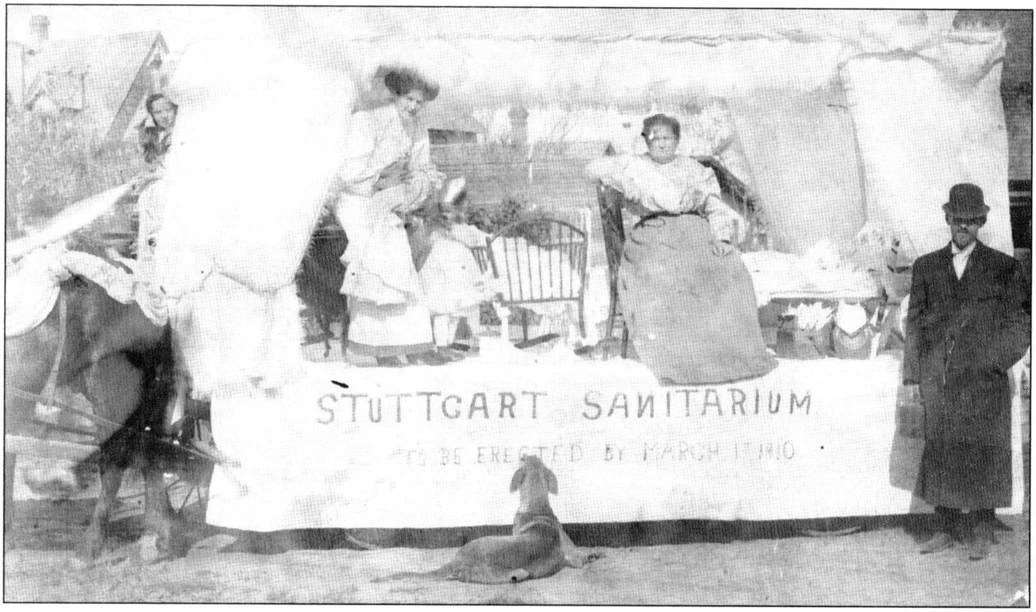

While the community in Stuttgart attracted several physicians, the city lacked any hospital for years. A 1909 parade carried the theme of upcoming progress in the form of the Stuttgart Sanitarium, a private hospital. The dog seems especially interested in the float.

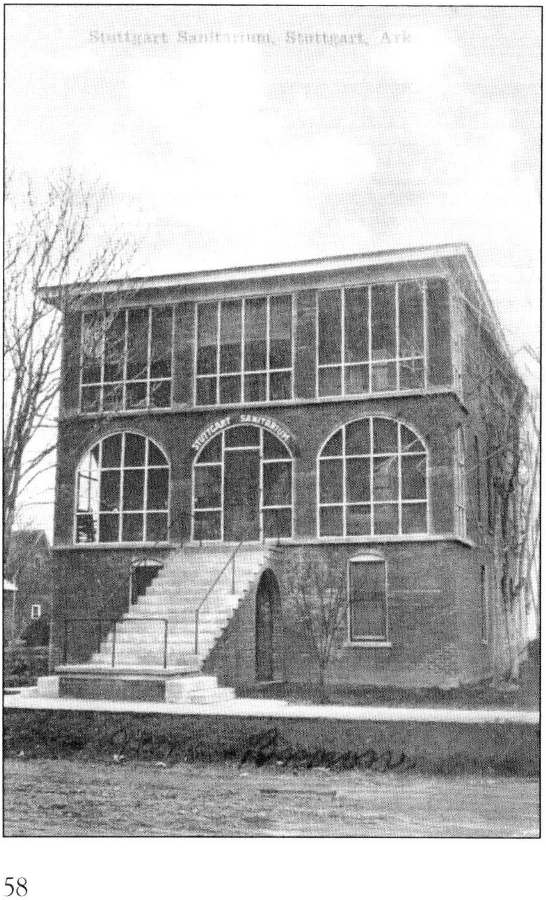

The private facility did indeed open, as did similar facilities in smaller Arkansas towns of the era. The Stuttgart Sanitarium is seen here in 1913. This postcard's sender writes, "Dear Grandpa are you sick? Ellen wrote that Grandma was dead. I am so worried. Please have someone write if you are unable. I have been quite sick but am better now."

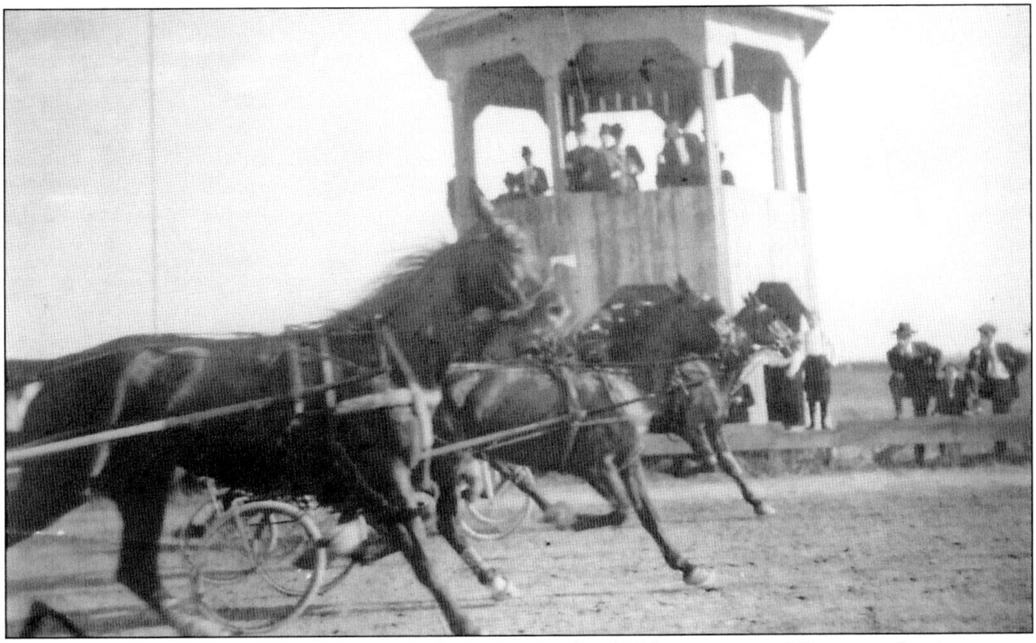

Seeking to expand the city's recreational options in the 1890s, a group of Stuttgart businessmen bought acreage on the south end of Main Street to create what was first just a driving park but later became the fairgrounds. Around 1900, businessman Phillip Reinsch purchased the Fairgrounds Park and turned it into one of the finest horse tracks in the state. Here horses race by the new judges' stand in a close harness-racing finish. The park was closed by the time of the Great Depression. (Courtesy of the Museum of the Arkansas Grand Prairie.)

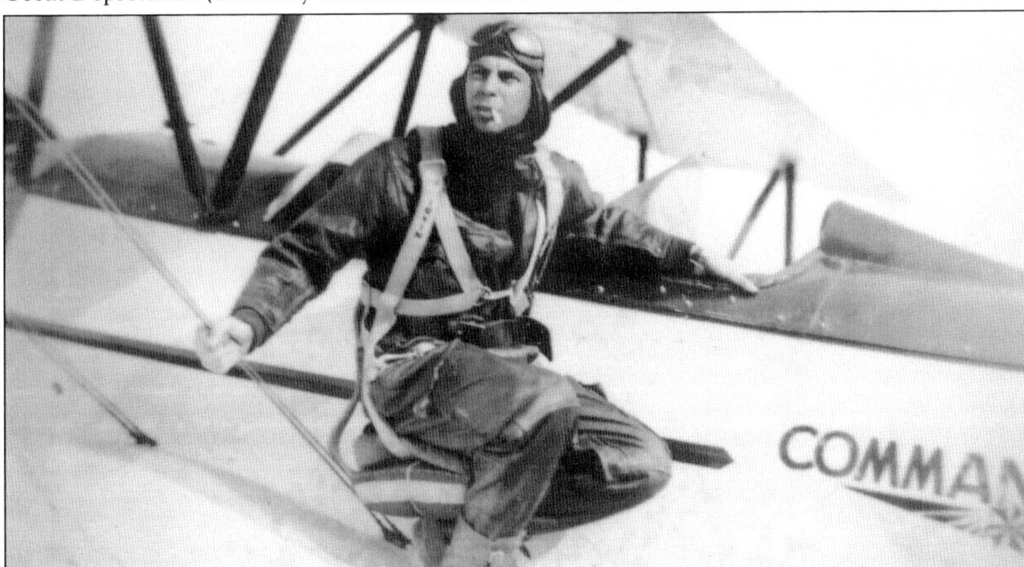

Stuttgart's contribution to aviation came in the 1920s with Buddy Rhodes, who was often seen flying over the prairie in his World War I–era plane, the *Command-Aire*. He once balanced on the wing of a plane in mid-flight and, in 1930, parachuted from 19,500 feet. When the barnstormer gave up stunt flying, he became renowned locally as an expert furniture maker. Rhodes died in 1980. (Courtesy of the Museum of the Arkansas Grand Prairie.)

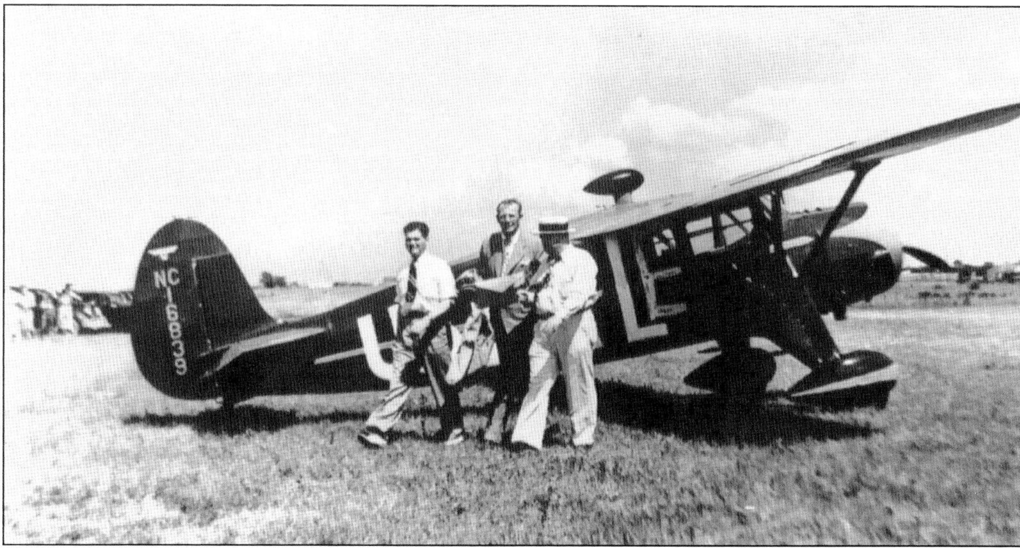

Stuttgart's reach to far-flung locales was boosted on May 19, 1938, when the first mail plane landed on the town's outskirts. Previously the mail had come in and gone out primarily by train. (Courtesy of the Museum of the Arkansas Grand Prairie.)

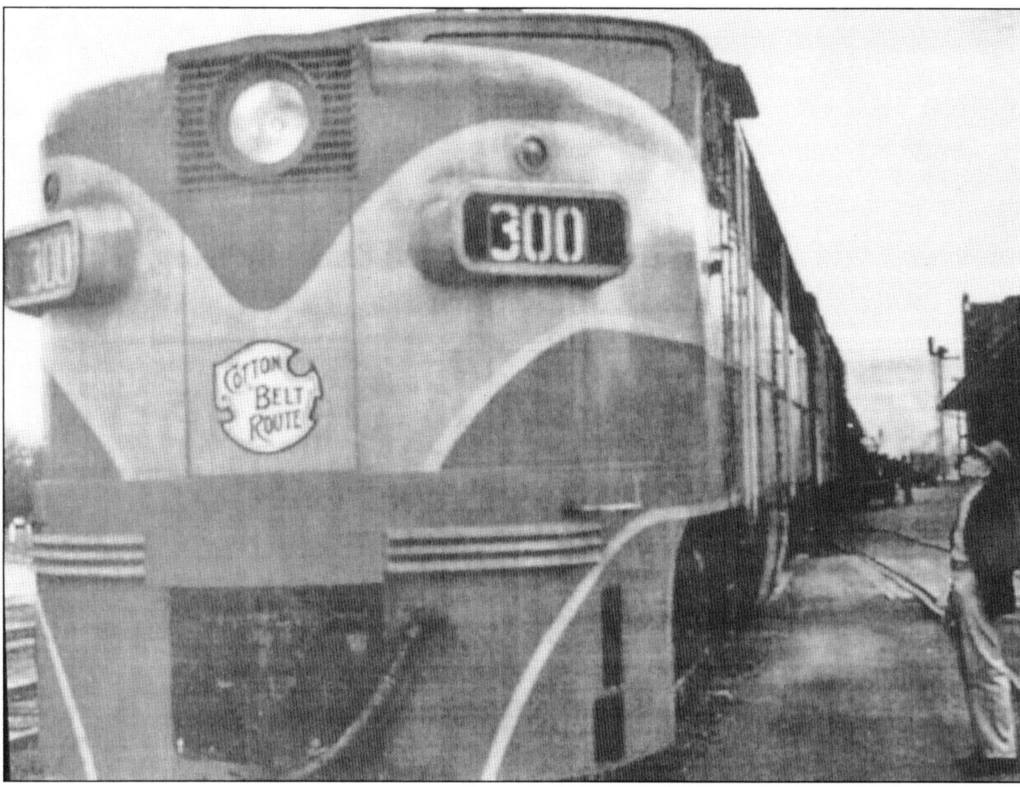

One transportation era rolled to a halt on November 30, 1959, when the St. Louis Southwestern Cotton Belt passenger train made its final stop in Stuttgart. Eighty years of passenger service had come to an end because of the public's preference for automobile travel. (Courtesy of the Museum of the Arkansas Grand Prairie.)

Visitors to Stuttgart today might stroll on the lawn of the courthouse for the northern district of Arkansas County, which was erected in a quasi–Greek Revival style in 1929. The building is one of the smallest courthouses in the state. The town of DeWitt hosts a facility for the county's southern district.

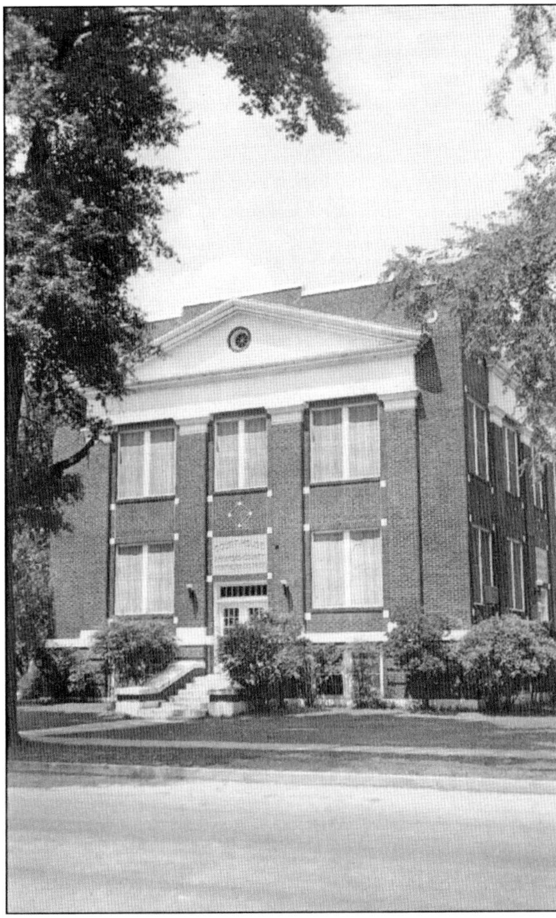

In the 1940s, before the rise of the big box stores, family-owned businesses like Conn Hardware and Furniture, located at the southeast corner of Third and Main, were downtown mainstays. This postcard was part of a mass mailing sent to potential customers in the surrounding area. On the reverse side, it lists sale items such as "45 lb. Cotton Mattress for $3.95, Simmons Metal Bed for $4.75," and a "Levee Shovel for $1.45." "Friendly Service–Cheaper Prices" was the store's motto. The business later relocated, but the original building remains today.

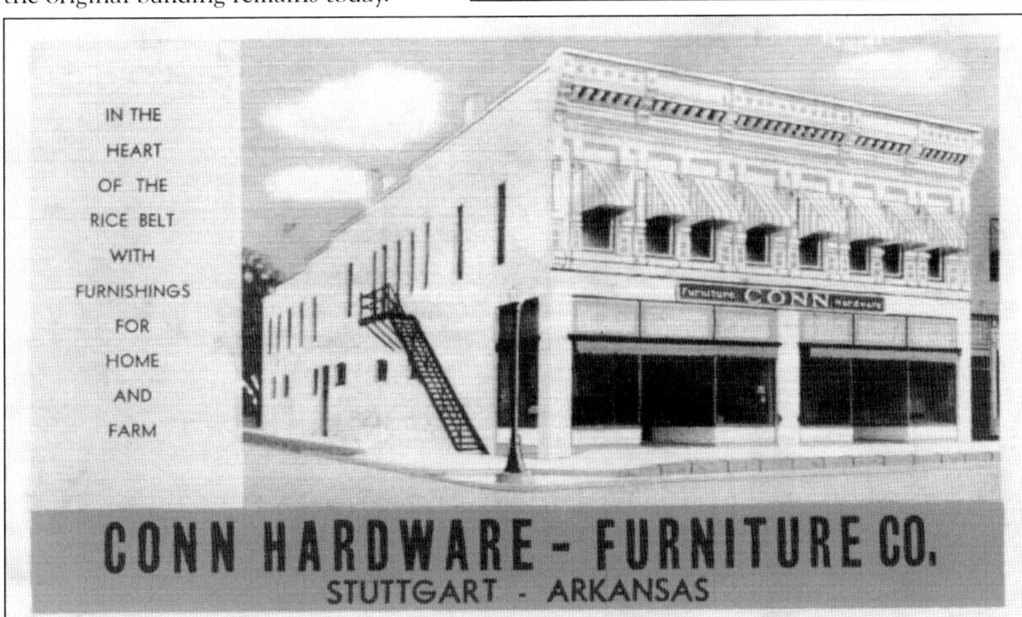

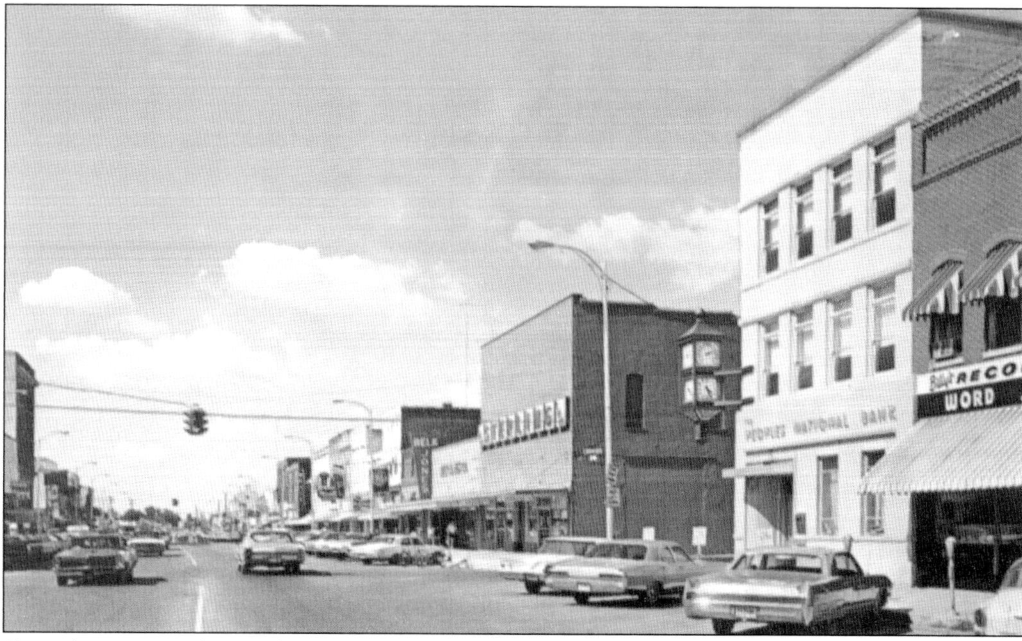

Over the course of more than a century, Stuttgart's Main Street has seen the tracks of pioneers in its dirt road; the wheels of wagons, buggies, and all manner of farm machinery; and finally automobiles continuing the history of small-town commerce. In the above *c.* 1970 view, Main Street is *the* place to shop, with a Sterling five and dime, Billy's Record Store, a Rexall drugstore, and Belk Jones department store. In the author's 2007 photograph, taken from the same angle, much has changed, as most of the area's retail trade has moved to the shopping centers at the edge of town, anchored by the town's Wal-Mart. Back on Main Street, Radio Shack operates in the old Sterling building; the Peoples' National Bank has moved on; and Billy's Record Store is no more. A vacant lot occupies the former location of Belk's. Even so, the street remains mostly intact and hopeful for a revival worthy of the colorful history that built the town.

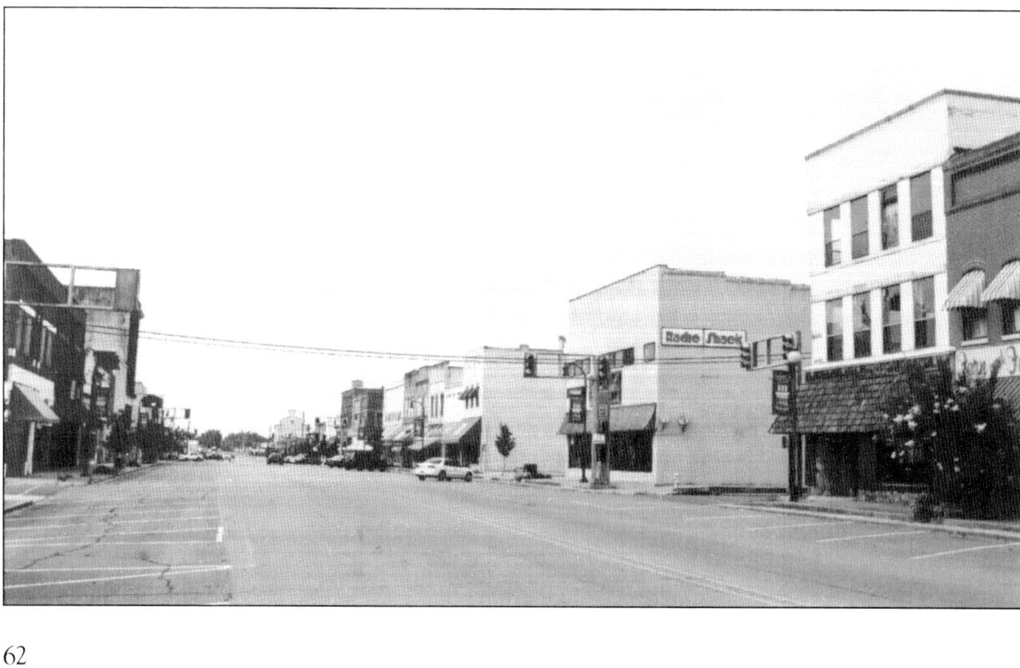

Three

SMALLER TOWNS, VILLAGES, AND HAMLETS

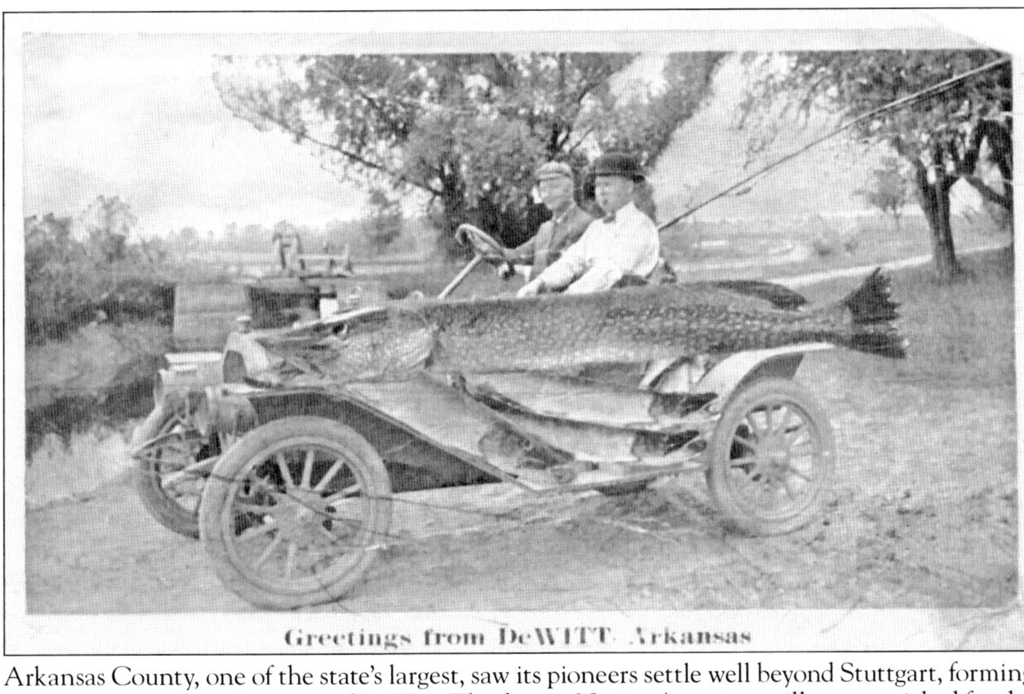

Arkansas County, one of the state's largest, saw its pioneers settle well beyond Stuttgart, forming communities such as the town of DeWitt. The former Native American village was picked for the county seat in 1852, replacing Arkansas Post. The site commissioners drew from slips of paper to determine who would have naming rights for the new town. Surveyor Adam McCool, an admirer of New York politician DeWitt Clinton, had the winning slip.

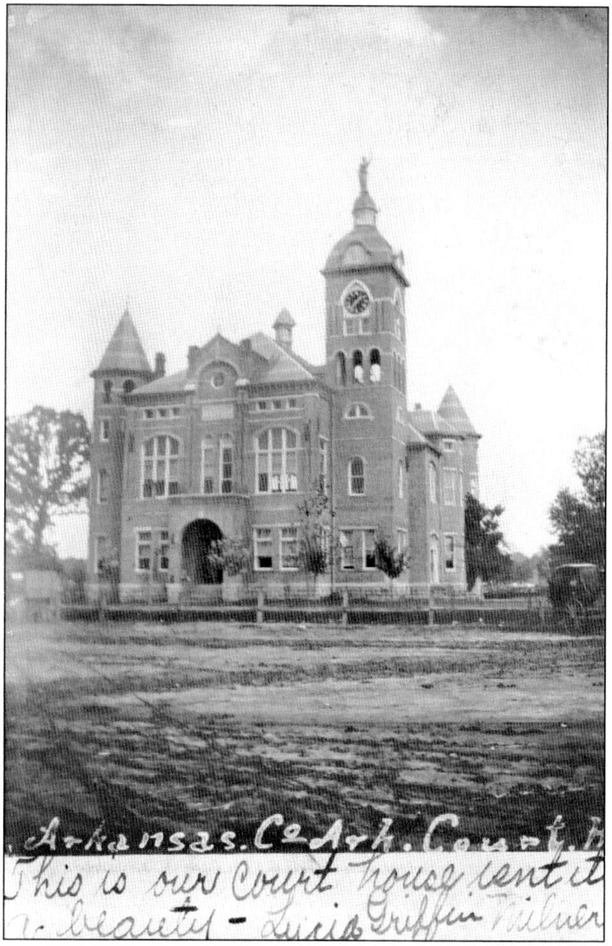

DeWitt came to share county seat honors with Stuttgart, some 25 miles to the north in the expansive Arkansas County. This 1909 postcard of the *c.* 1880s building carries the message, "This is our court house, isn't it a beauty? We are at DeWitt now housekeeping & like the place so much."

This 1909 view, taken from a distance up the wide, tree-lined dirt street, gives a sense of the massive size of the DeWitt courthouse. The lawyer sending the card to a young lady in Memphis writes that he "just last night got thru with the last of three cases that I had to try, one right after the other. Had a hung jury in one and won the other two cases."

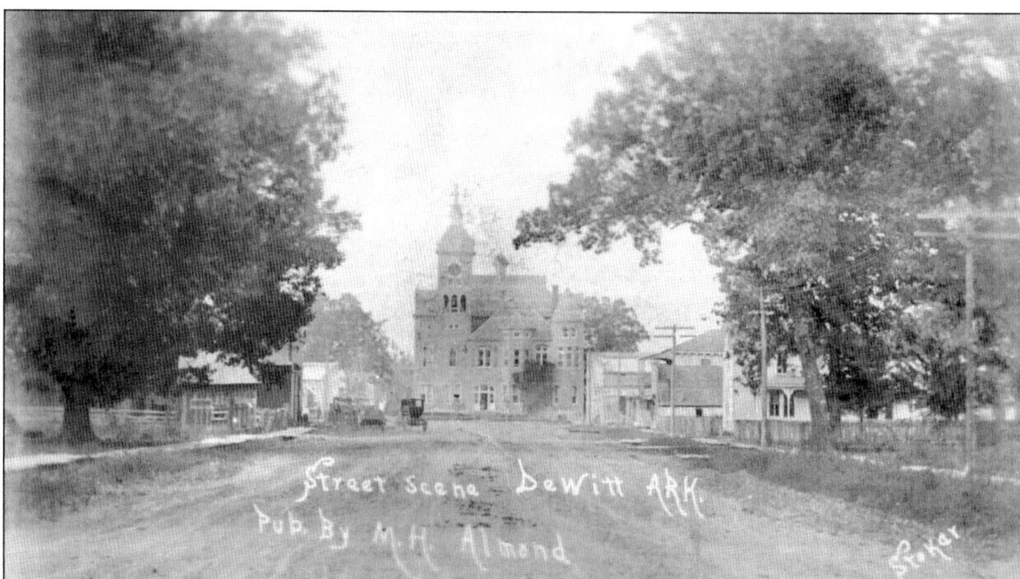

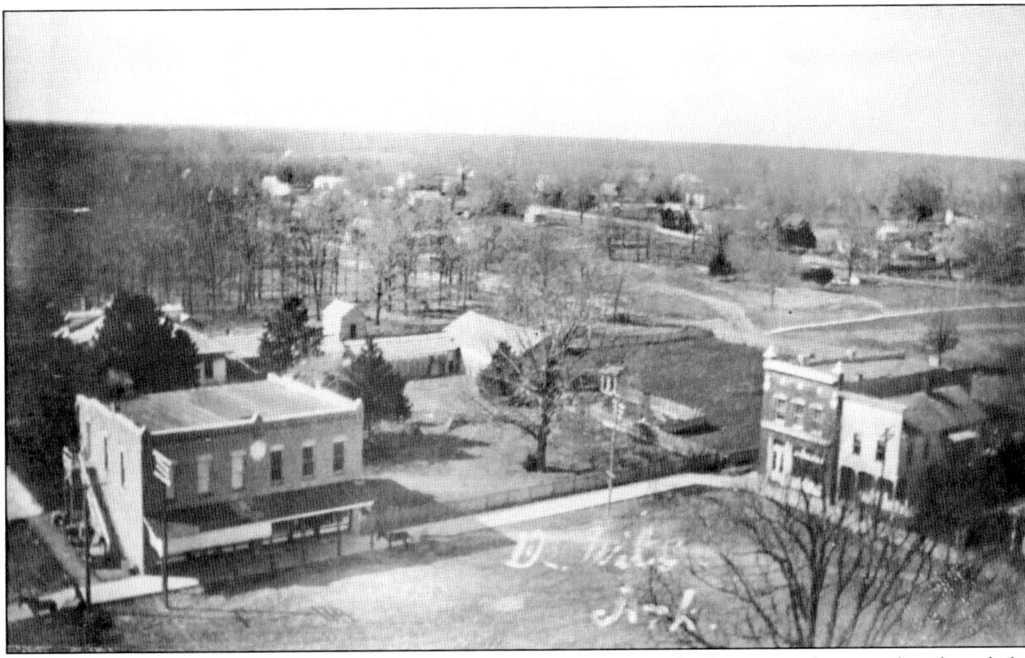

This 1908 view from the courthouse tower looks down upon the business district that lined the square surrounding the courthouse. "The clock has just struck 11," a young woman named Lizzie wrote on the back of the card. The population of DeWitt was around 800 at the time.

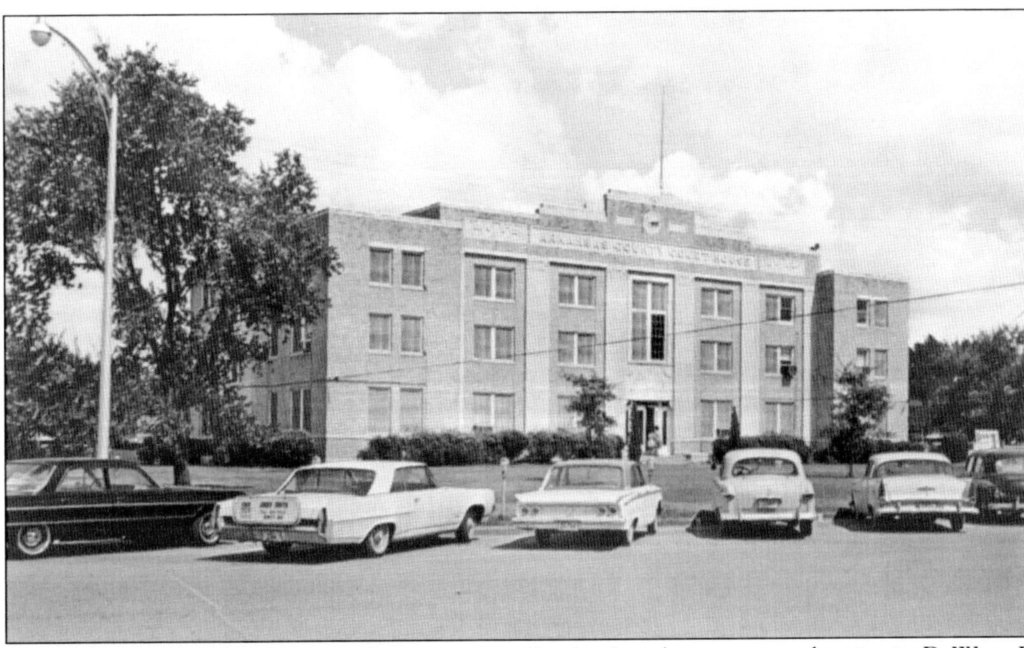

Pictured around 1960, this courthouse is actually the fourth to occupy the site in DeWitt. It was erected in the WPA's Moderne style in 1932, in an era when a number of the state's historic courthouses were replaced. It holds land records dating to 1796.

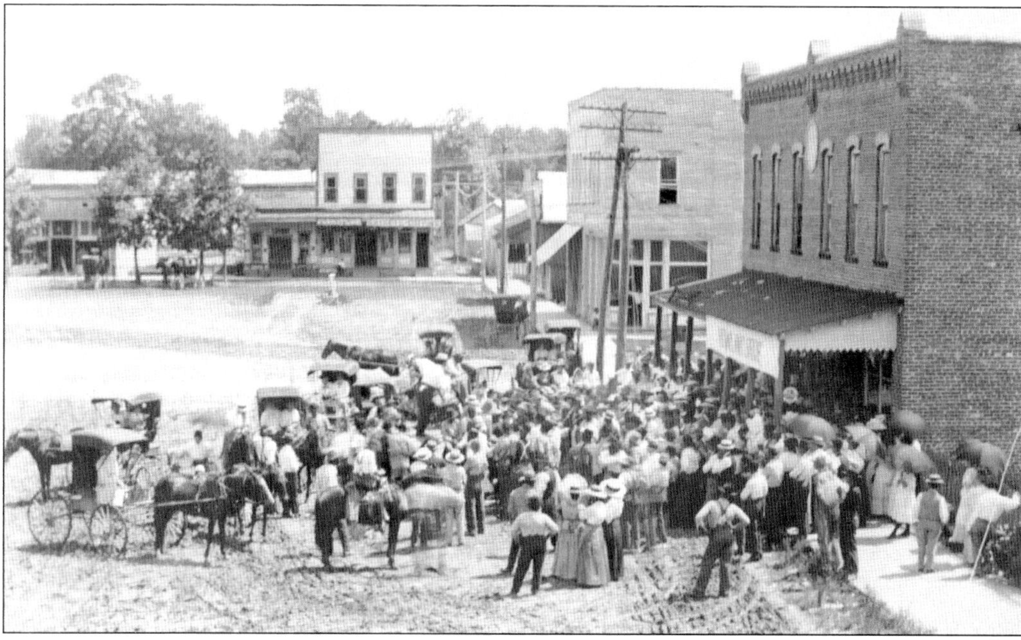

A crowd gathers in front of the store building seen from the courthouse tower on the previous page, for a demonstration of a new Singer sewing machine about 1910. Across the square, the wood-frame store with four windows bears a sign reading "Furniture, Caskets & Coffins," in a time when the dead were often prepared at home for burial.

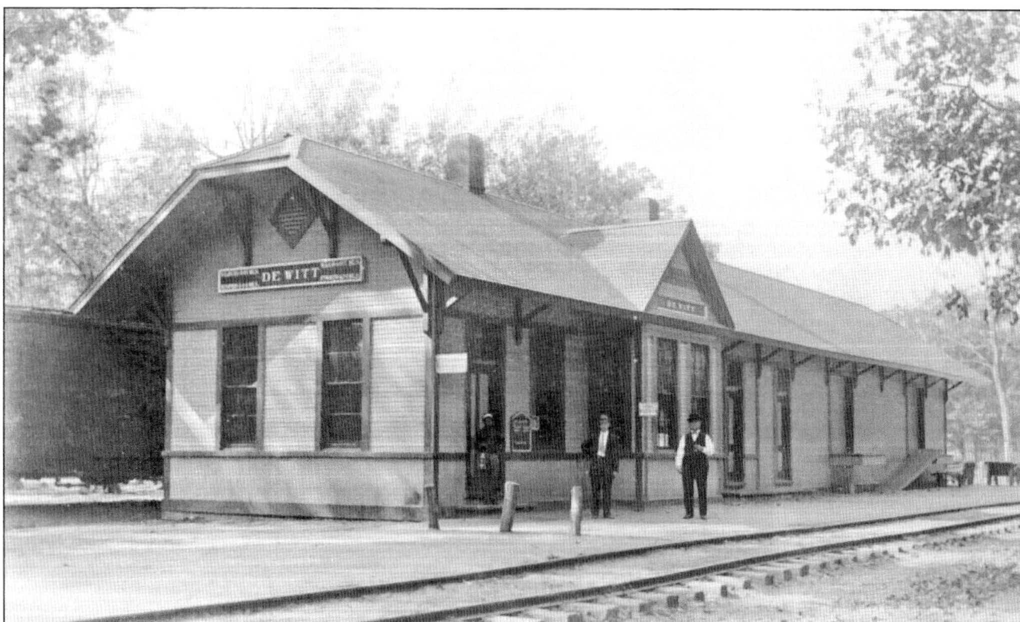

DeWitt prospered in large part because of the railroad connecting it to Stuttgart and points nationwide for the shipment of lumber and farm products. On this c. 1910 postcard, a man with a watch in his hand waits for an expected train. The sign on the end of the depot states distances to various cities: "Waco 467 mls," "Memphis 144 mls," "St. Louis 401 mls," and "Ft. Worth 424 mls."

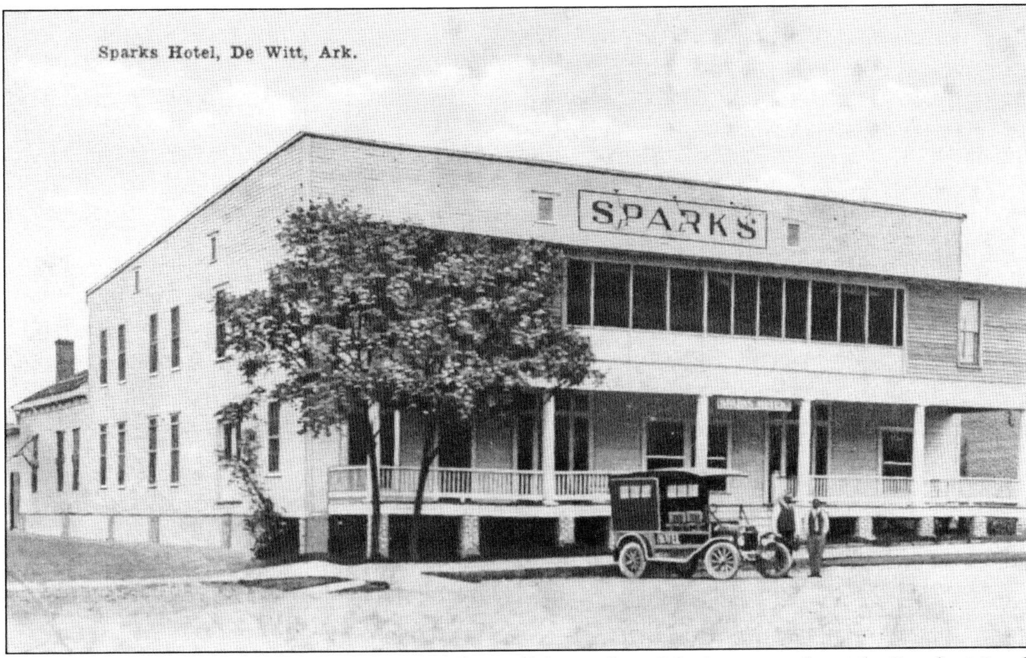

A visitor arriving in DeWitt by train might well have found lodging at the tidy Sparks Hotel, seen here around 1915. The car parked in the front belonged to the hotel and picked up guests and their baggage at the train station.

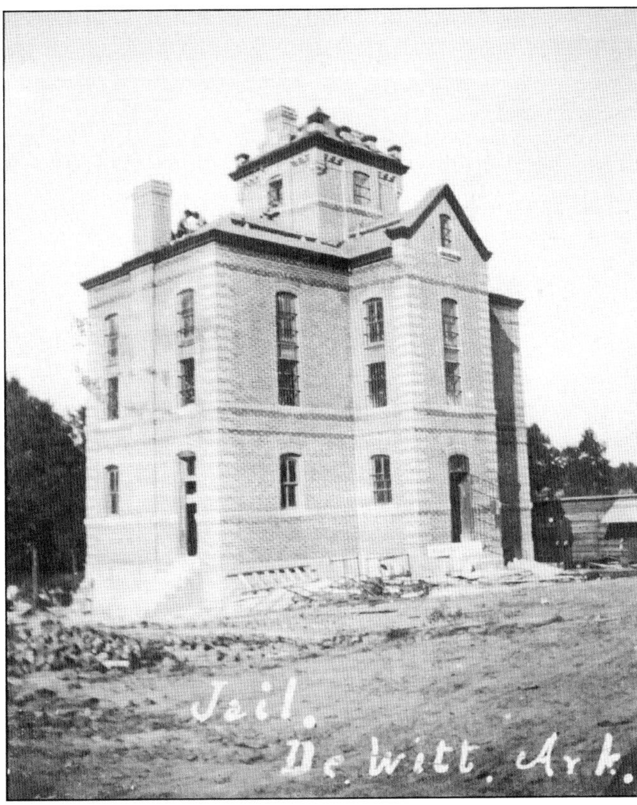

Those who misbehaved in DeWitt could find their lodging not at the Sparks Hotel but at the new jail, nearing completion in 1908. The note on the reverse, sent to Gulnora McGuire of Little Rock, remarked, "[Turn] over and you will see the pride of Arkansas County, but we never use it. Everybody's good." The writer was looking forward to "another party at Dr. Winkler tomorrow night—expecting a fine time."

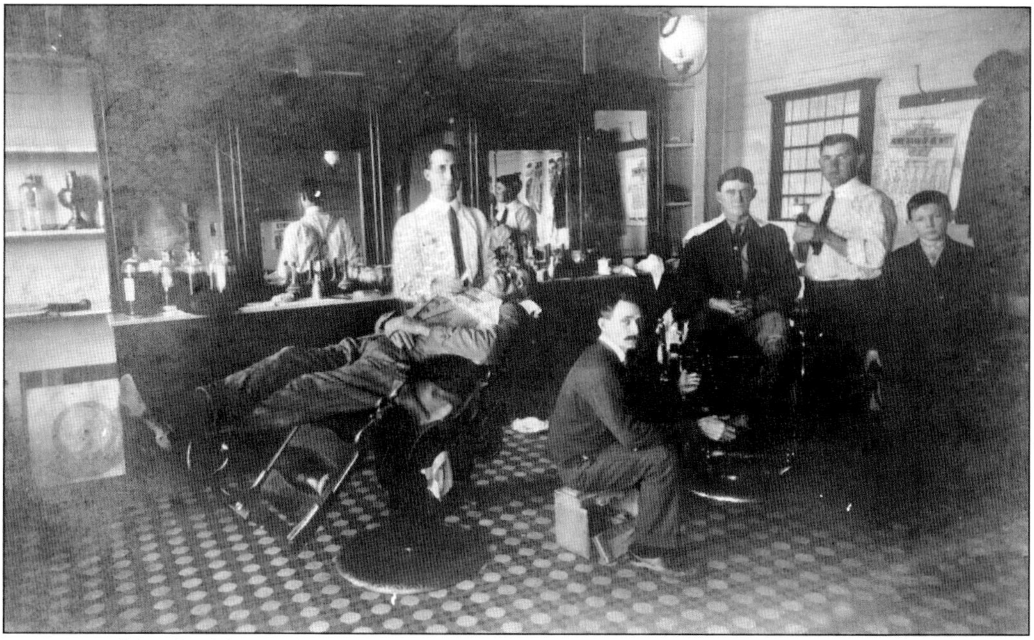

Visitors and locals alike would have patronized this barbershop, located on the courthouse square. The calendar on the wall to the right is from the Home Bank of DeWitt for the year 1913. The man in the chair to the right has his shoes shined while also getting a haircut.

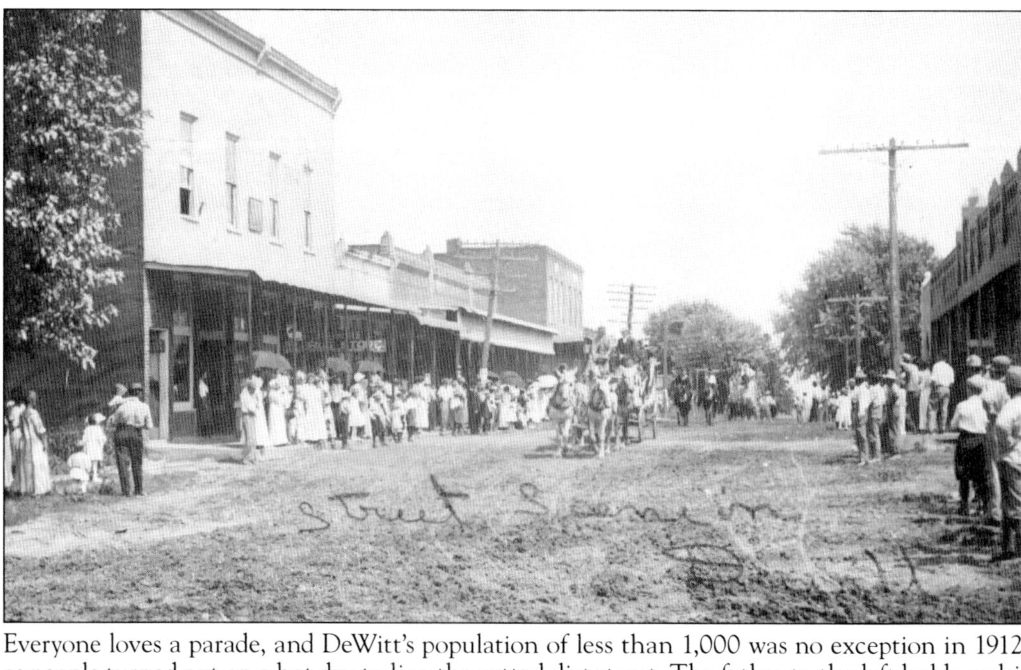

Everyone loves a parade, and DeWitt's population of less than 1,000 was no exception in 1912, as people turned out on a hot day to line the rutted dirt street. The father to the left holds up his child to get a better view, in a timeless pose for parades even a century removed.

A young woman named Hetty Smith wrote on a postcard of her DeWitt workplace in 1908, "I work upstairs as Stenographer & Abstractress for Judge Allen. . . . Just returned from a week's camp hunt—had a delightful time, it was composed of young people of the town."

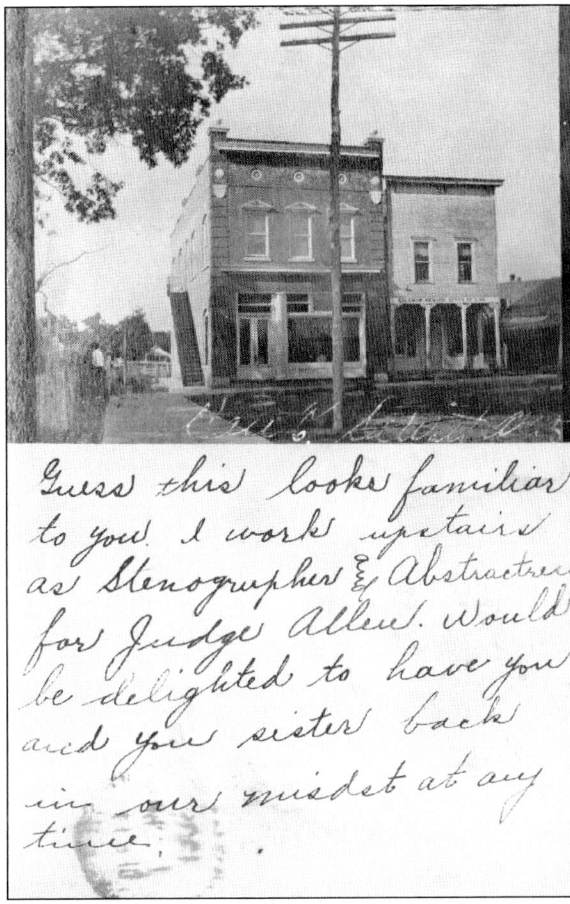

Local photographer Dayton Bowers recorded many scenes of life in early DeWitt; his cards are marked "Established 1881," apparently in reference to the beginning of his business. This photograph, taken around 1910, shows the local ice factory, which provided blocks for homeowners' and grocers' iceboxes in the era before modern refrigeration.

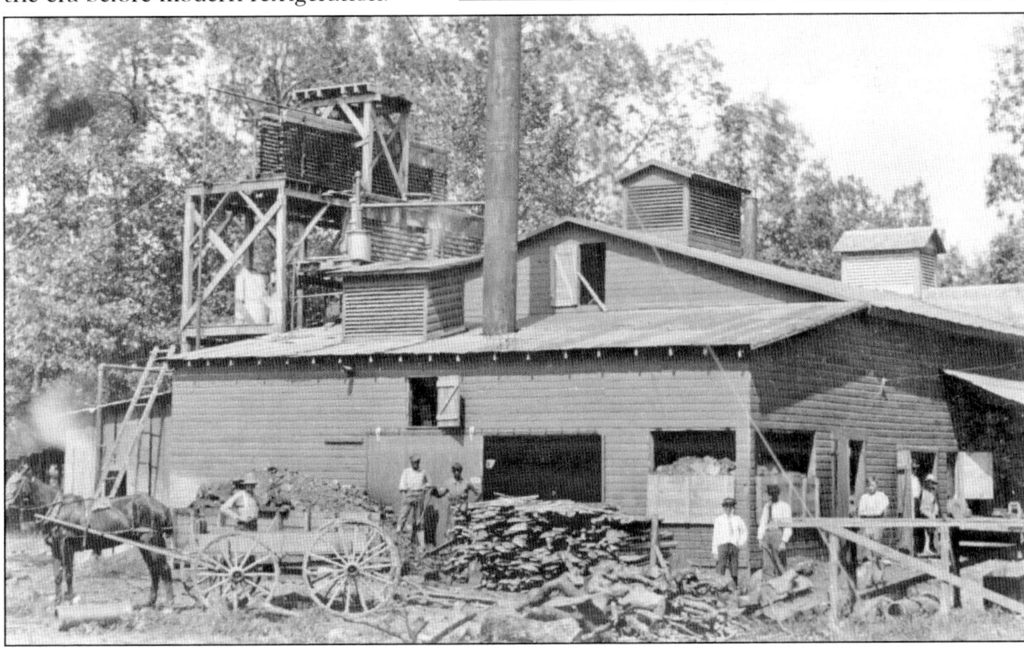

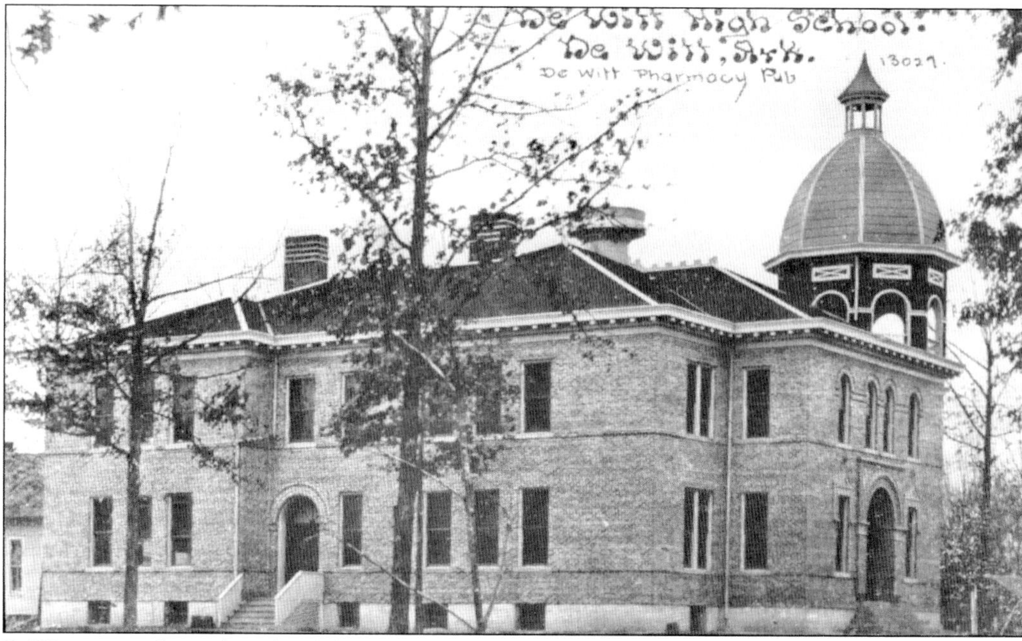

DeWitt erected a striking brick high school for white students in the early 1900s; it is seen here in a postcard from around 1915. At the time, a teacher earned a little over $300 for a school year of about 110 days. Arkansas had only passed a compulsory school attendance law in 1909, as schools competed with the harvest season on the surrounding farms in Arkansas County.

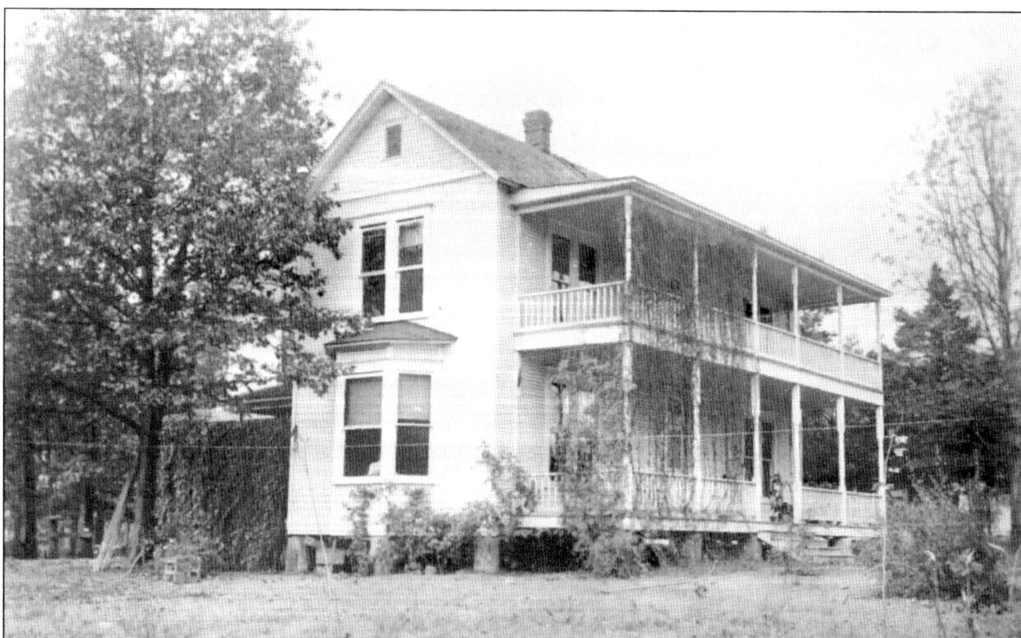

The houses in DeWitt tended to be somewhat more modest in size than some found in the larger city of Stuttgart to the north. The success of local photographer Dayton Bowers, whose work ended up on a number of postcards, allowed him to build this two-story home in DeWitt.

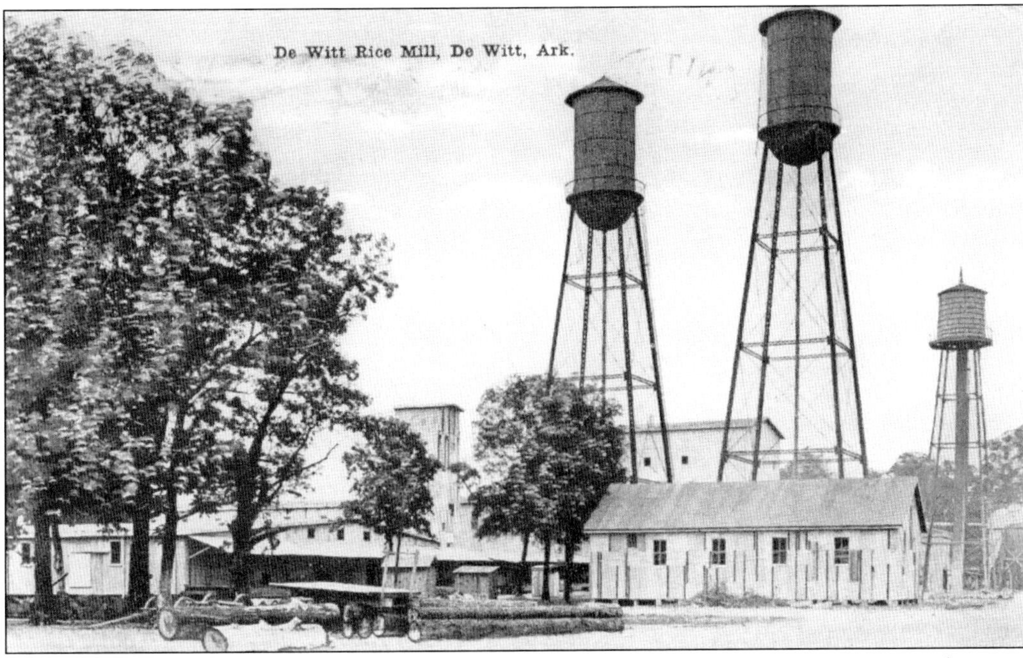

As rice production expanded into the southern part of Arkansas County, DeWitt gained its own rice mill in 1908. This postcard's message to Illinois reads, "We are enjoying our visit very much, wish we could stay all winter, lots of birds and flowers and sunshine. We enjoyed the butter, it's very scarce here."

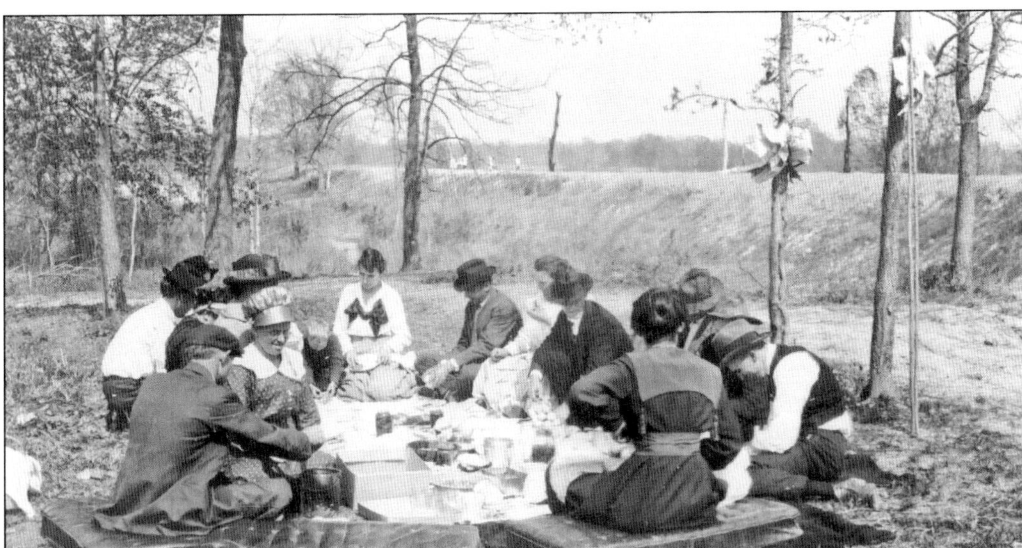

The town of St. Charles, located on the White River in eastern Arkansas County, had a quaint atmosphere markedly different from that of the farming communities to the west. Sitting on a bluff above the White River, St. Charles became the setting for a picnic on a Sunday afternoon in 1925. Several of the picnic diners are seated on what appear to be seat cushions removed from automobiles. Today St. Charles is the center for hunting and fishing in the White River National Wildlife Refuge, which wraps around part of the town.

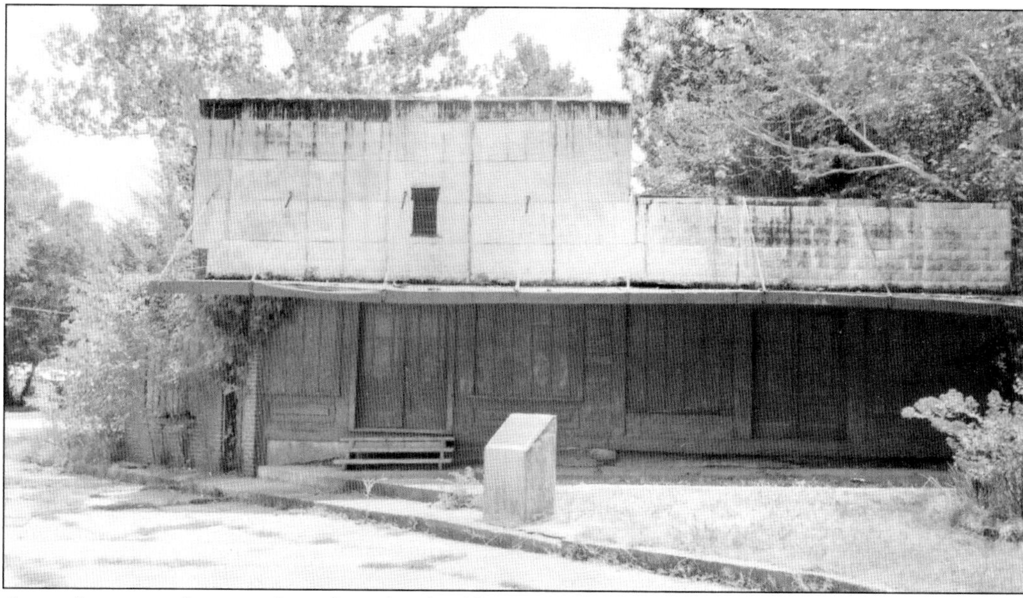

According to its historical marker, this building was the J. Deane Hardware store, which began serving the area in 1890. During the steamboat era, St. Charles was a thriving riverboat community, and this shop was its largest retail outlet. First managed by founder Joe Deane, later by his son Ballard, and finally by Ballard's widow, Estelle Walton Deane, the store closed its doors in 1976. (Photograph by Ray Hanley.)

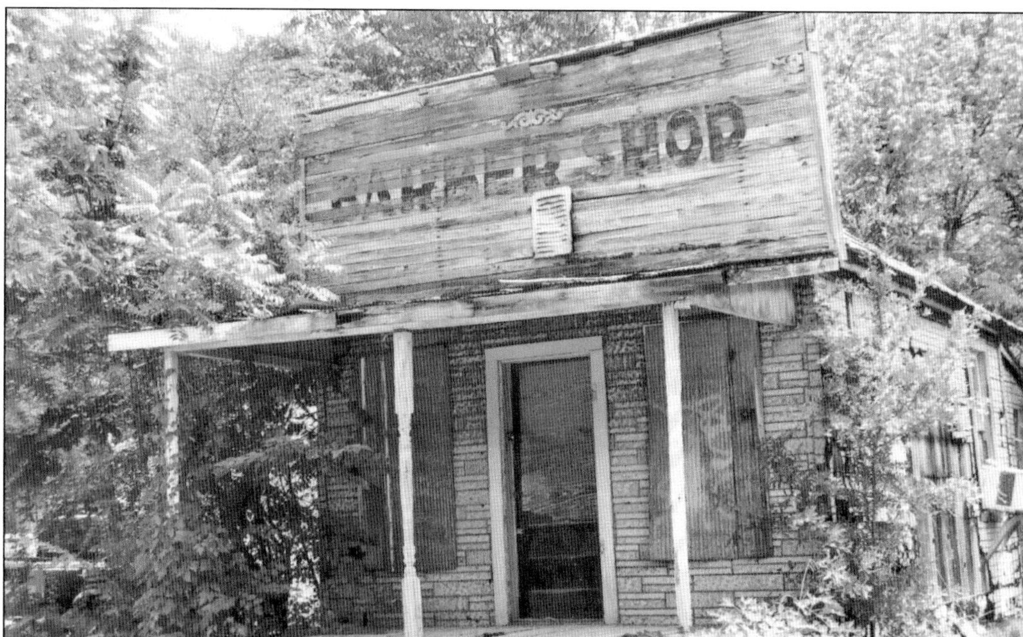

In its heyday, men flocked to the St. Charles Barber Shop to get their "ears lowered," their mustaches waxed, and their beards trimmed or shaved. While waiting for their turn in the ornate barber chair, customers could smoke, chew tobacco, gossip, tell jokes, and play checkers or dominos. In that bygone era, barbershops served as men's clubs where women dared not enter. (Photograph by Ray Hanley.)

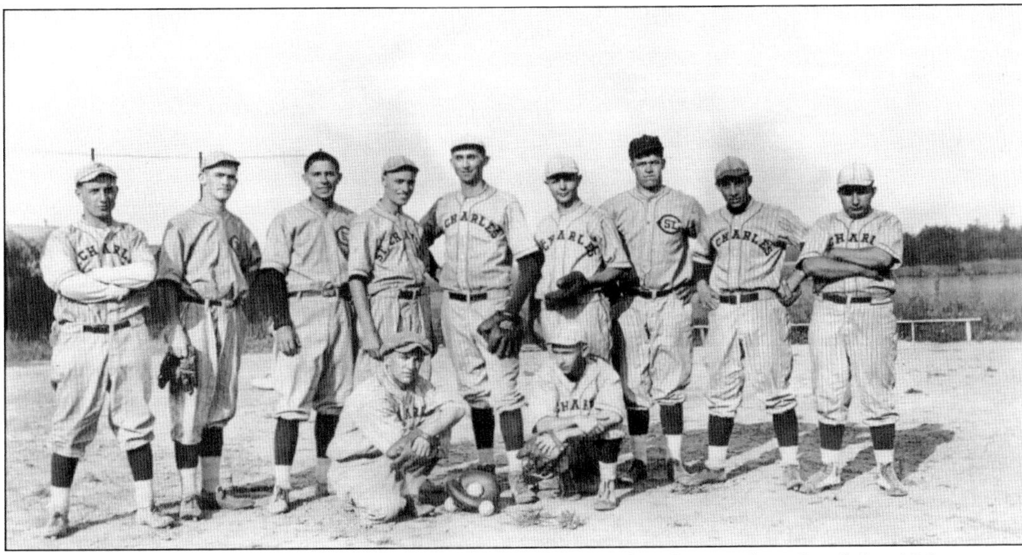

The St. Charles baseball team poses around 1920. From the closing decade of the 19th century through the Roaring Twenties, baseball fever spread like wildfire, sparking the golden age of the small-town game. Local business leaders often paid for uniforms and equipment, while fans sat on wooden benches and cheered for their local heroes. Barnstorming—traveling across the country and playing exhibition games—was common. These much-anticipated road trips often took young men away from home for the first time in their lives.

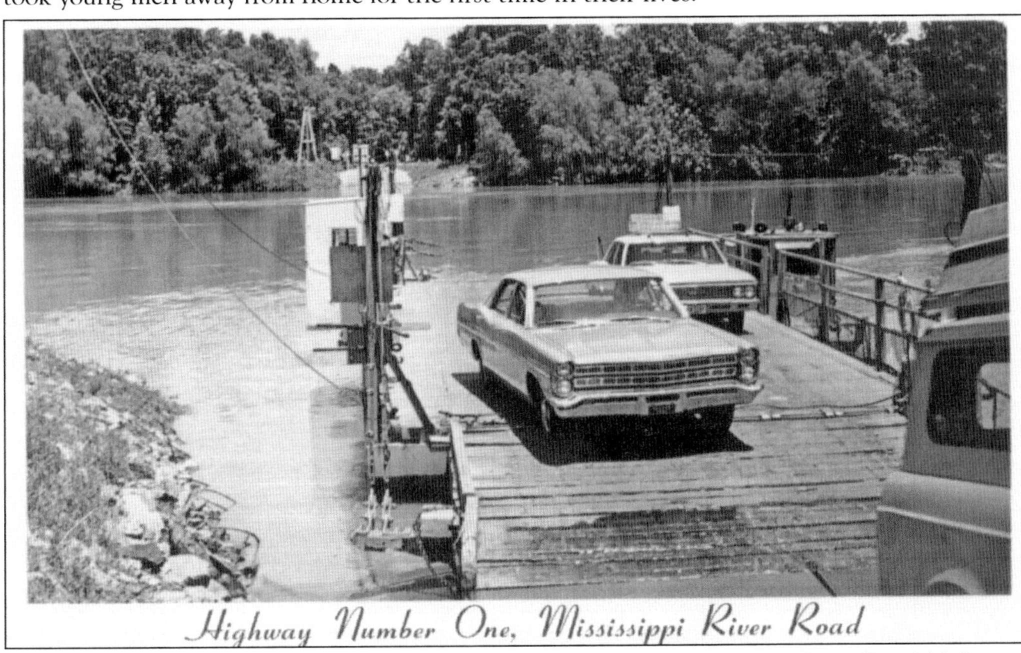

The St. Charles ferry travels the White River about 1962. The Mississippi River Road (Arkansas Highway 1) handled traffic from the Helena, DeWitt, and Stuttgart area and made a crossing of the White River at St. Charles. "The tourist or casual traveler always has a thrill in this manner of crossing one of the most interesting streams in the area," asserts the caption on the reverse side of this image. There was no fee for the ferry ride. Today a modern highway bridge spans the waterway, a short distance downstream.

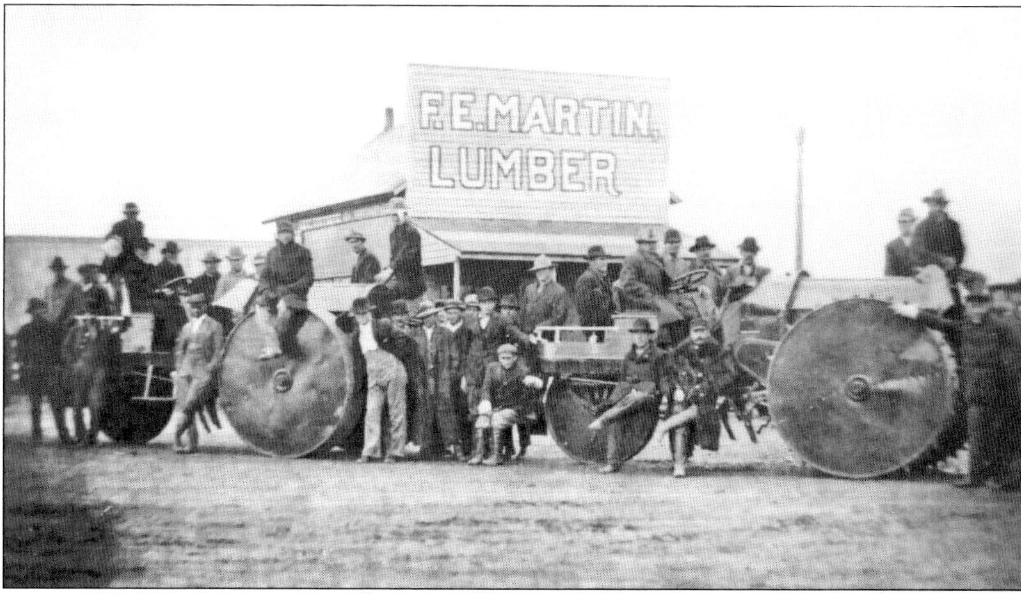

In the small Grand Prairie village of Gillette, men pose in front of F. E. Martin Lumber around 1920 with the first two steam-powered traction engines used to pull farm equipment in the surrounding rice fields. Settlers migrated to the area from Fulton County, Illinois, in 1881. The town's name originated in 1892, when the first post office was named in honor of railroad executive Francis M. Gillette. In November 1906, the Arkansas County Court approved a petition incorporating the town of Gillette.

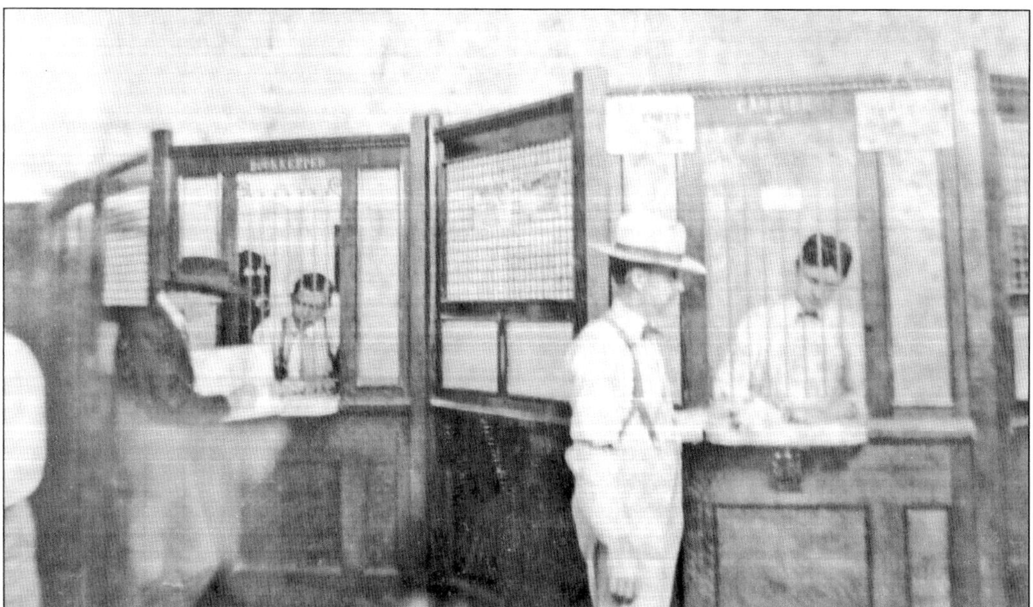

In 1920, a few years after this photograph of the interior of the Bank of Gillette, the town recorded its highest-ever population of 1,175 residents. The community fell on hard times in the late 1920s with the flood of 1927 and the Great Depression. Many residents lost their homes and farms, the bank closed, and businesses went bankrupt. A decade later, Gillette underwent an economic revival as sawmills, stave mills, and handle factories relocated to the area.

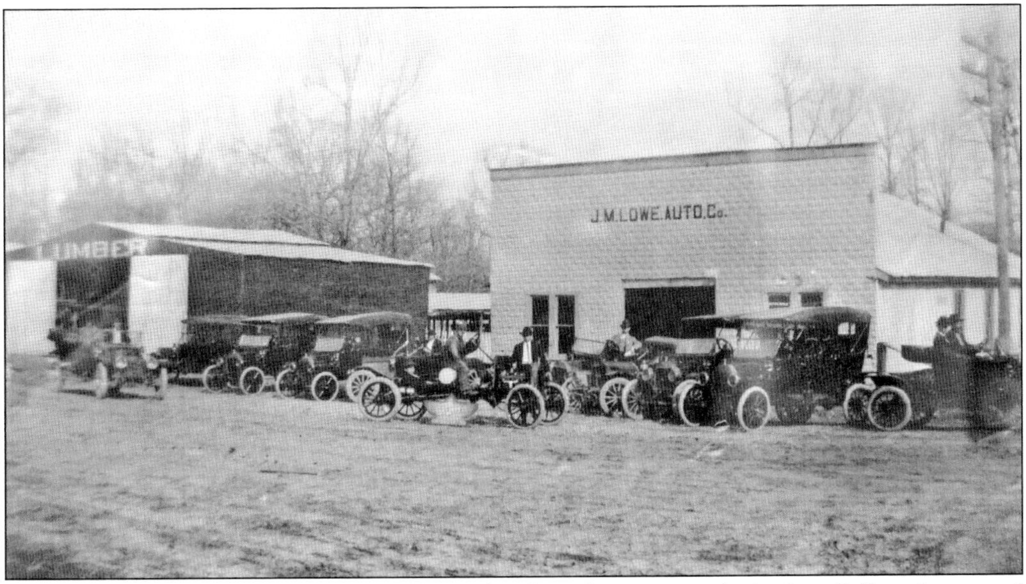

The J .M. Lowe Auto Company was Gillette's first horseless carriage dealership. Selling for around $800, the Ford Model T put Arkansas on wheels. By the early 1920s, increasing traffic led to the establishment of the Arkansas State Highway Commission. License fees and a gasoline tax were enacted to fund road improvements. Service stations, garages, roadside diners, and tourist courts began to appear along the roads in the more populated sections of the state.

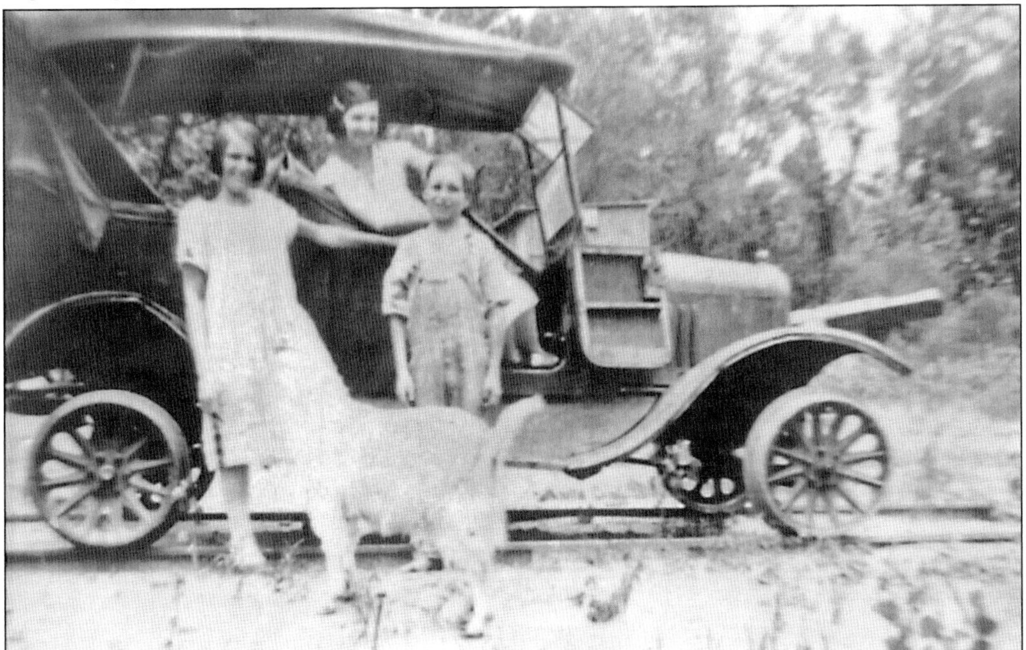

The "Flood Gate Special" was a Ford Model T fitted with wheels that enabled it to run on railroad tracks. In this c. 1920 image, the smiling young woman seated at the wheel is Grace Strong Malcomb. Mrs. Art Hightower (left) and an unidentified friend stand in front of the Tin Lizzie, as Henry Ford's modern marvel was affectionately nicknamed. The three were residents of Gillette.

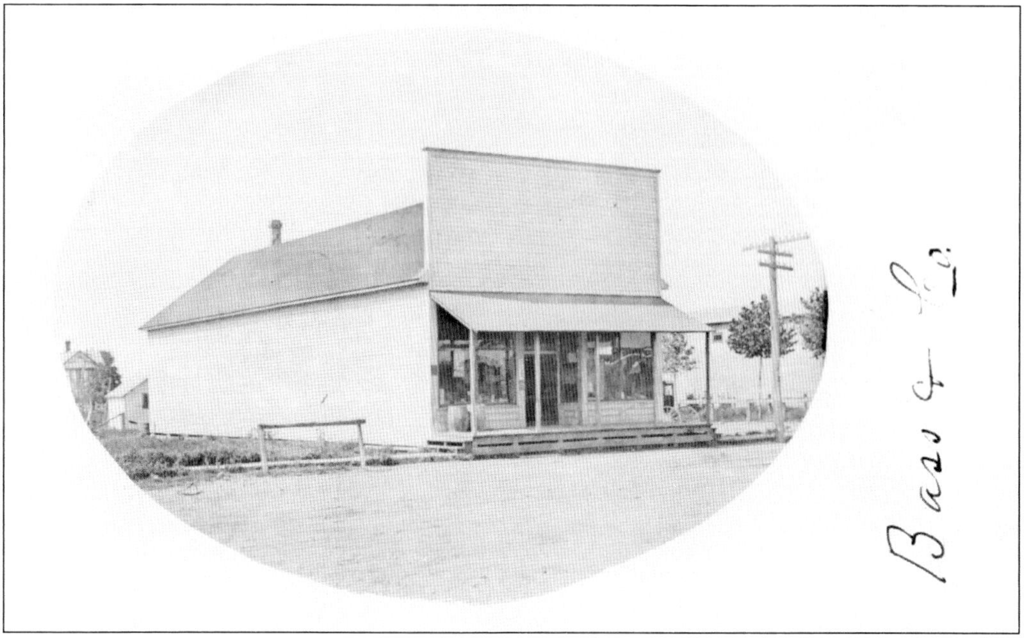

Gillette's Bass and Company, seen above about 1910, offered a wide assortment of groceries, household and hardware items, clothing, boots, shoes, hats, caps, and other merchandise. "Dear Eve, Let this show you I think of you even if I don't write a letter," urges the message. "Am still busy. . . . This store has some attraction for me. Can you guess? More later. Heaps of love." Below, a customer stands at the counter of Bass and Company while signs overhead advertise "Dinner Biscuit" and "Lewis Lye" soap. The store survived the great flood of 1927, and the building now houses a tavern.

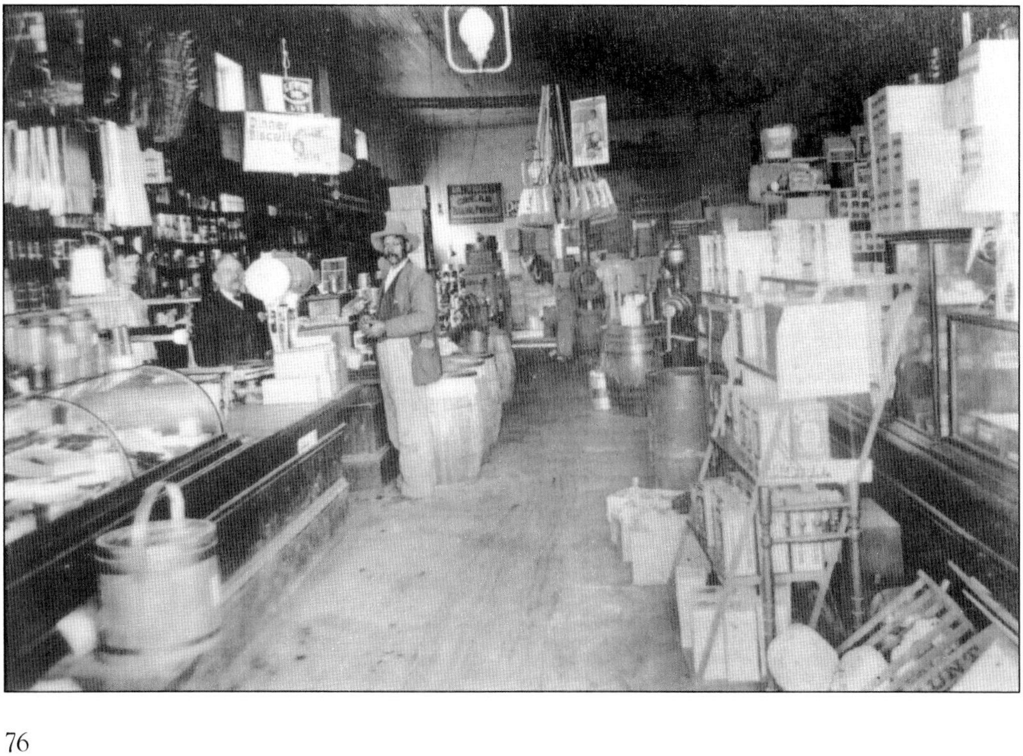

Rural communities took pride in their school buildings, as did Gillett. The structures were often featured on postcards that could be purchased at the local drugstore for a penny apiece. In 1913, the year this card was mailed to Table Grove, Illinois, Arkansas state law mandated a school year of 107 days. The average teacher's salary was $273 a year, or less than $3 per day.

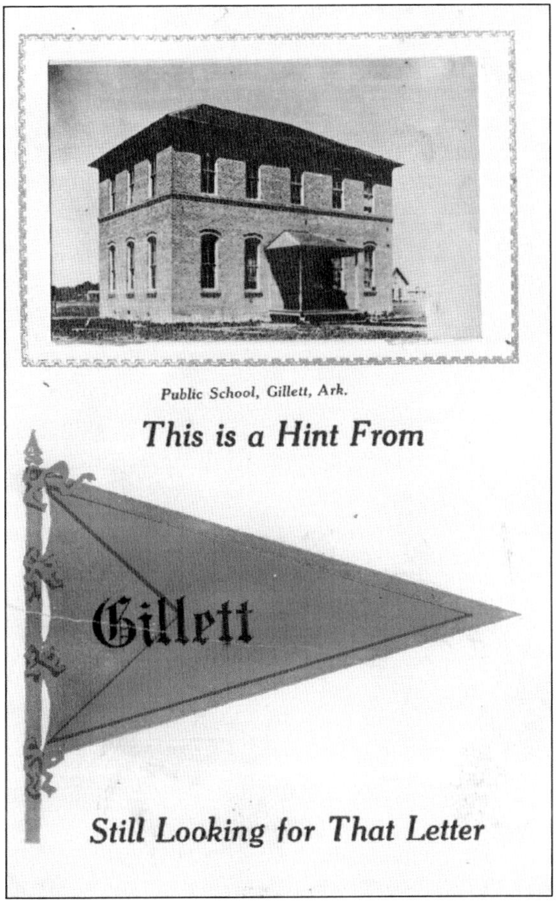

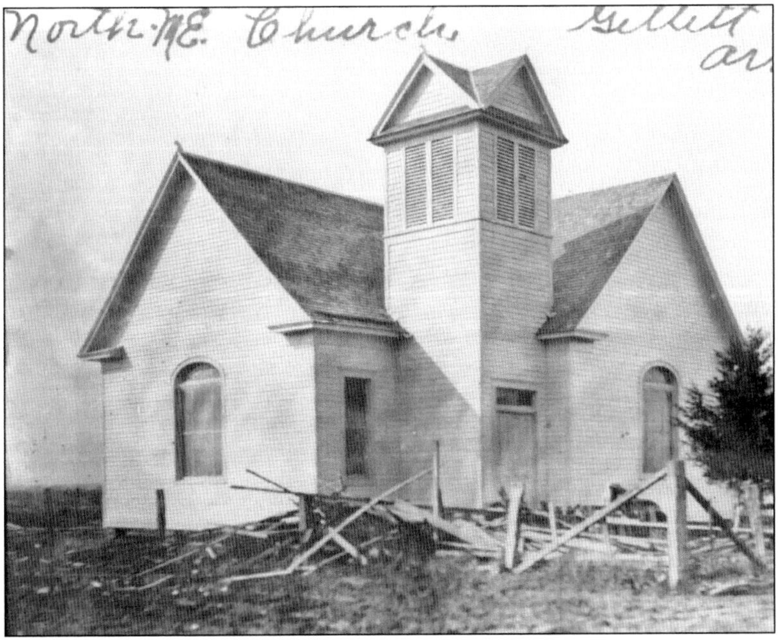

Gillette was dotted with various houses of worship, including the North Methodist Episcopal Church. "Dear Kid," pleads the message, "why in the name of girlie don't you answer my letter? Hope you are all OK. I am purty well. Am going to a dance at the hall tomorrow night. Wish you were here. You had better answer 'fore long or I will think you have forgotten me."

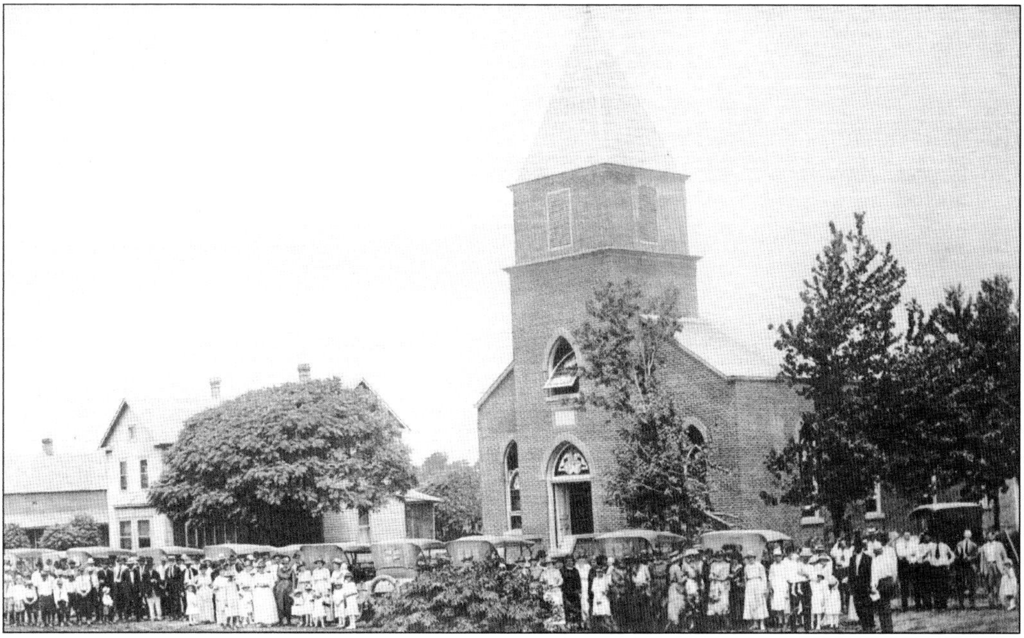

The congregation of St. Paul's Church poses in front of the building following Sunday services around 1912. "Dear Anna," reads the message from Mrs. J. F. Kraft, "this is a photo of our church here. The minister is standing at the extreme right with his little girl. Paul will be confirmed Easter. We are all well and getting along fine. We are living on a nice farm for 2 years." Perhaps the two-story house on the left was the church's parsonage.

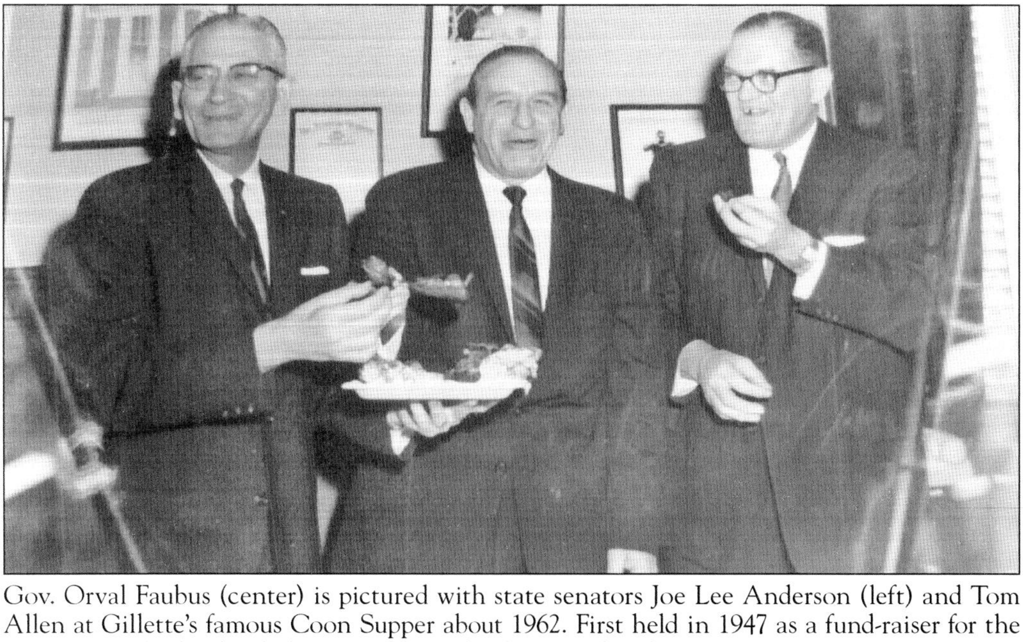

Gov. Orval Faubus (center) is pictured with state senators Joe Lee Anderson (left) and Tom Allen at Gillette's famous Coon Supper about 1962. First held in 1947 as a fund-raiser for the community's high school, the annual event has become the ultimate "meet and greet" for anyone seeking or holding statewide political office in Arkansas. Each year on the second weekend in January, the community more than doubles its population, and over 800 pounds of raccoon meat are consumed. (Courtesy of Arkansas Post State Park.)

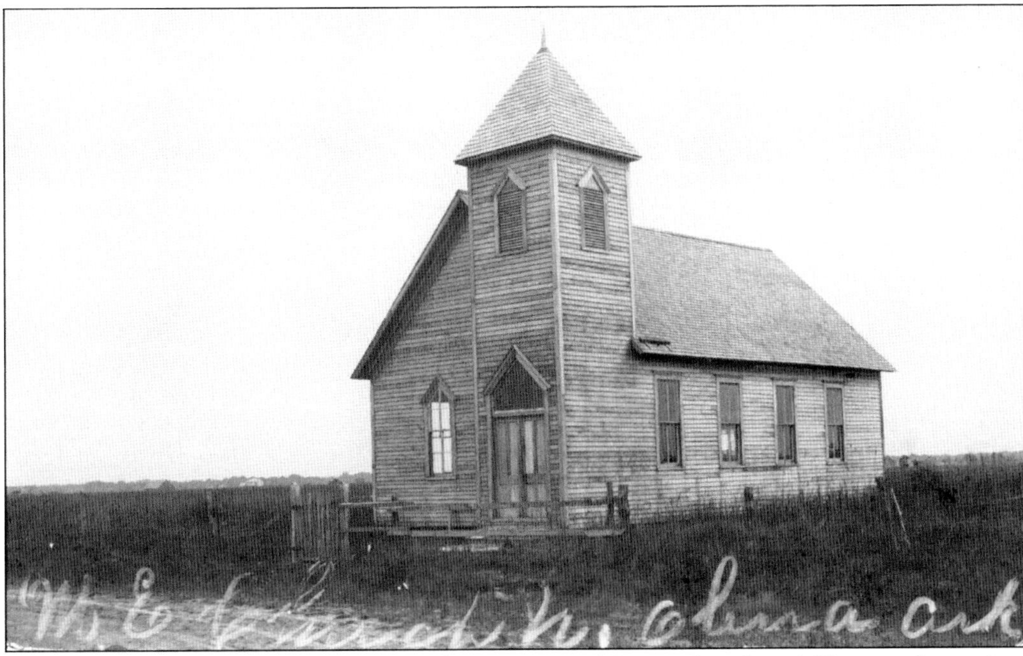

The Methodist Episcopal church near the tiny Grand Prairie hamlet of Olena is shown here around 1912. On long-ago Sunday mornings, the house of worship was surrounded by many horse-drawn vehicles and a few Ford Model Ts as its members gathered to lift their voices in song and hear their pastor's "hellfire and brimstone" sermon.

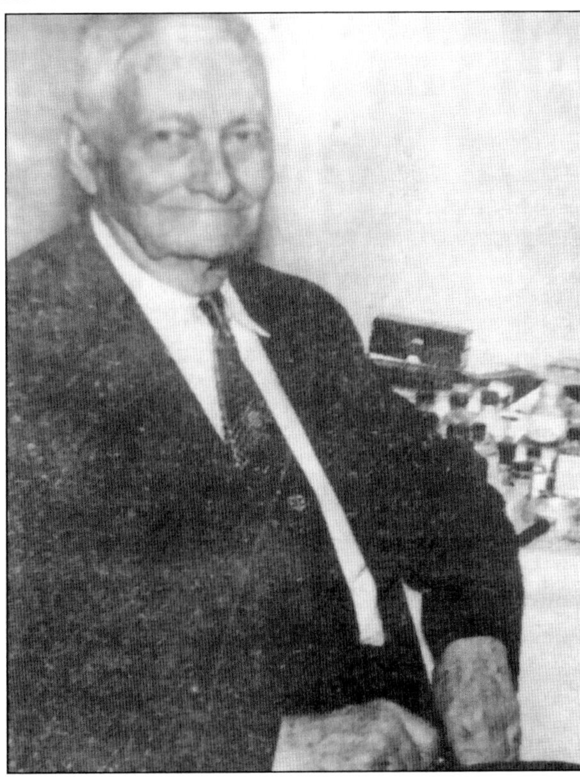

Dr. H. C. Riley practiced from his home office in the Bayou Meto community for 54 years, retiring in 1962. During his career, he delivered more than 3,500 babies—mostly in the homes of the rural areas he served—and often reached his patients by horseback. In the early days, he received $1 for a day call and $2.50 for a night visit; his records from 1916 show that his fee for delivering a baby was $7.50. (Courtesy of the Museum of the Arkansas Grand Prairie.)

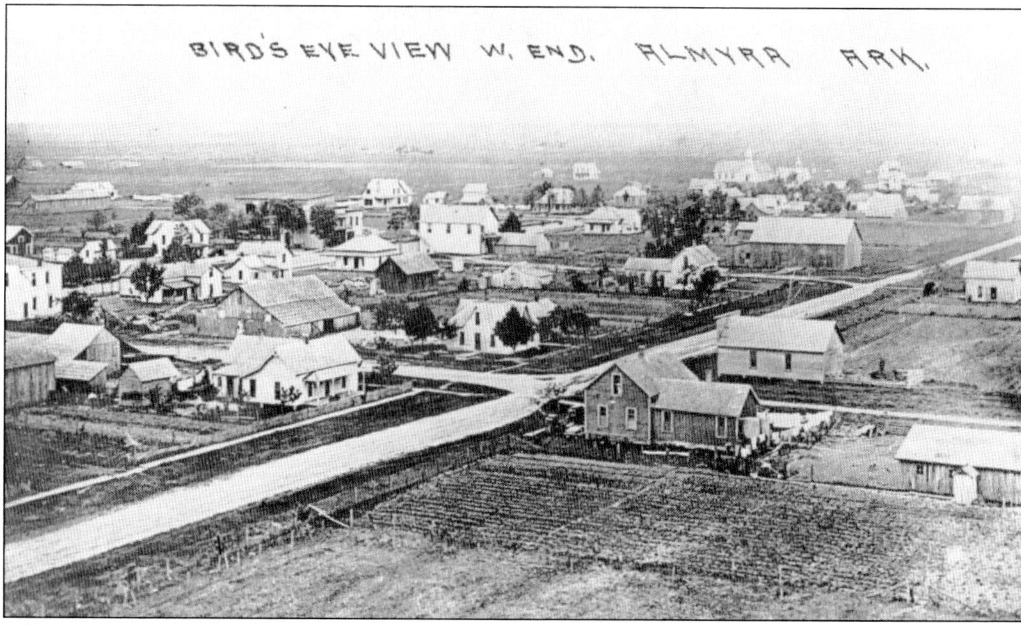

Almyra, located a dozen miles east of Stuttgart, is captured above in a 1912 bird's-eye view of the west end of town. Note the large garden beside the house on the right. The message reads, "Thought I would send you more cards in the mail so you would not get so lonesome. Hill." The thriving farm economy of the Grand Prairie region ensured that even the smallest communities had train service; the railroad came to Almyra in 1891. Mailed to a girl in Hornsby, Illinois, the c. 1909 postcard below reads, "Dear Friend Chrissie, I like this country fine. I wish you were here too. I am missing you. You folks want to eat plenty of rice next summer. Me and John going to raise plenty for you folks. We live on wild geese and ducks now. Do they still have dances? No dances here." The sender, "Fritz," clearly longed for home and sweetheart.

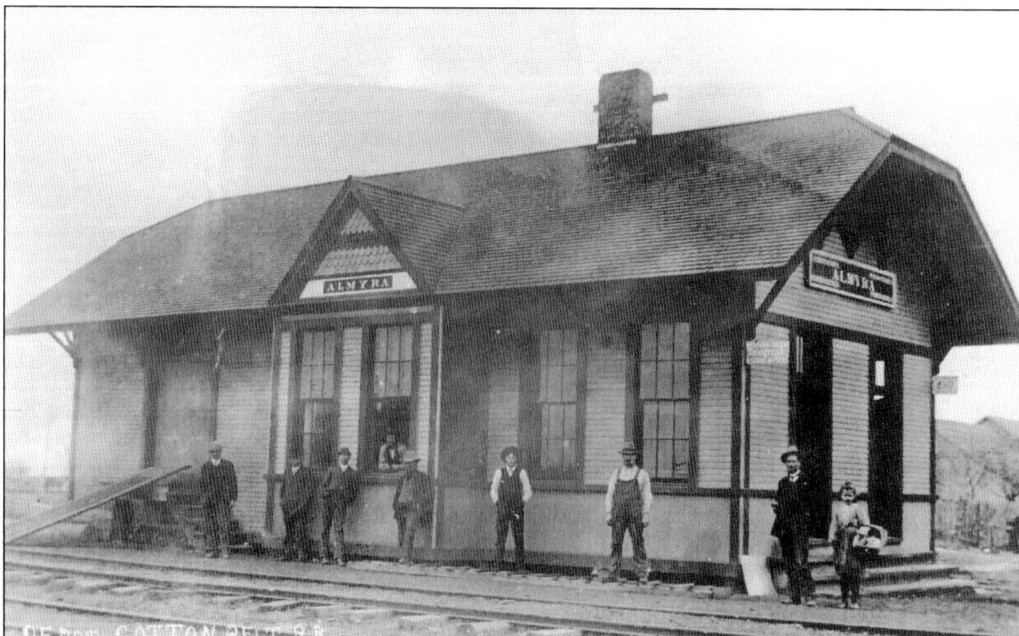

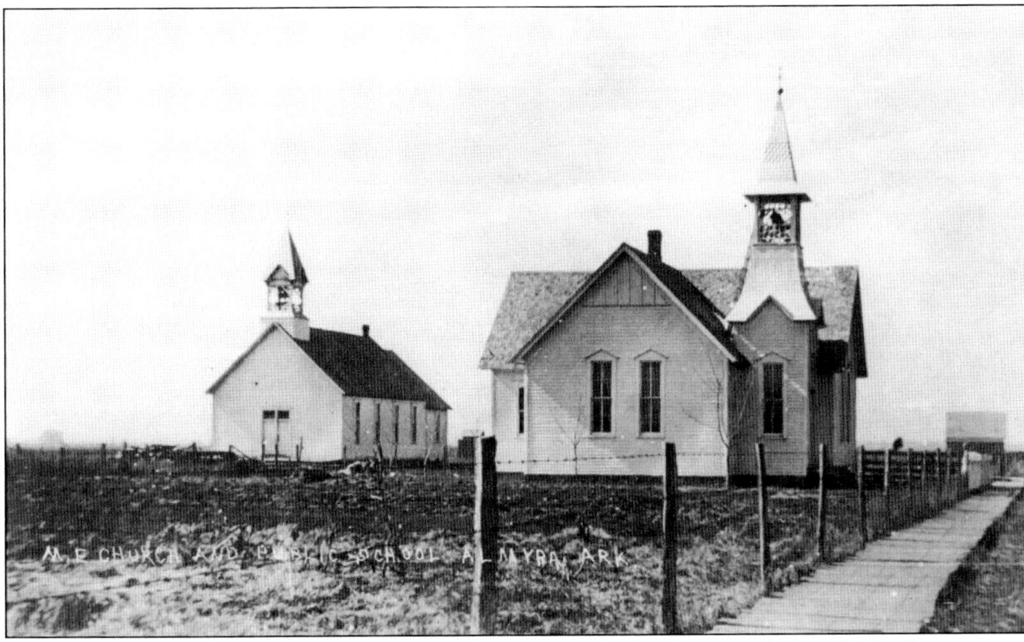

Almyra's public school building stood next to the Methodist Episcopal church; both structures had belfries. In this *c.* 1905 photograph, note the boardwalk in front of the house of worship, allowing a clean approach from wagon to church when traversing muddy roads in one's Sunday best. School and church were central to the social life of a rural farming community.

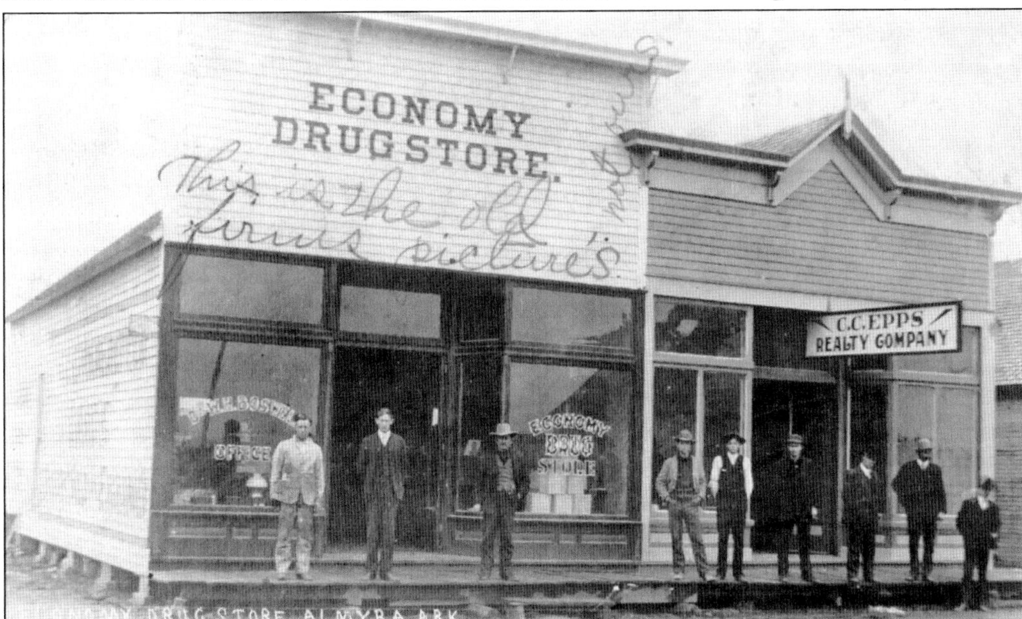

The residents of Almyra shopped at the wood-framed stores lining the dirt Main Street such as Economy Drug. This 1908 message to Indiana offers an insight into entrepreneurial initiative: "Dear Grandma, This is a picture of the drug store we bought here in Almyra. One of Benton's brothers runs it, Benton still stays in the bank, think this going to be a good business. Much love, Effie."

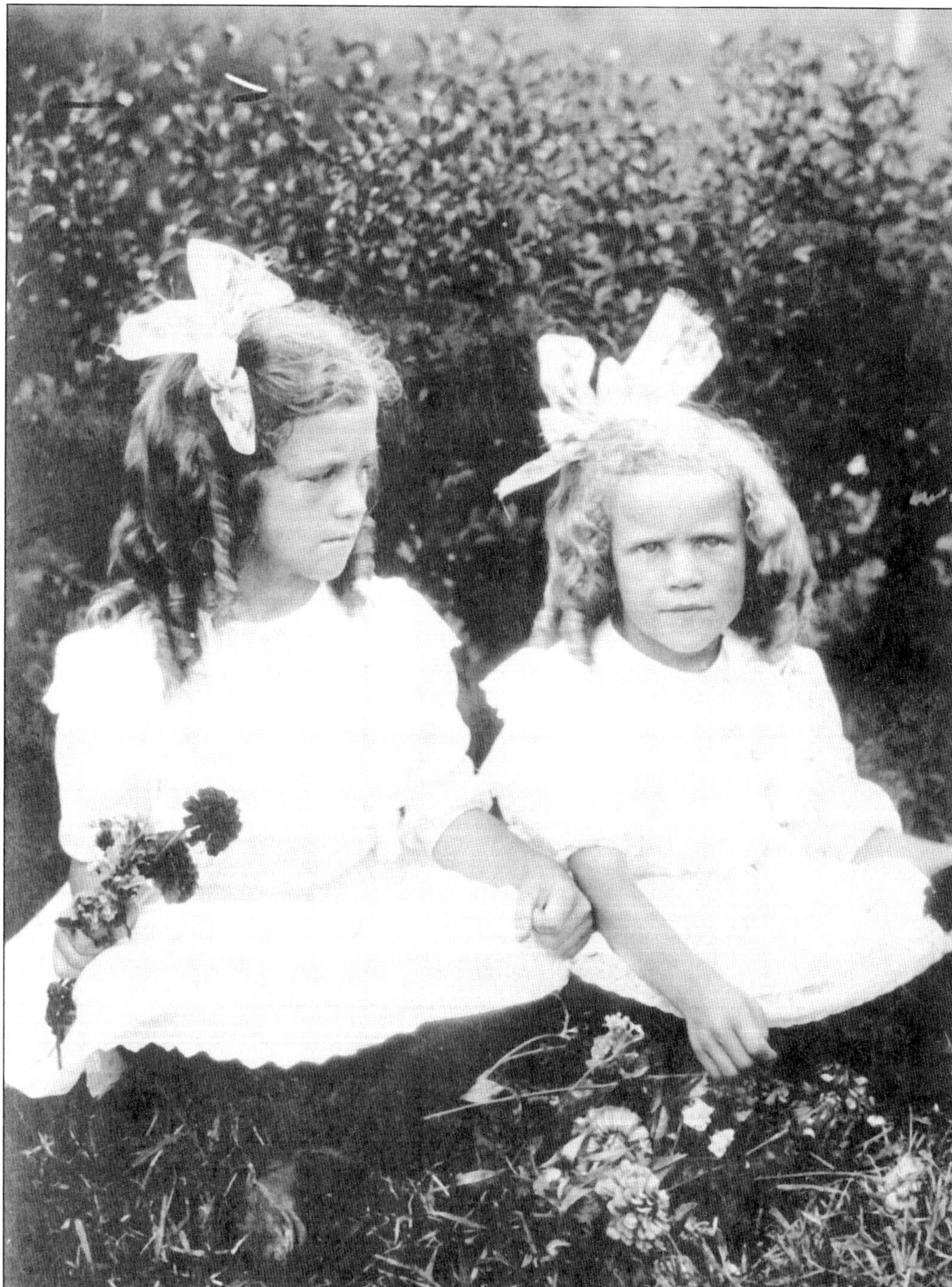

"Ruth (younger) and Naomi Moore, next door neighbors to our home in Almyra," reads this postcard. The view portrays two girls dressed in their Sunday finery after perhaps attending one of the town's churches. They clutch freshly picked flowers. A century later, we are left to wonder what the older girl was thinking as she focused her attention on her little sister rather than the photographer. The dropped flowers, clenched fist, and tense expressions may provide clues.

By 1915, Almyra had replaced the white frame schoolhouse, seen on page 81, with a red brick structure, where these young women pose with an older person, possibly their teacher. The average Arkansas schoolteacher's salary was approximately $350 per year at the time.

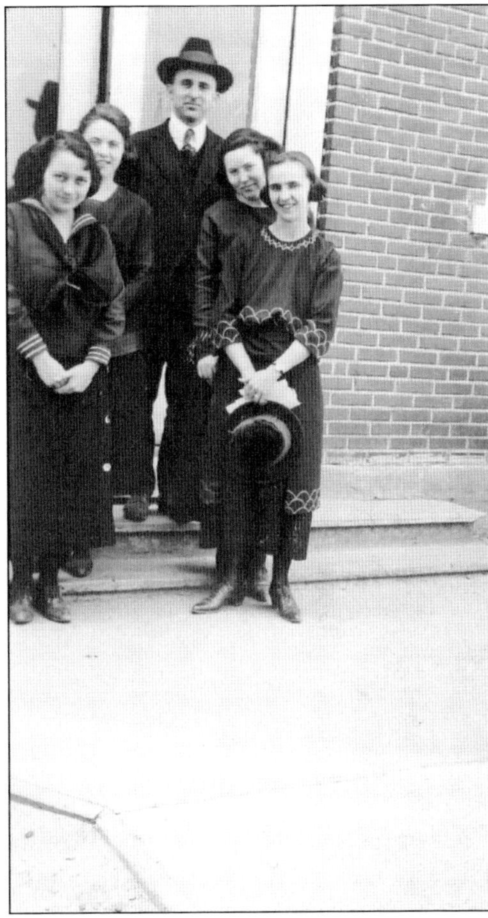

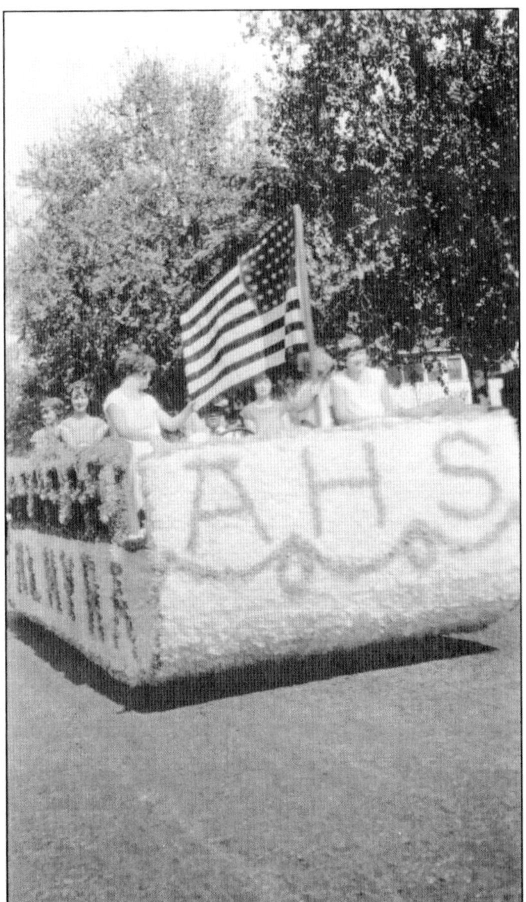

Almyra High School sent its float to Stuttgart in 1925 as a part of the Rice Carnival, an annual festival that had begun in 1909. The celebration was a yearly event through 1928.

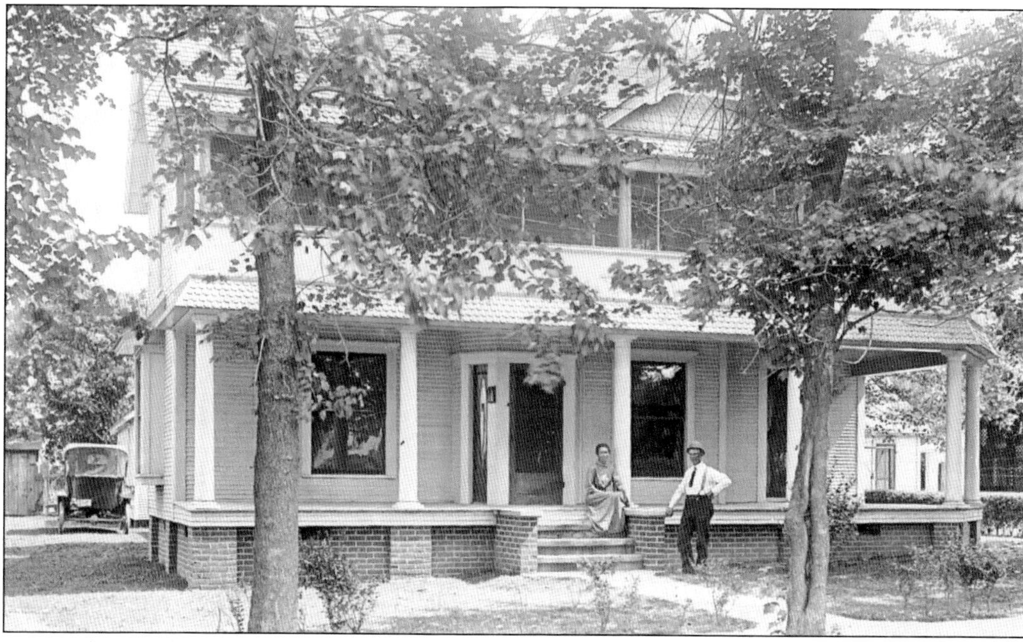

An unidentified couple poses in front of their new home, perhaps the largest in Almyra, in 1914. The screened veranda upstairs would provide a comfortable, mosquito-free spot for an afternoon rest. "Dearest Effie: I am having the time of my life—never at home as you can see. All very well. Love, Pearl."

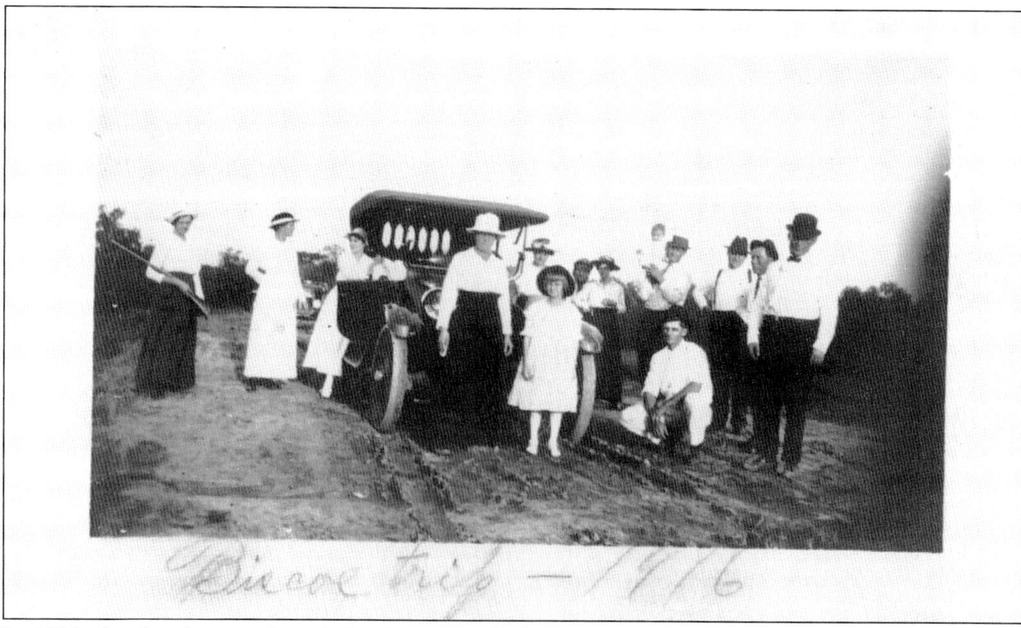

In 1916, the deeply rutted roads leading out of Almyra were often impassable after a heavy rain, but the way seemed manageable for a trip to Biscoe in the next county. "Fred is putting a self starter on the Ford today for my birthday. Is a cold spell, 16 degrees above zero this morning. Irene is at school, a show here tomorrow we want to see," read a message from "Grace" to Mrs. J. R. Chambers in Biscoe.

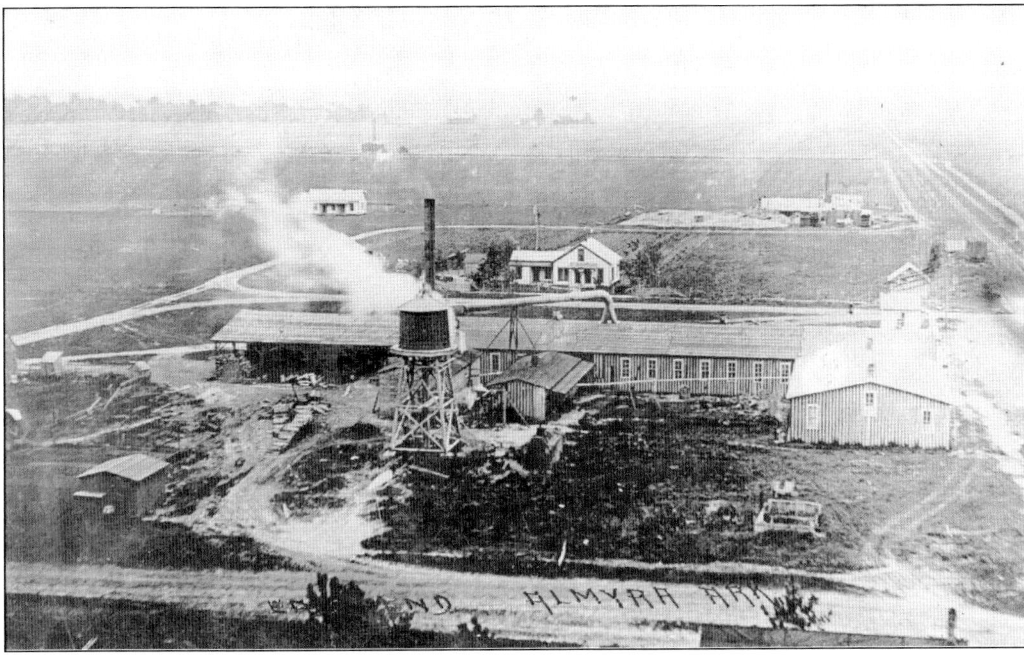

Almyra supported a thriving lumber business early in the 20th century, as virgin hardwood timber was logged in Arkansas County. The sawmill above was perhaps photographed from atop a nearby water tower. Some of the mill's output was likely sold by the Arkmo Lumber Company. In the view below, taken in 1912, two men stand in the doorway of the Almyra business while another sits in the window. The card's message reads, "Dear Friend Sarah, I like my new house first rate. I am going to school at Almyra. Like to go. Am in the second grade. Hope you are getting along in school. Write and tell me all about the girls. Nice warm day. Your Friend, Fern."

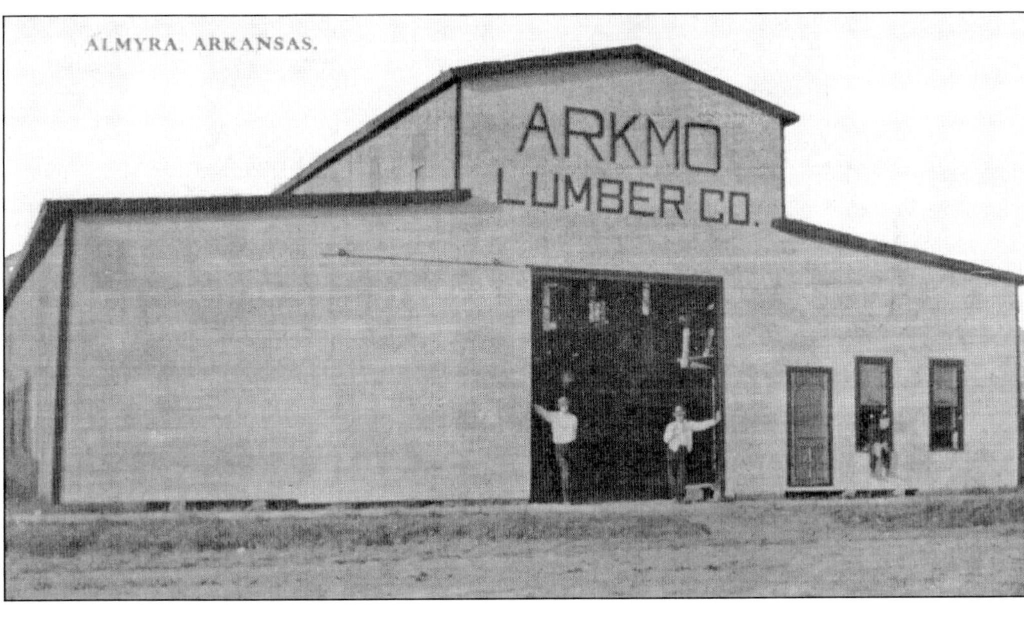

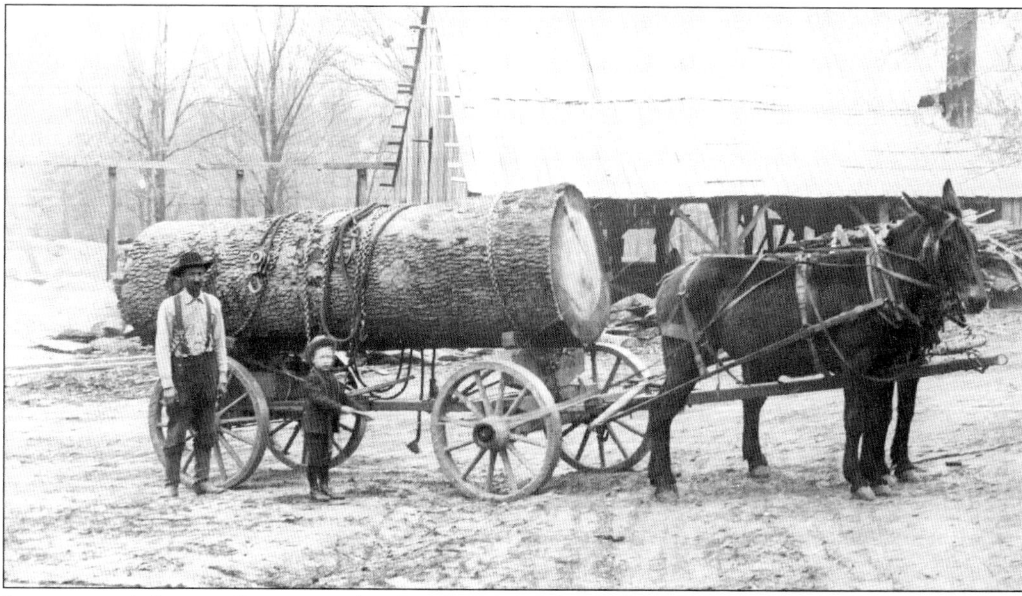

Logging in Arkansas County in the first decade of the 20th century was mostly on a small scale, with families seeking to supplement their income with a few massive logs like the one seen here at a sawmill. It took great labor by man and beast to cut this massive ancient oak log, a legacy of the primeval forests that exist only in isolated tracts today such as those in the White River Wildlife Refuge. Dayton Bowers took this photograph somewhere in the southern part of Arkansas County.

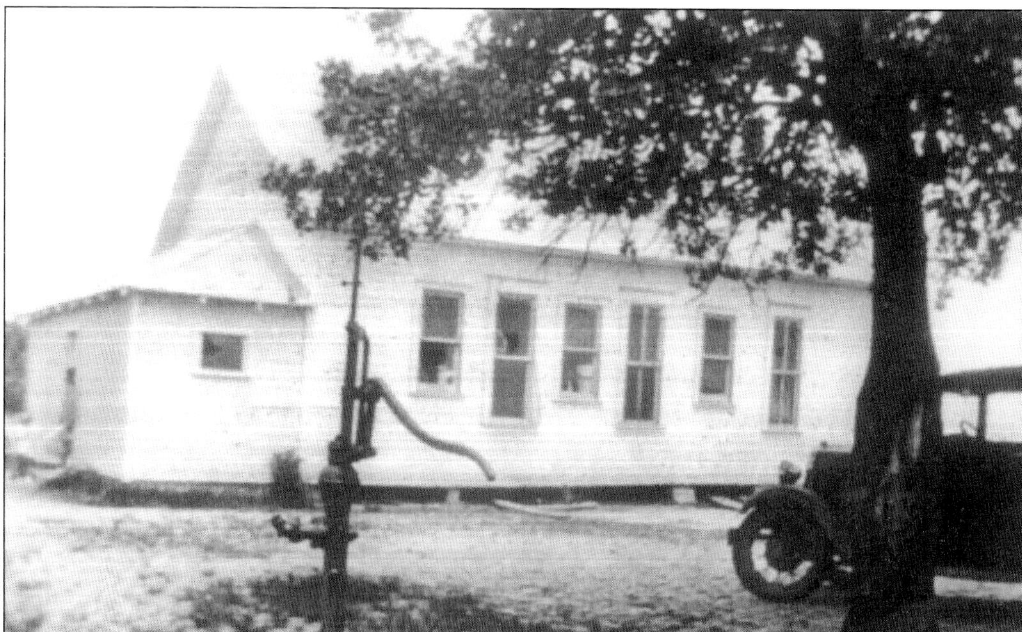

Prairie Union is a tiny community south of DeWitt on State Road 152. In 1920, the hamlet boasted this one-room schoolhouse with a pump in the yard to supply drinking water. The Model T under the tree most likely belonged to the schoolteacher, who, if earning the state average, was paid $476 for a 124-day school year. (Courtesy of the Museum of the Arkansas Grand Prairie.)

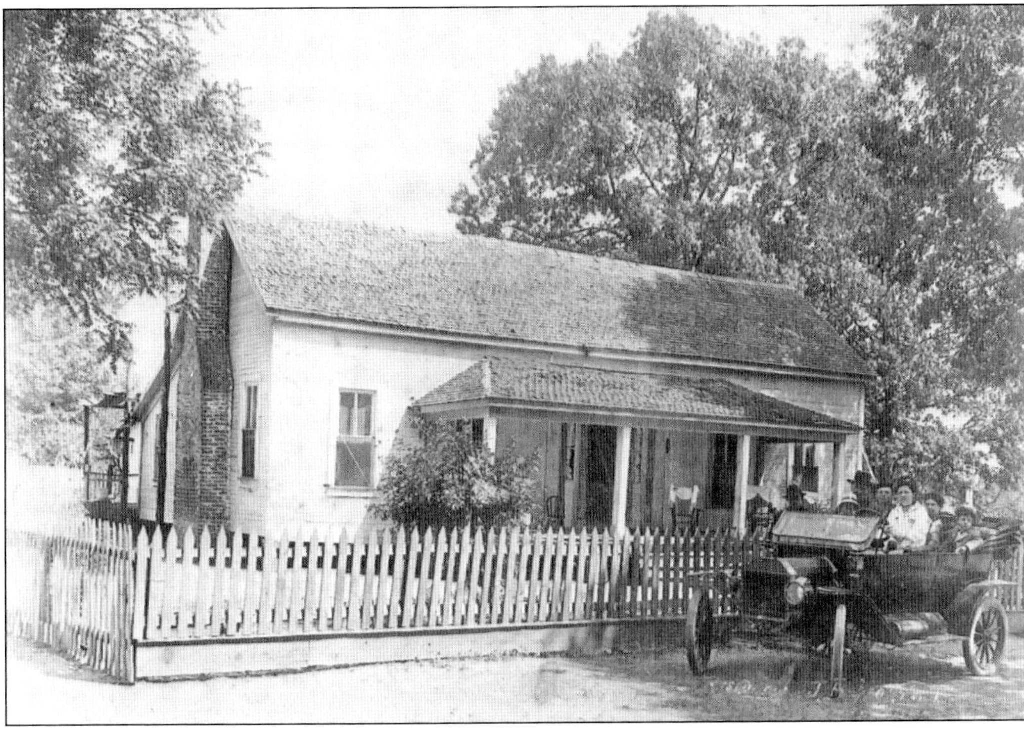

The hamlet of Ethel sits on remote State Highway 17 on the eastern edge of Arkansas County. In 1915, it was home to the John Barry Horton family, seen above parked in front of their trim home adorned by a picket fence. In the 1941 photograph below, students from Ethel's Oak Flat School pose with their teacher. The smiling teacher is Syvella Jones, who made about $592 for a 147-day school year instructing this energetic group of 20 children. (Above courtesy of Sue Noble, granddaughter of John Barry Horton.)

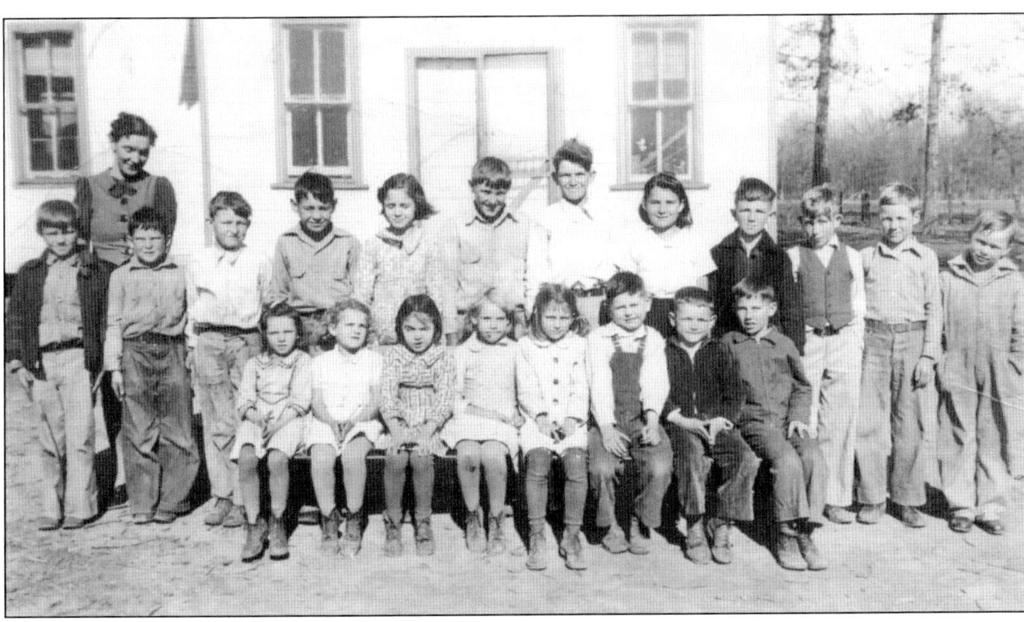

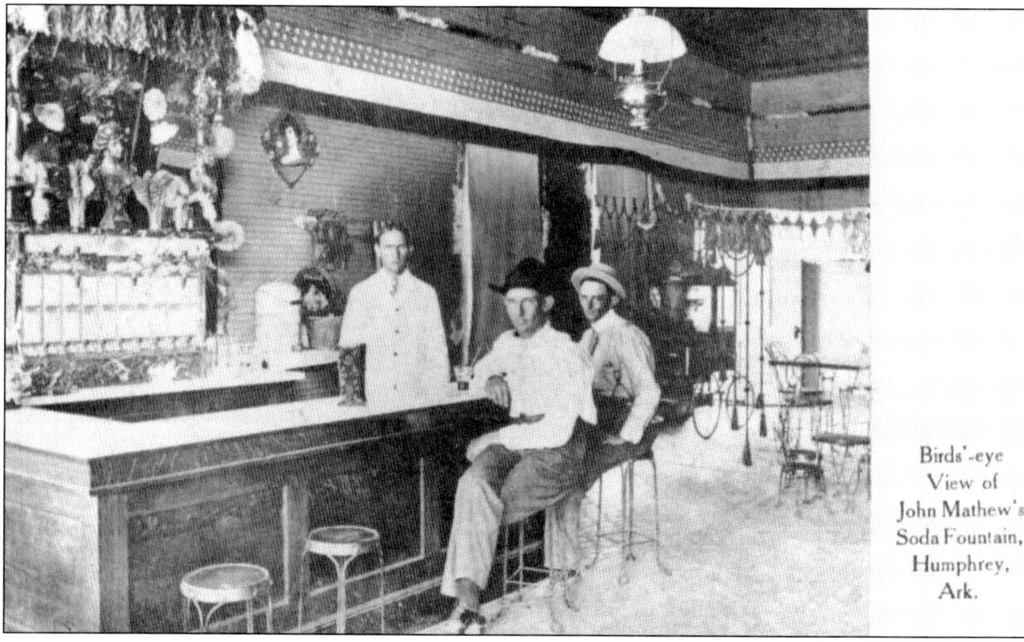

John Mathew's Soda Fountain was a popular place to satisfy one's sweet tooth in the small town of Humphrey, located on the western edge of Arkansas County. One customer wears a cowboy hat while the other sports a "straw Katie," a popular fashion trend with young men. Perhaps the man behind the marble-topped counter in the above *c.* 1910 image is owner John Mathew. Peterson's Motel and Café, located on Highway 79 just west of Humphrey, was a typical roadside "mom and pop" lodging and dining establishment. In the *c.* 1940 photograph below, the older man and woman behind the lunch counter are possibly the owners, Mr. and Mrs. Peterson. The community was named in honor of Andrew Humphrey, chief of the U.S. Army Corps of Engineers.

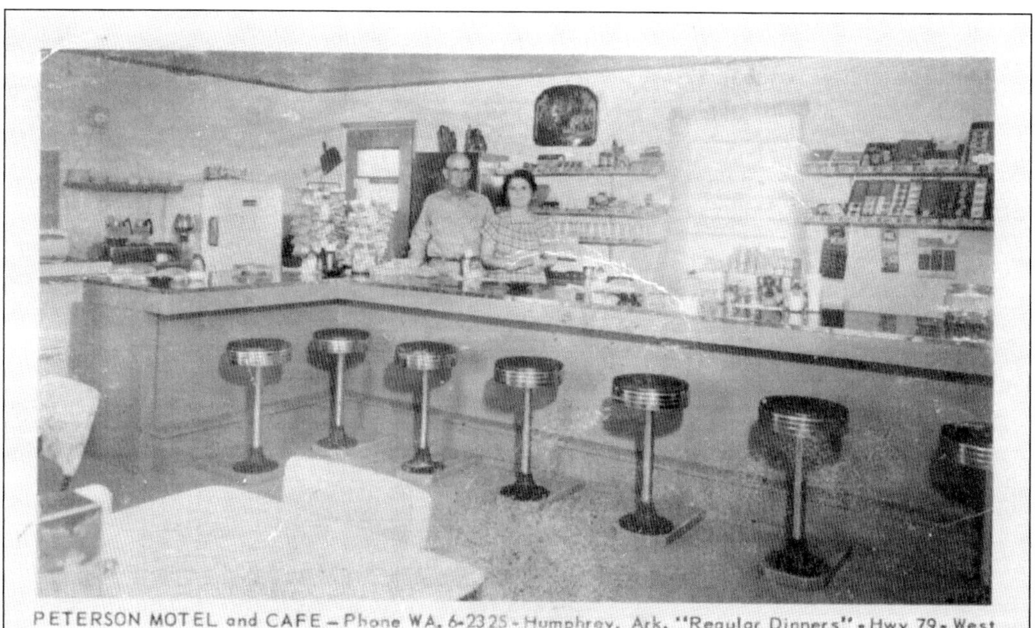

Four

The Bounty of the Grand Prairie

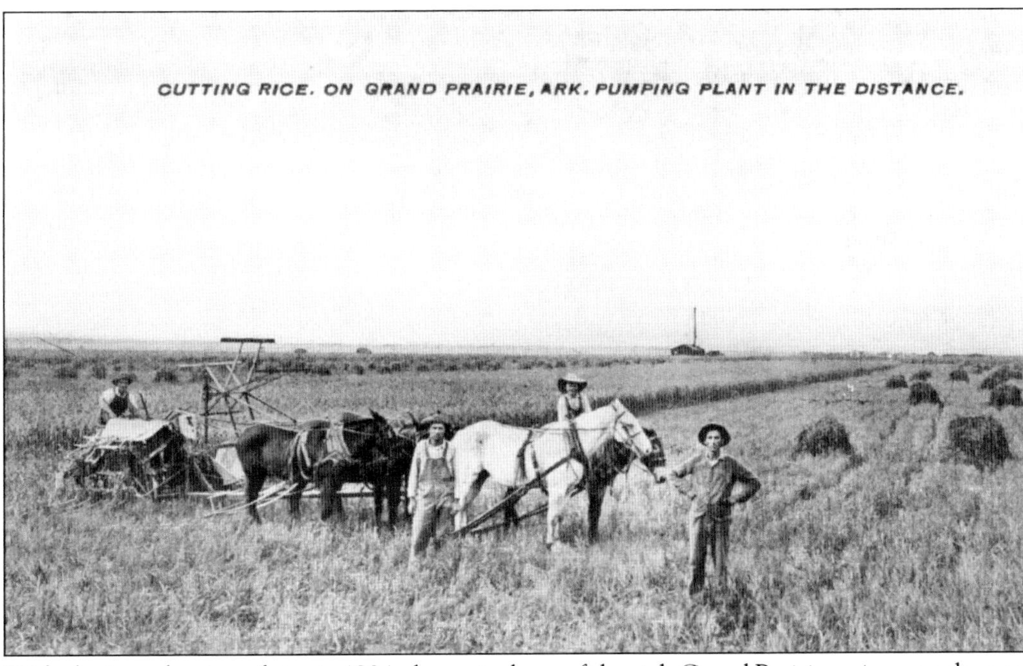

With the introduction of rice in 1904, the agriculture of the rich Grand Prairie region was changed forever. Early production relied on horse-drawn harvesting equipment and heavy manual labor. Growing rice required great quantities of water, much of which was supplied by pumping stations like the one seen here in the distance. As the 19th century rolled into the 20th, farms spread out across Arkansas County, growing not only rice but corn, hay, and a variety of livestock. Soybeans, introduced in 1925, would become the second-largest crop in the county.

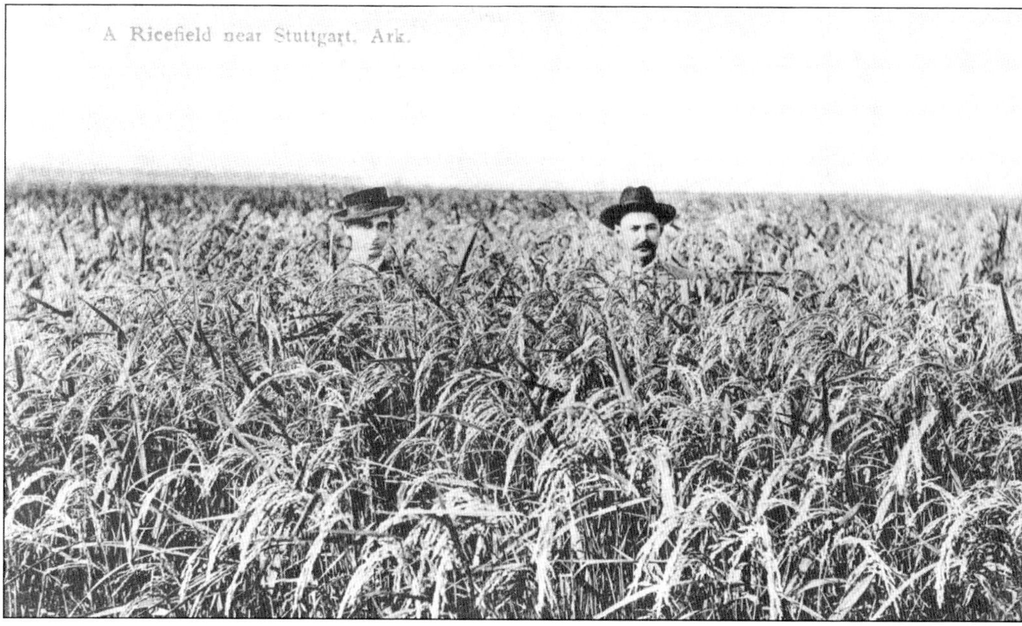

Rice had been grown for home use in Arkansas as far back as 1819, according to pioneer naturalist Thomas Nuttall. The first serious commercial attempt that succeeded was undertaken on 70 acres in Lonoke County in 1904. Soon afterward, W. E. Hope experimented on a 9-by-27-foot plot at his Arkansas County home, using water from his house well. The endeavor was a smashing success, and local farmers followed suit; by 1909, the crop was being showcased on postcards. Above, two men pose neck deep in a rice field ripe for harvest, while below a child is seen "Comin' Thro the Rice" around 1910. In the early days, rice buyers went to the fields, evaluated the crop, and gave farmers a price. The price varied greatly—from $1.40 per bushel in 1905 to a high of $3.50 in the aftermath of World War I. By 1924, the price had fallen to $1.59, and in 1930, with the coming of the Great Depression, it dropped to 90¢ per bushel.

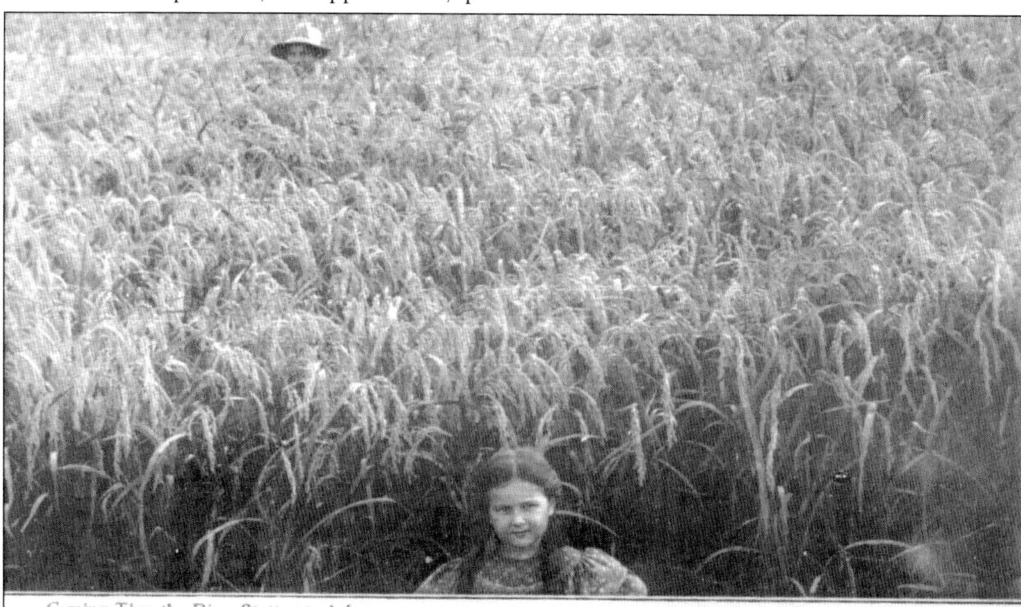

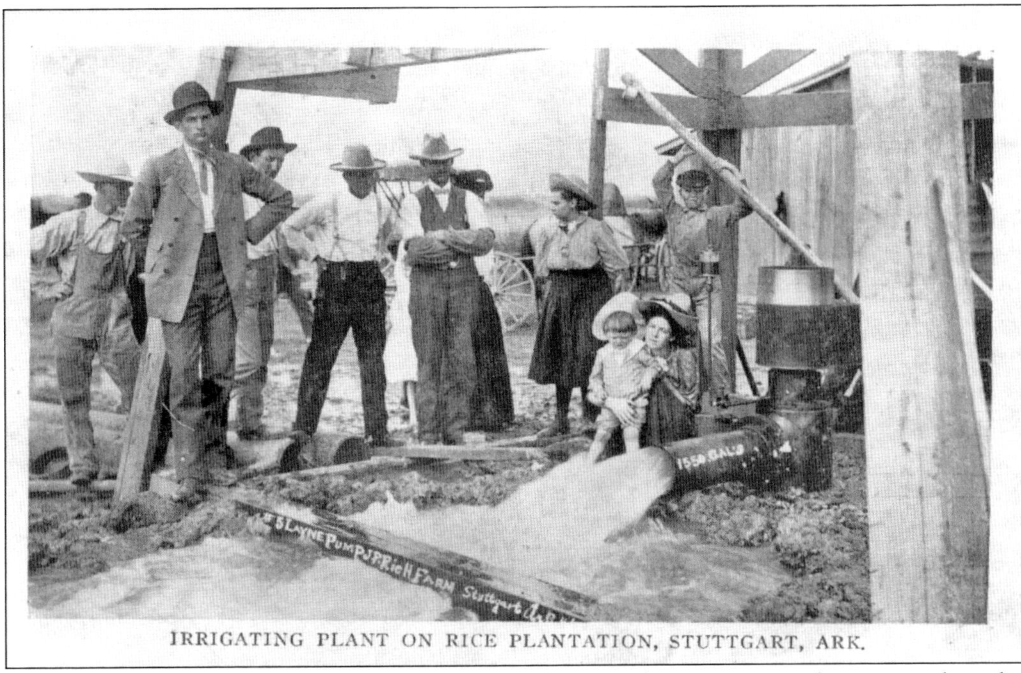

Above, a well taps into the region's abundant underground water as a mother tries to keep her young son from getting his Sunday clothes wet and muddy in 1908. "I am going to rice plant now and then I am going to take a drive out on the prairie," states the postcard's message. As early as 1905, technology allowed wells reaching 90 feet below the earth to bring up the water that made rice such a huge success across the Grand Prairie. Below, the opportunity to go wading in the knee-deep irrigation water of a rice field brings smiles to the faces of four youngsters around 1915. (Courtesy of the Museum of the Arkansas Grand Prairie.)

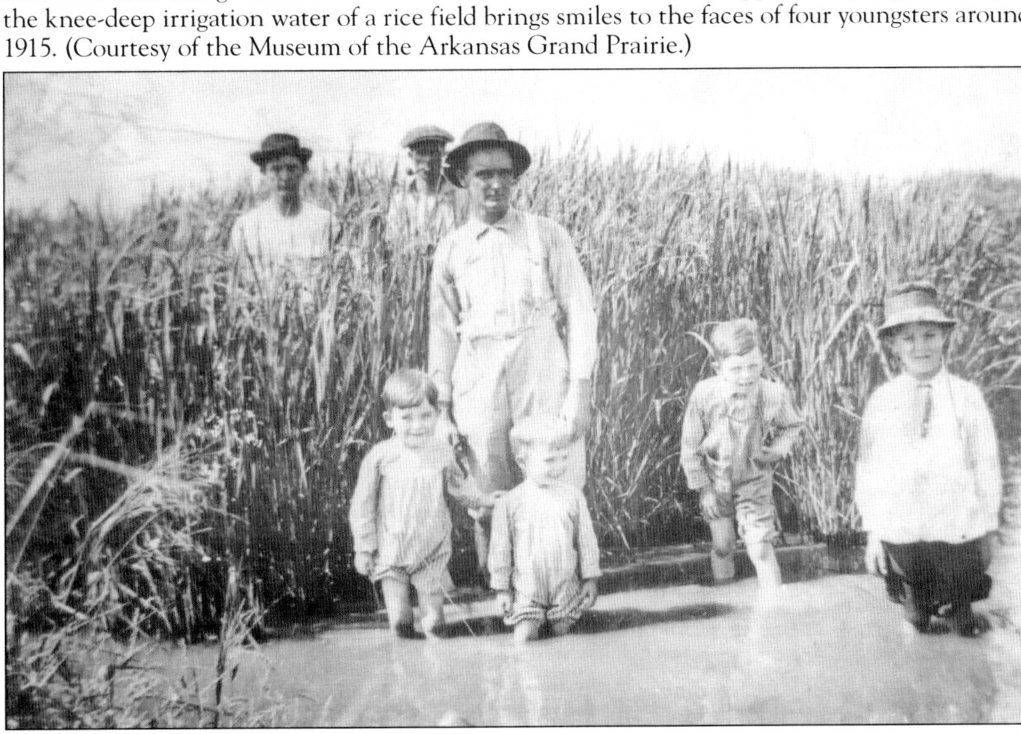

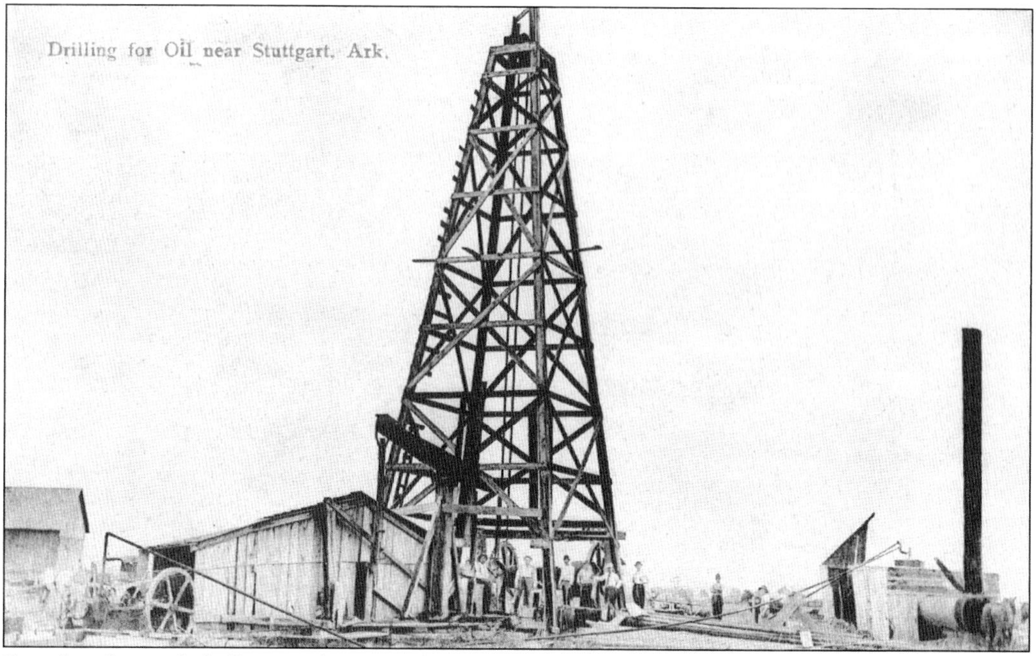

For a brief period, drillers on the Grand Prairie had dreams of striking oil, but the gushers never produced anything but water. This card's 1909 message, penned by young Morris Burns, reads, "I am in fine shape, gained 16 1/2 pounds. I find Stuttgart and community is primarily filled up with the most sociable and polite people I ever dreamed of." He also speaks of his new "rig": "It's going to skin everything around here, and I've sure got a 'cutter' of a girl to ride in it." Praising the area, Burns invites his friend to come to Arkansas: "I would sure show you some fine people, good farms, large tracts of unbroken prairie, and endless forest."

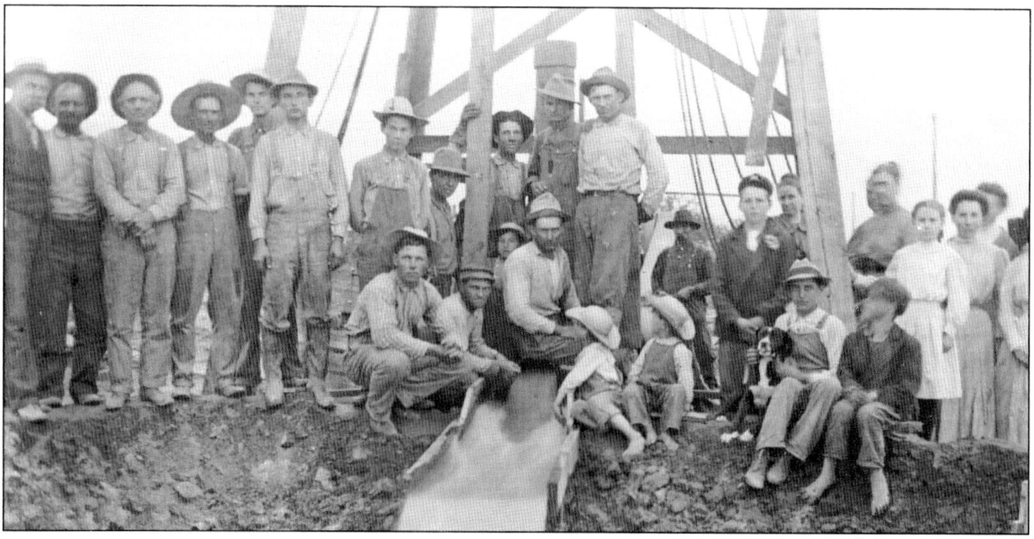

Adapting drilling technology from the oil industry, like this wooden derrick in 1910, enabled early Grand Prairie rice farmers to drill deeper wells to irrigate their crops. These workers, joined by family and friends, pose to commemorate their successful quest for liquid gold. According to the Museum of the Arkansas Grand Prairie, it takes 65 million gallons of water to raise 100 acres of rice, necessitating conservation measures in recent years.

The expanding fields of rice demanded better technology to reach the millions of gallons of water needed, and local inventor J. E. Shutt of Stuttgart rose to the challenge. Working first with wooden and later with the iron pumps shown here, Shutt and his son Howard obtained a number of patents, manufacturing their pumps in Texas and Oklahoma for the Arkansas rice crop but also for other uses in the nation's farm belt. (Courtesy of the Museum of the Arkansas Grand Prairie.)

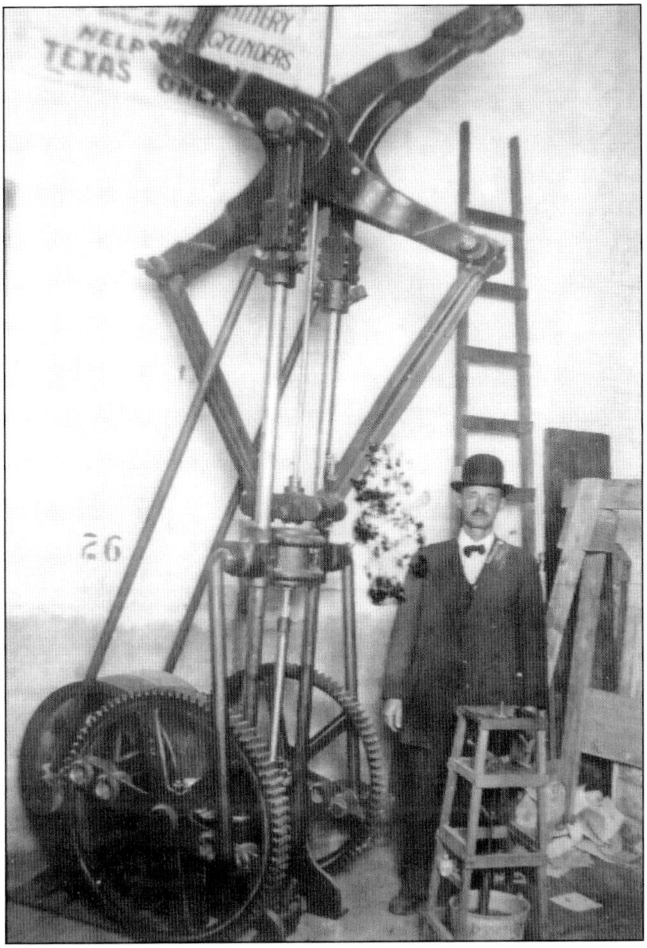

In the early years of rice production, the equipment was primarily drawn by mules. These plows, displayed in Stuttgart by the H. E. Rhodes and Sons Company, were needed to prepare the fields for planting. (Courtesy of the Museum of the Arkansas Grand Prairie.)

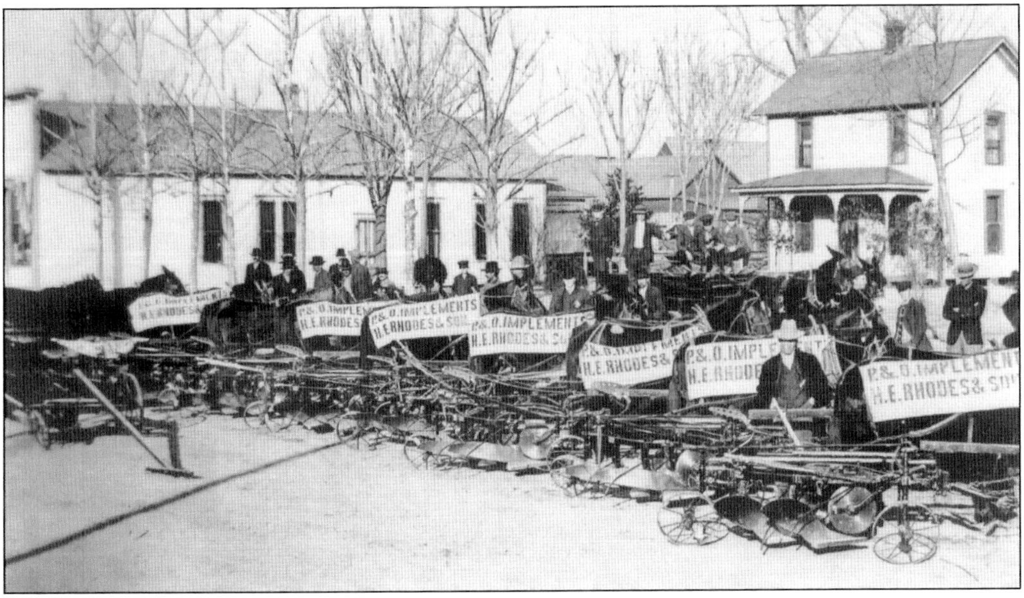

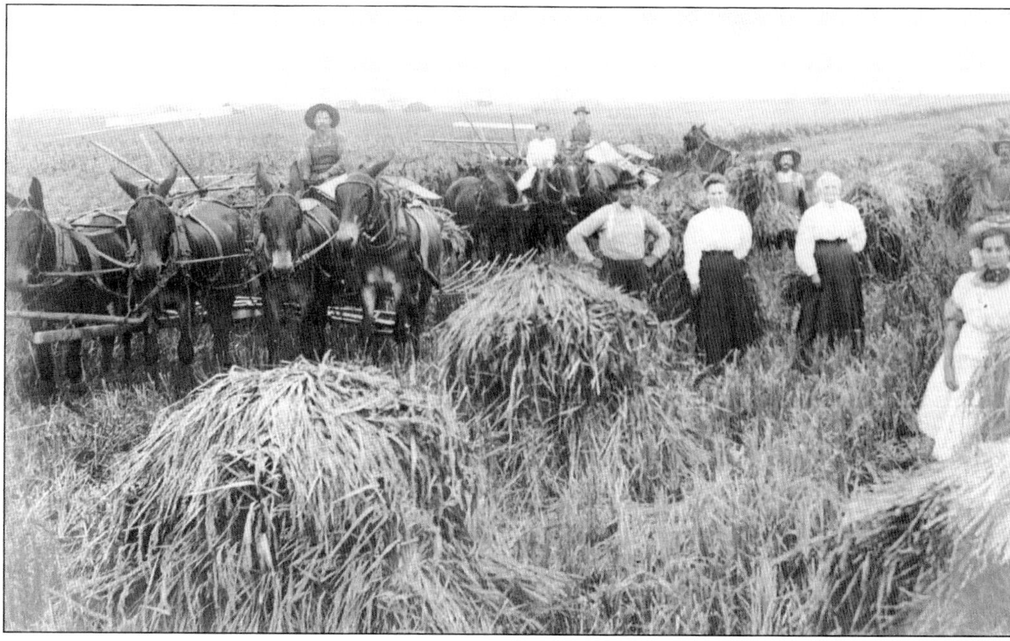

Rice was harvested by machines that cut the crop into bundles and dropped it on the ground. Field hands then stacked it in shocks to dry. In the photograph above, the women posing near the shocks most likely did not share in the stacking duties. Field hands, seen below taking a break from their labors, "mug" for the camera amid shocks of rice drying in the sun. The work was hard, the hours were long. The owners of the farm are possibly riding in the horse and buggy below. (Courtesy of the Museum of the Arkansas Grand Prairie.)

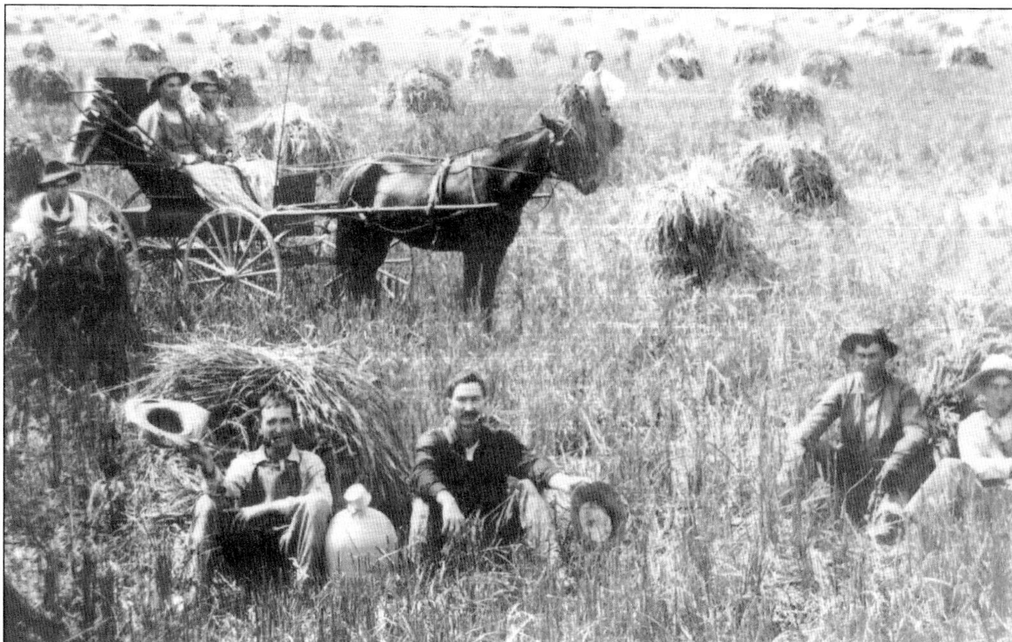

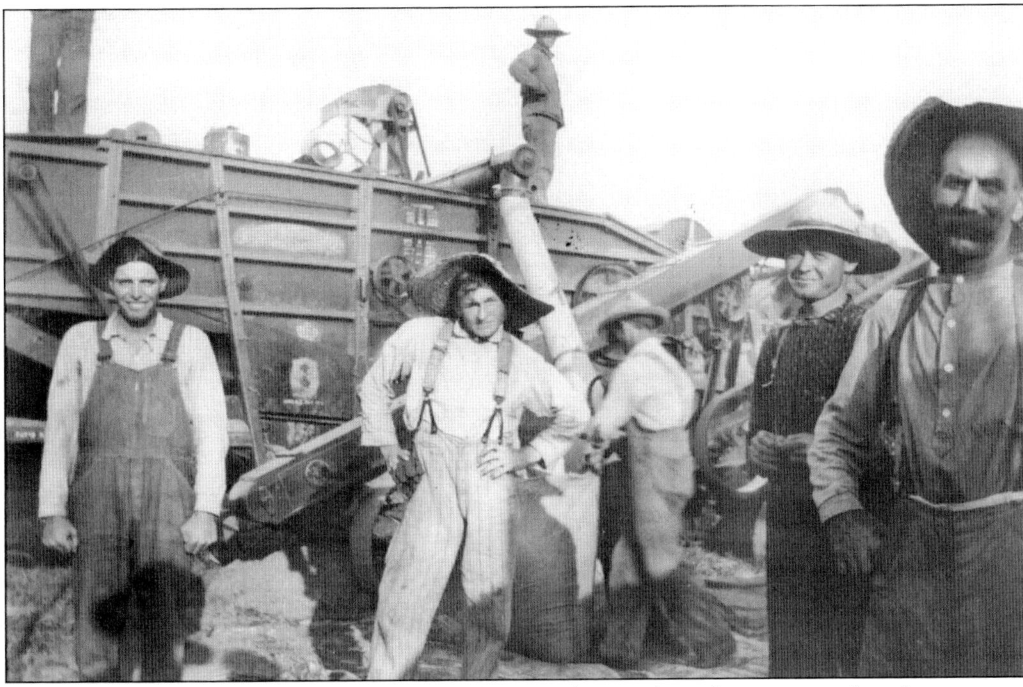

After drying for about 10 to 20 days, depending on the weather, the rice was placed in a steam-powered thresher, like the one above, that separated the stalk from the rice. In the early years of production, the small sizes of most farms—coupled with the expense of a threshing machine—put ownership of such equipment out of reach. Groups of farmers often shared a threshing machine or relied on traveling machines owned by someone specializing in that aspect of the business.

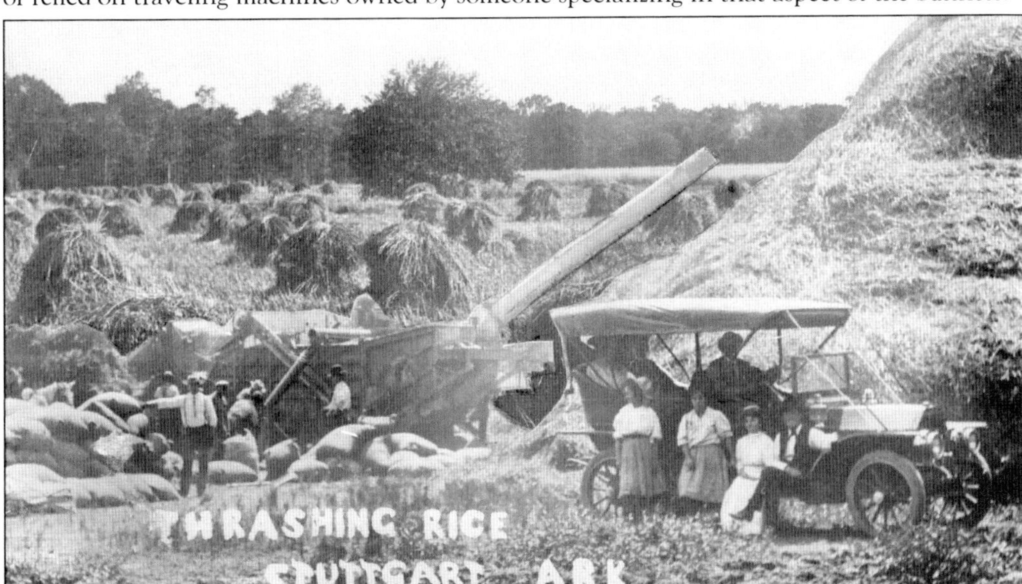

During the threshing process, workers caught the rice in burlap bags as it came out of a funnel. When the bags were full, large needles and twine were used to sew them shut. The bags were then loaded into wagons for transport to the processing mills. A group of women, three of them seated on the Model T's running board, traveled to a rice field to watch the process about 1912.

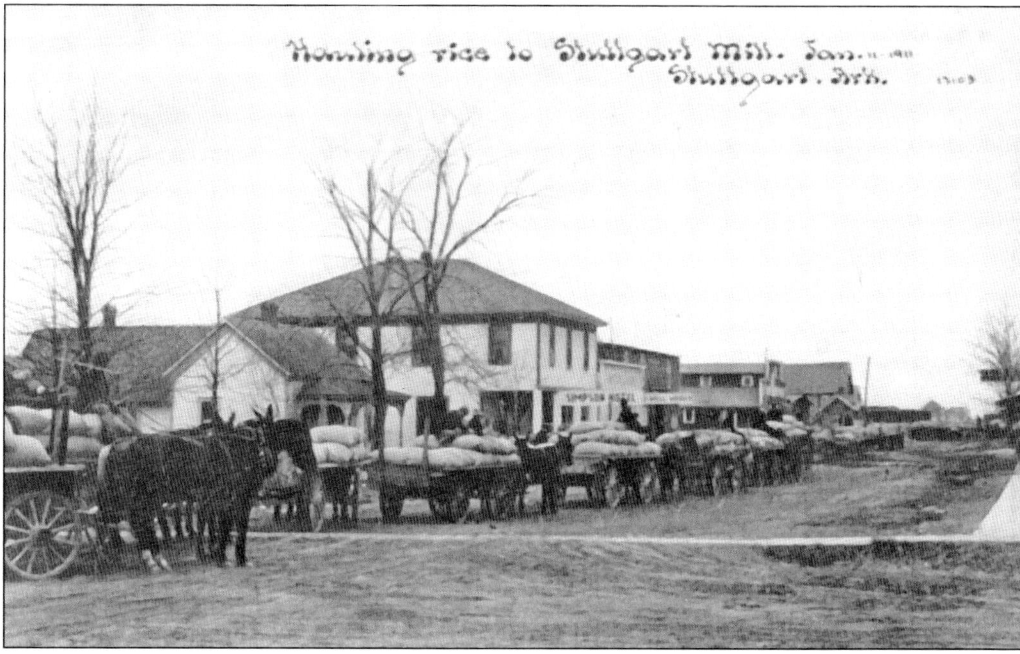

Even in the early days, the lines at the rice mills were long, as seen on both of these postcards. After the rice was bagged, the sacks were loaded 25 to a wagon—twice that many if two mule teams were used—and hauled to the processing mill. The mill's job was to take the hulls off the rice, separate the perfect kernels from the less than perfect while saving some brown rice for packaging, and then take several layers of bran off the rest to make polished rice. The rice was then re-sacked and shipped to market. The photograph above was taken around 1909. Penciled on the 1911 postcard below is the following: "It sure is a sight to see the rice fields around here. We come down to look after Father's Plantation."

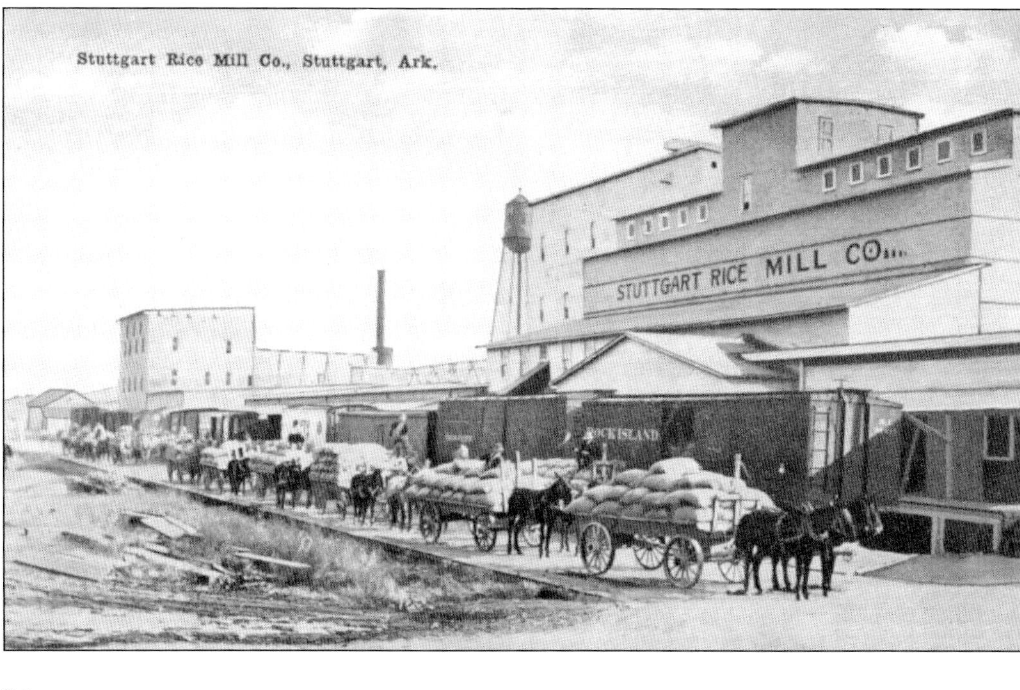

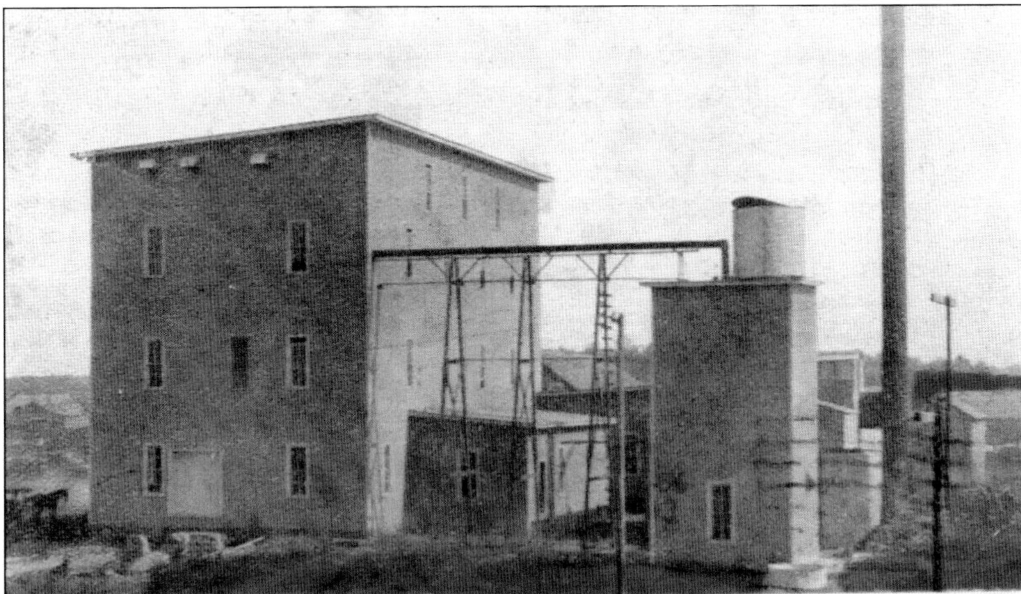

B222F9 First Rice Mill in the State, Stuttgart, Ark.

The state's first rice mill, pictured above around 1908, was established at Stuttgart in 1907 by a group of the community's leading farmers and businessmen led by William M. Price. Their vision helped make the town the Rice Capital of the World, as merchants, lawyers, and other professionals flocked to the Grand Prairie to profit from supporting the farmers. The view below shows the Stuttgart rice mill about 10 years later, greatly expanded from its earlier dimensions.

Stuttgart Rice Mill Co., Stuttgart, Ark.

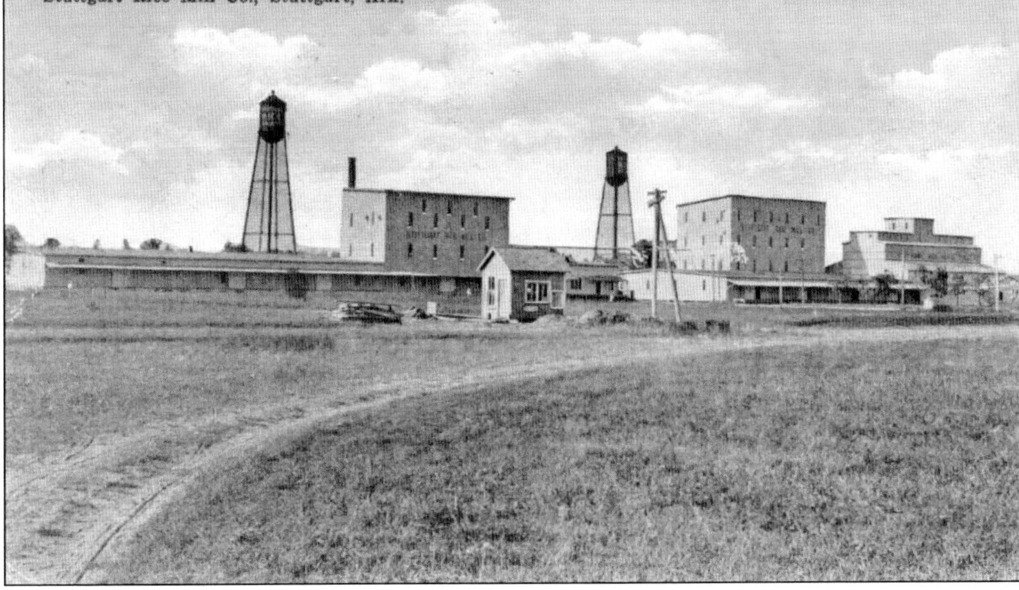

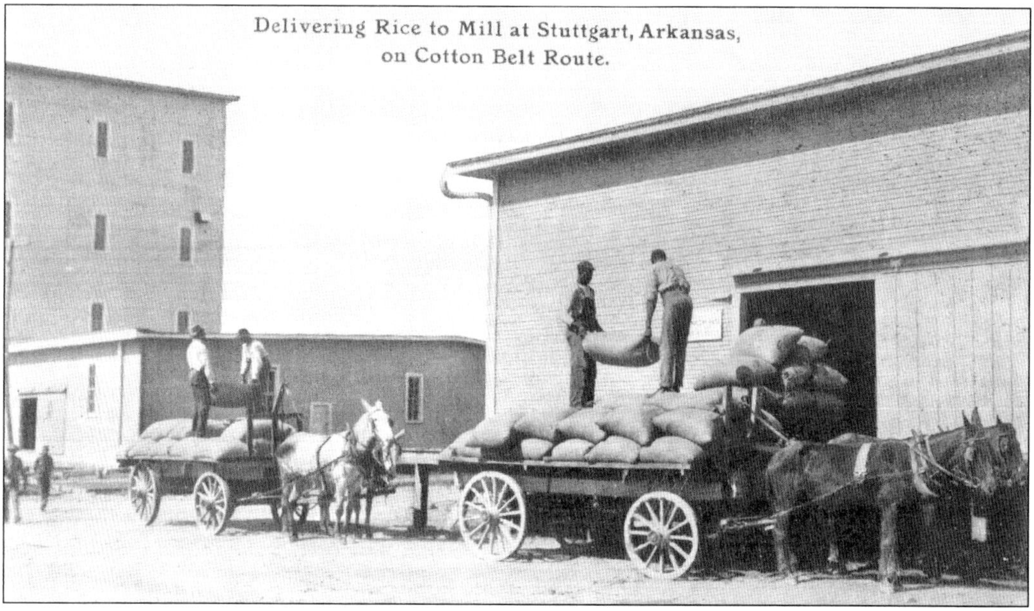

Workers unload sacks of rice at a Stuttgart processing mill in 1913. Each burlap bag (commonly called a tow sack) was designed to hold 180 pounds or four bushels of rice. Field hands, however, would often cram as much as 200 pounds in them. By 1916, the cumbersome bags were being phased out in favor of storing rice in bulk until it was processed. This card was mailed to Glen Brothers, a farm equipment supply house in Rochester, New York, bearing the message, "Gentleman, Kindly forward me your 1913 catalogue and planting guide. Yours truly, A. O. Watson, St. Louis, Mo."

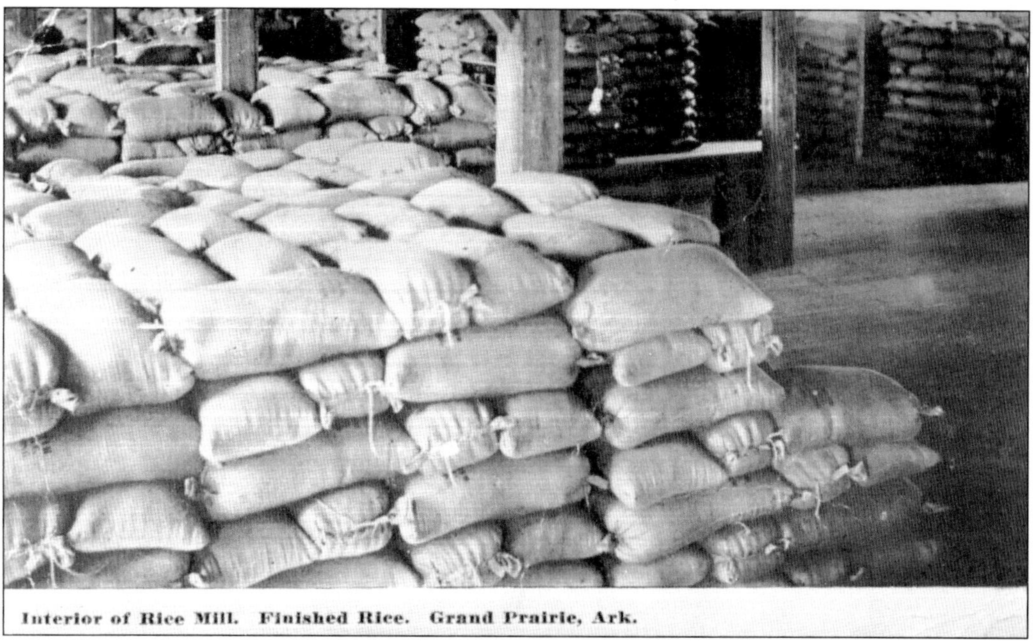

After processing at the mill, the rice was loaded into sacks that were sewn shut with twine. The bags were stacked, as seen here, awaiting shipment by rail to often distant markets. Without today's modern forklift equipment, these sacks of processed rice had to be re-stacked multiple times by hand before reaching their final destination.

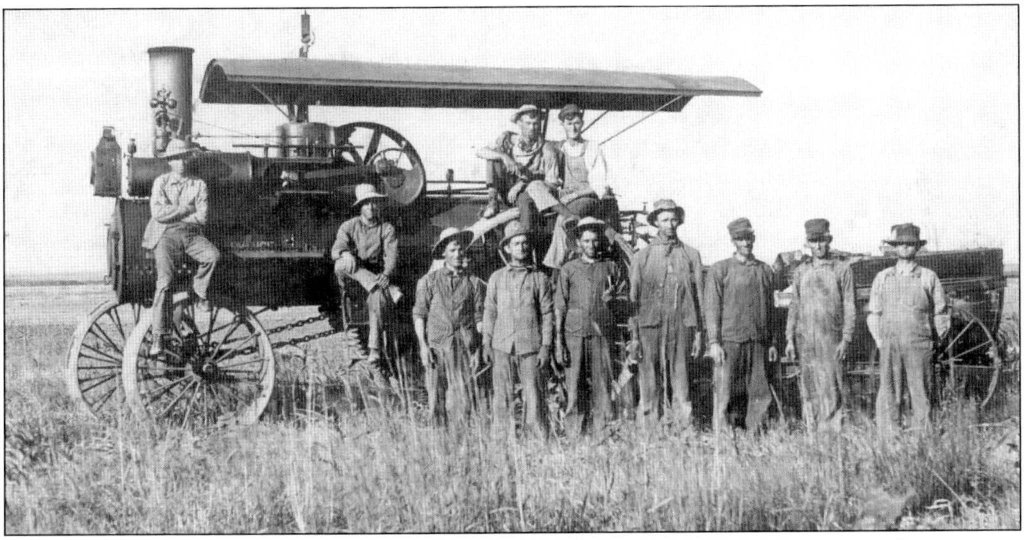

Rapid increases in the use of advancing technology helped spread the footprint of rice across Arkansas County upon what had been virgin prairie only a few years earlier. Seen above in 1909, near the tiny hamlet of Rule, is a Case steam traction engine, first sold in Arkansas County in 1906. The engine could pull all manner of equipment through the often muddy ground. A fully restored Case steam traction engine sits on the grounds of the Museum of the Grand Prairie, admired below by nine-year-old Joey Hanley of Little Rock. The great machine weighed 25,000 pounds and could cover as much ground as 18 men working with 54 horses. Its boilers were fueled by coal and 70 barrels of water a day; it could complete its daily field course of 15 to 20 miles at 2.5 miles per hour. Another of the great iron machines, restored and on display inside the museum, is equipped to allow children to climb aboard for a farmer's view from behind the steering wheel.

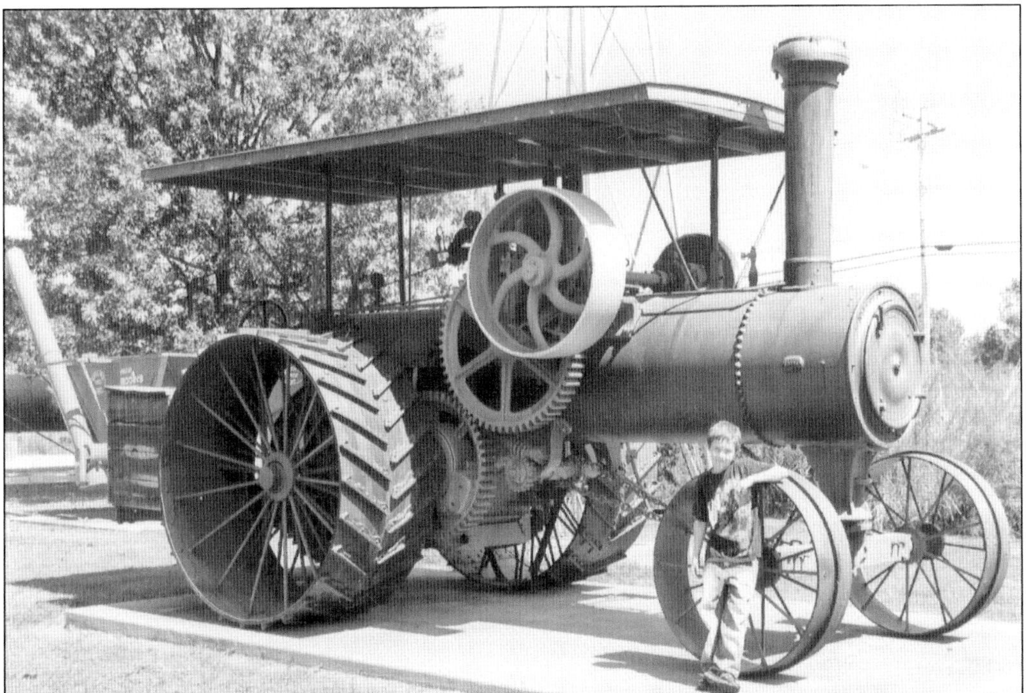

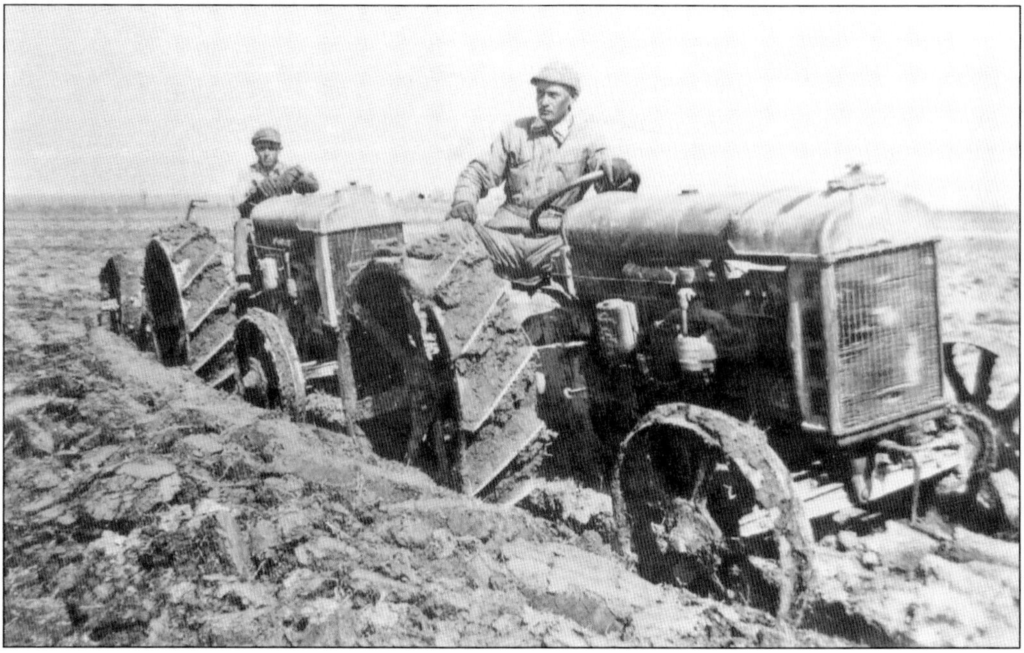

The Carlson Take Off tractor was invented by Stuttgart rice farmer George Carlson, who along with his brother formed the Carlson Tractor Power Company for the purpose of manufacturing and selling the machines seen above. The first models were built at the Pine Bluff Iron Works in 1922 and were later produced in Little Rock. The powerful, more dependable machines further expanded rice production on the Grand Prairie. Pictured below around 1915, a huge Case steam engine pulls a wide disk plow, preparing the prairie soil for the planting of rice. The machine easily handled a task that was reserved for horse-drawn equipment less than a decade earlier. (Courtesy of the Museum of the Arkansas Grand Prairie.)

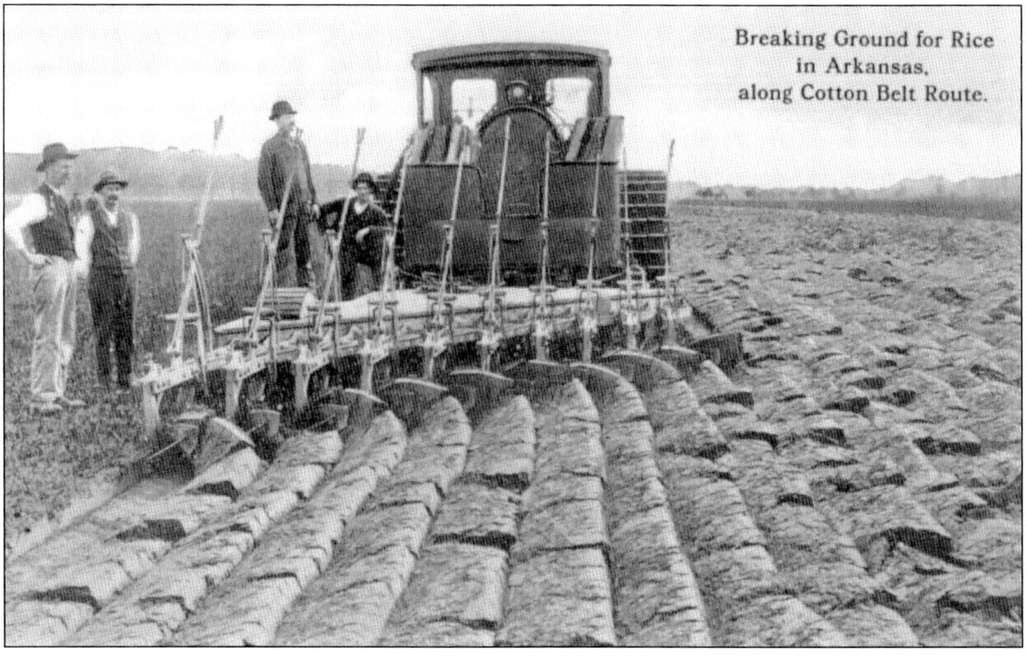

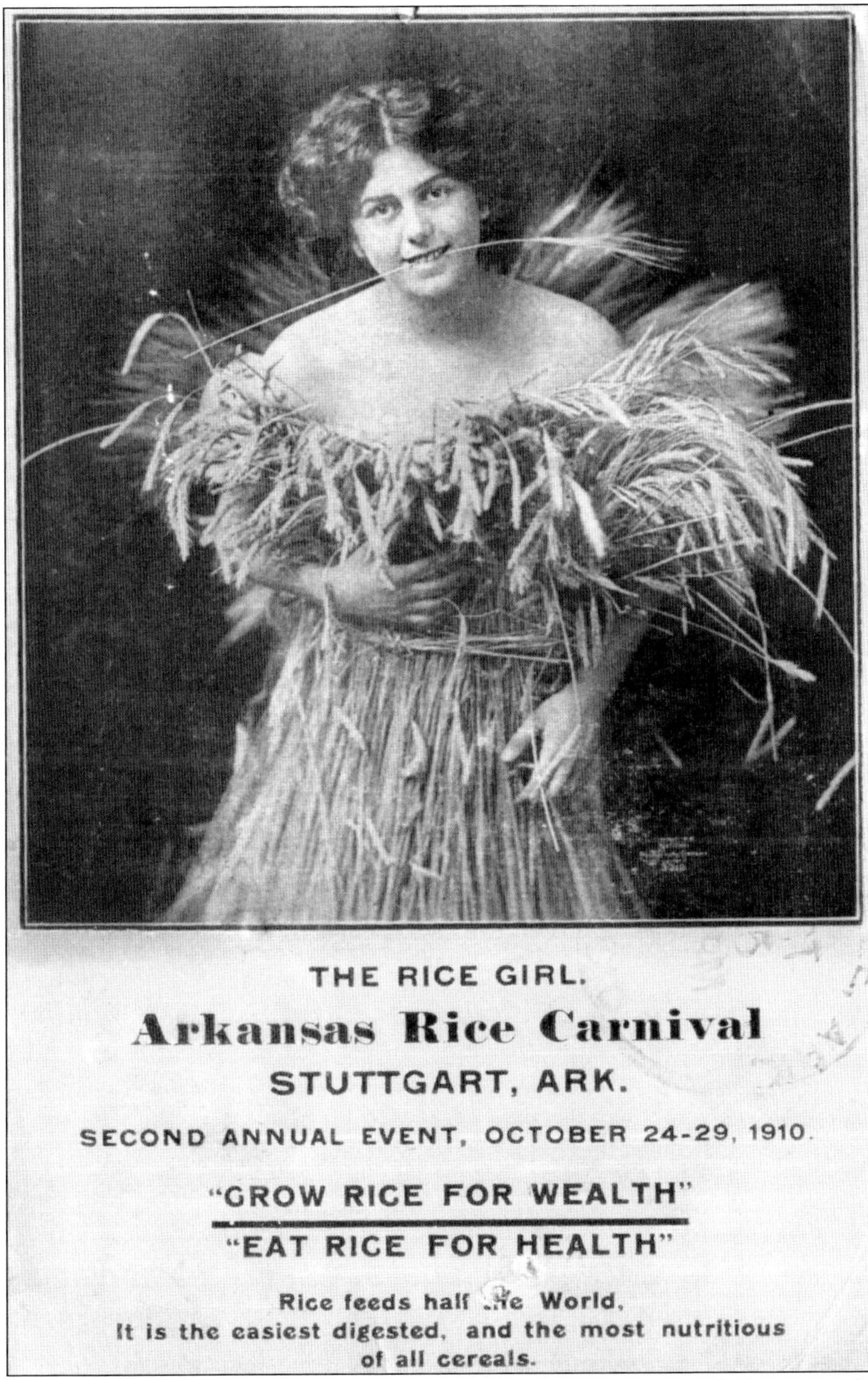

The Arkansas Rice Carnival was initiated as an annual event in 1909, only five years after the commercial growing of rice put Stuttgart on the map. The Rice Girl was featured in the second year of the carnival, clad in a shock of rice.

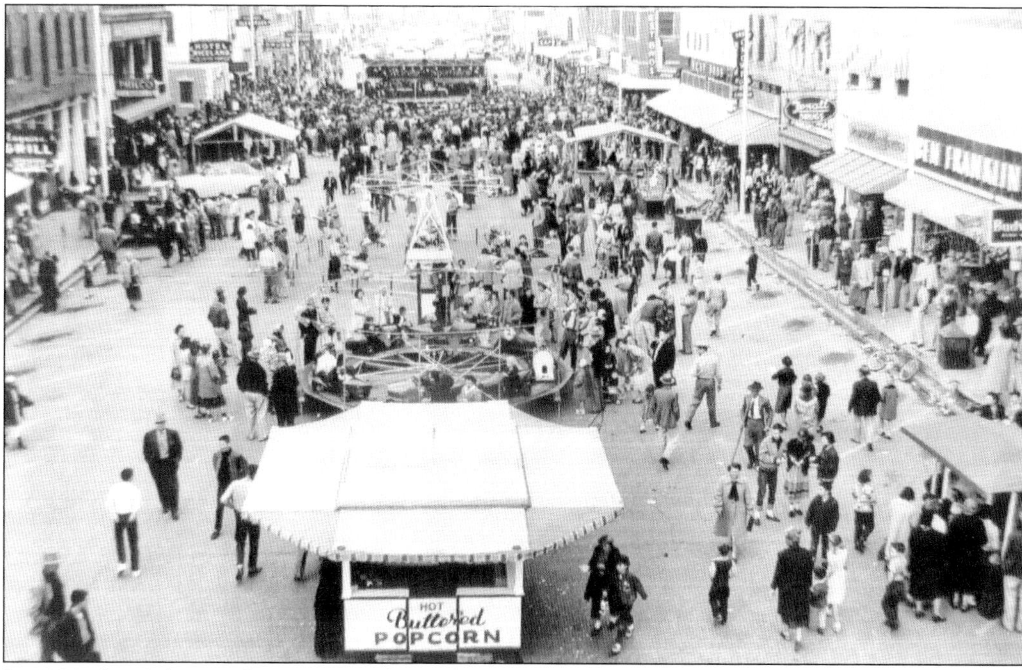

In 1929, the Arkansas Rice Carnival was discontinued because of the Great Depression but was started again by around 1940. Downtown Stuttgart was closed to traffic to make way for carnival rides and food booths. Visible along the thriving Main Street corridor are the Esquire Grill, a Philco appliance dealership, and the Hotel Riceland on the left, while on the right are a Ben Franklin store, Rexall Drugs, and a West Brothers department store. In recent years, the Rice Carnival has been halted in favor of the Wings over the Prairie festival held each Thanksgiving weekend.

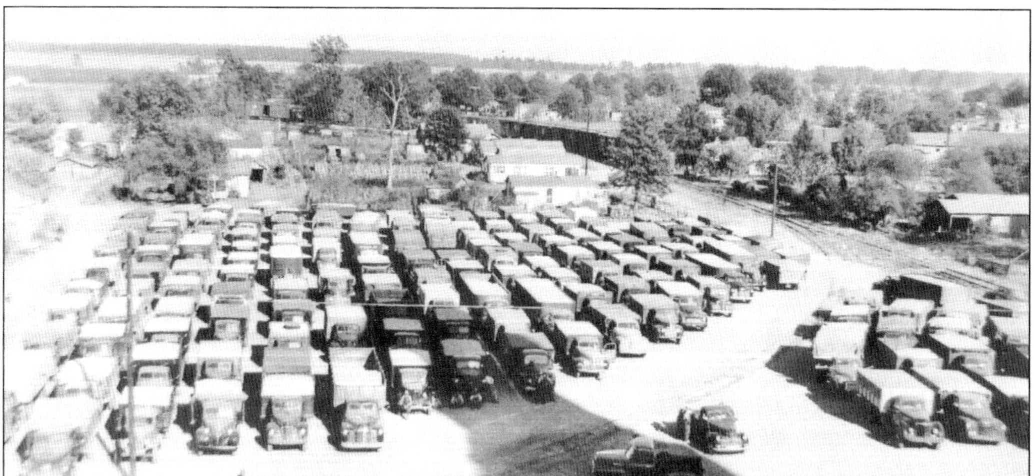

By the 1940s, the wagons that once brought bags of threshed rice to the processing mills had been replaced by trucks like those massed in front of the Producers Rice Mill, a cooperative formed during that same decade. Stuttgart is the headquarters for Producers as well as Riceland Foods, another cooperative formed by local growers and businessmen in 1921. The Stuttgart-based companies are the world's largest millers and distributors of rice; both were contracted to ship the crop to the war-torn citizens of Iraq in 2003. (Courtesy of the Museum of the Arkansas Grand Prairie.)

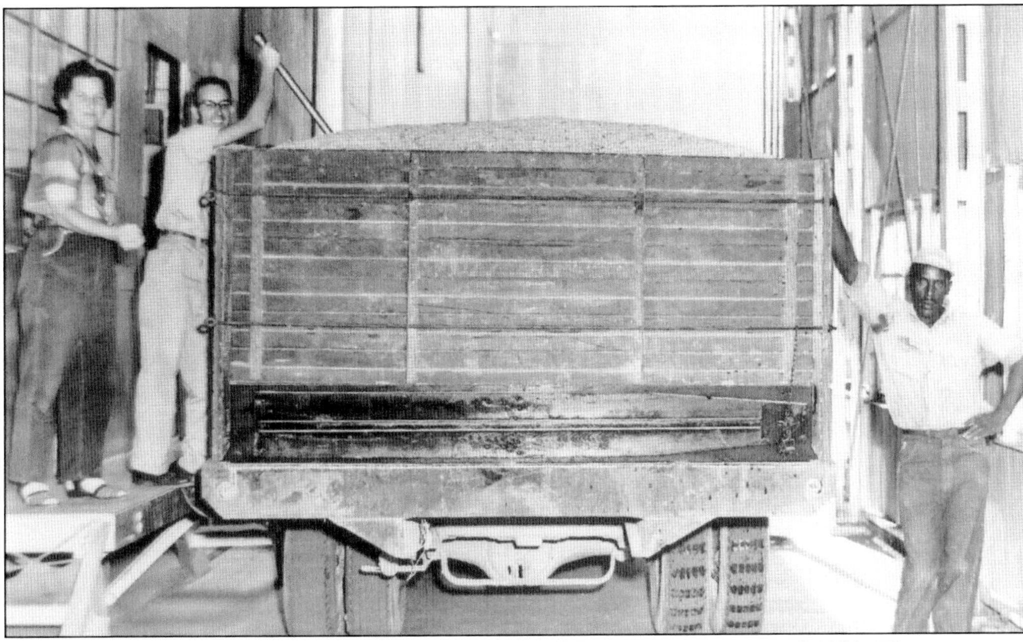

A truck is ready to have its rice unloaded at the mill for processing around 1950. The woman in jeans is most likely there as part of the work crew rather than as a spectator to rice production, as in earlier years. (Courtesy of the Museum of the Arkansas Grand Prairie.)

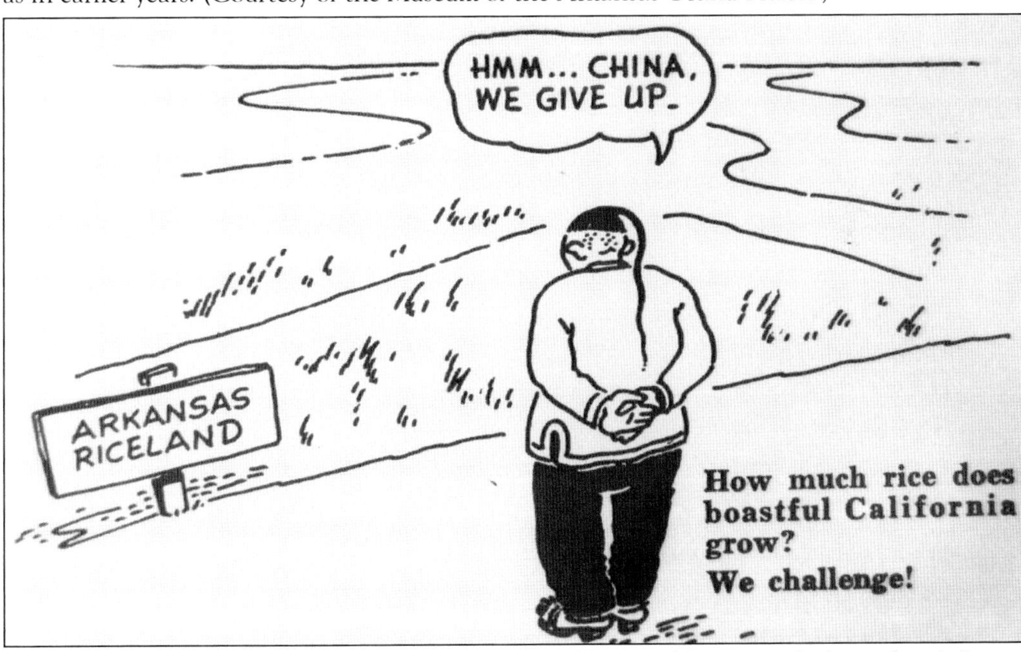

In this c. 1940 postcard view, a Chinese man gazes at the Grand Prairie and admits that Arkansas has outpaced China in rice productions. Today Arkansas is a national and international leader in rice production. The state devotes 1.4 million acres to the crop—43 percent of the nation's rice acreage. Arkansas is home to the world's largest rice processing and export company, Riceland Foods, a 9,000-member, farmer-owned cooperative located at Stuttgart, where Arkansas rice farming began over a century ago.

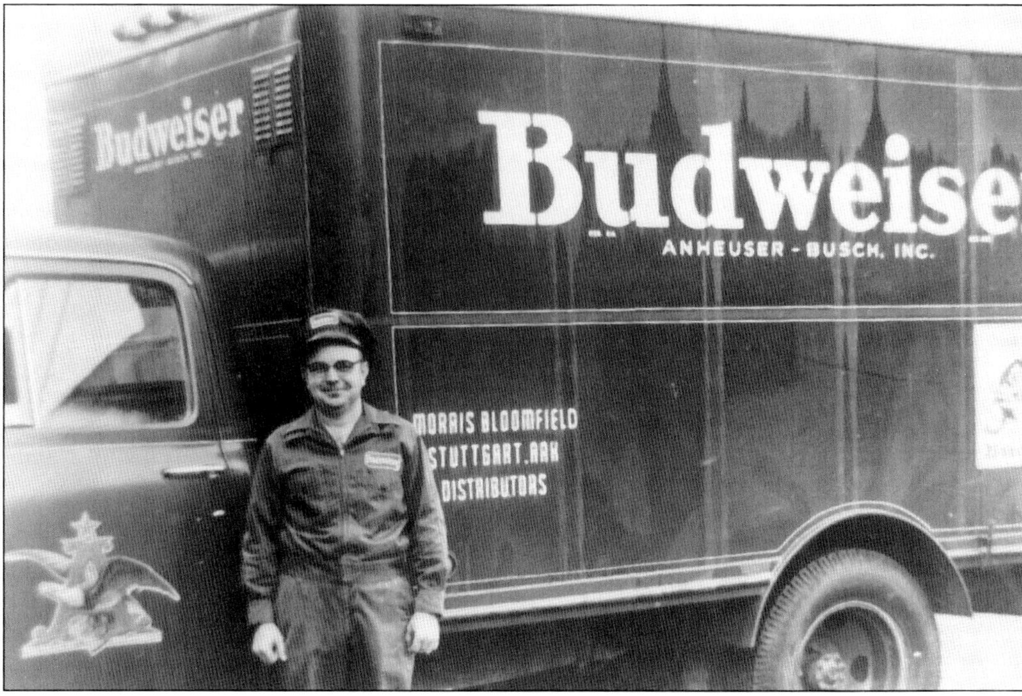

The *c.* 1950 photograph above might have carried the caption, "Rice isn't just for eating anymore." The Budweiser advertisement below, from the 1936 Rice Carnival souvenir program, proclaimed, "Anheuser-Busch buys 25% of all American rice used in brewing." Arkansas-grown rice was likely a key ingredient in the beer transported by Morris Bloomfield's distributor truck in Stuttgart. (Courtesy of the Museum of the Arkansas Grand Prairie.)

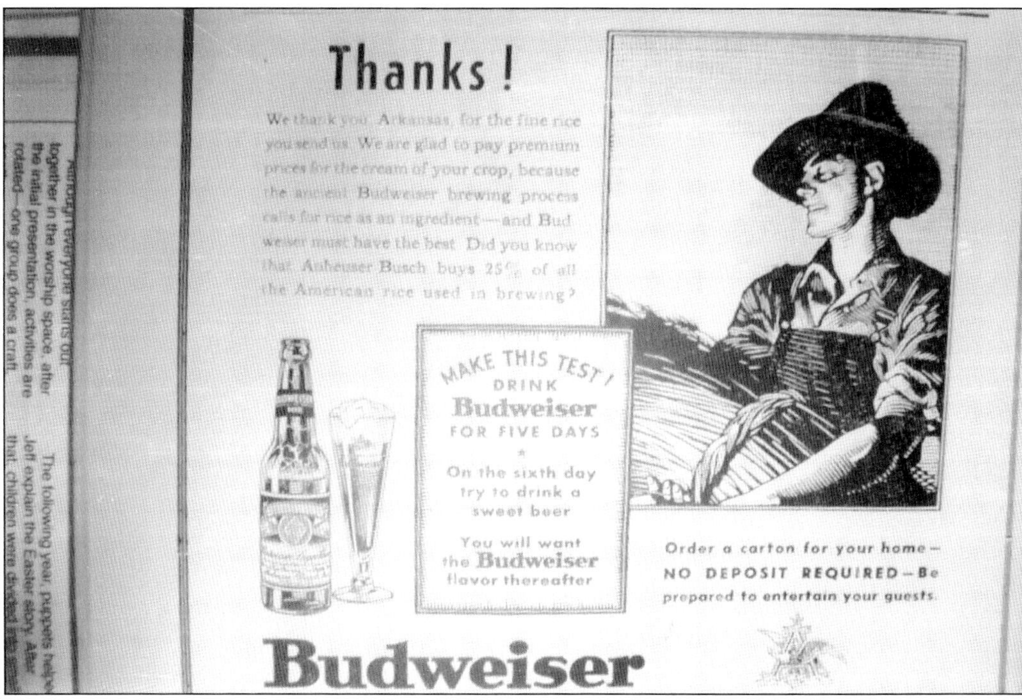

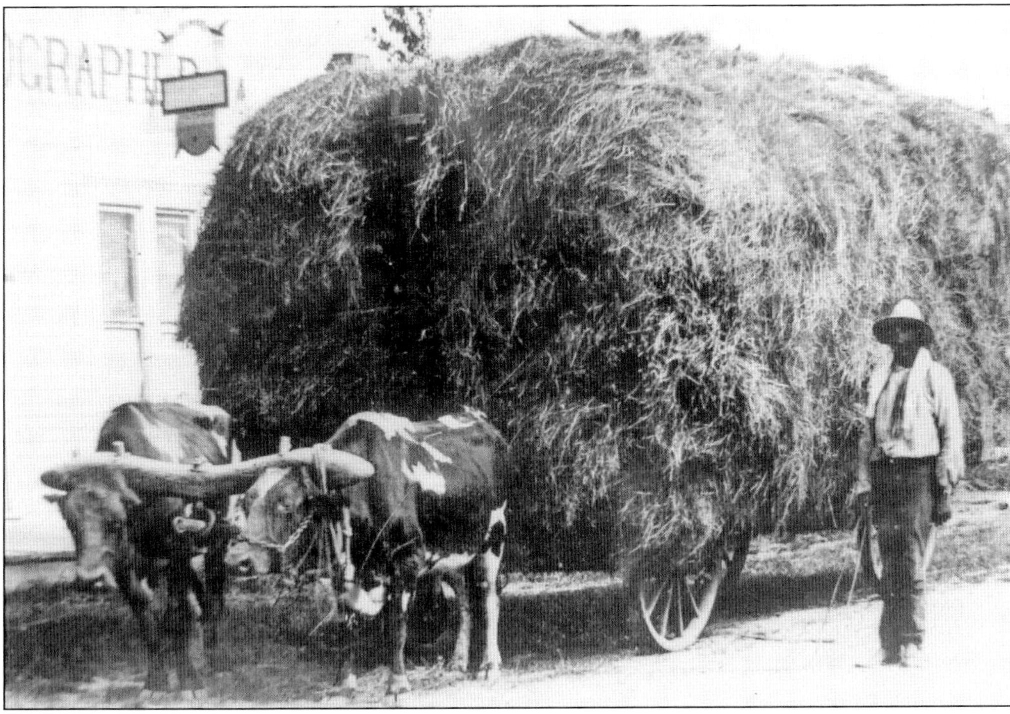

Before rice became the dominant crop on the Grand Prairie, Arkansas County was billed in some newspapers as "the Hay Capital of the World." In 1900, some 4,000 bales a day were shipped by rail from Stuttgart during the haying season. Above, hay is piled atop a wagon drawn by oxen, likely for local use, around 1905. Below, a couple and a little dog sit atop a wagon hauling more neatly baled hay in 1911. (Above courtesy of the Museum of the Arkansas Grand Prairie.)

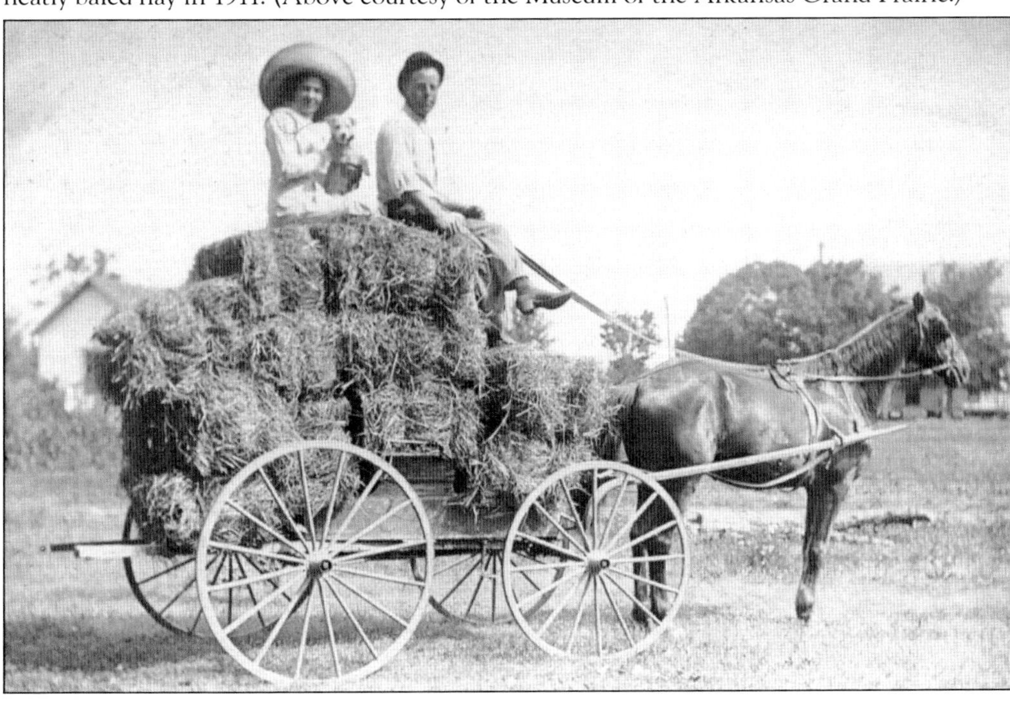

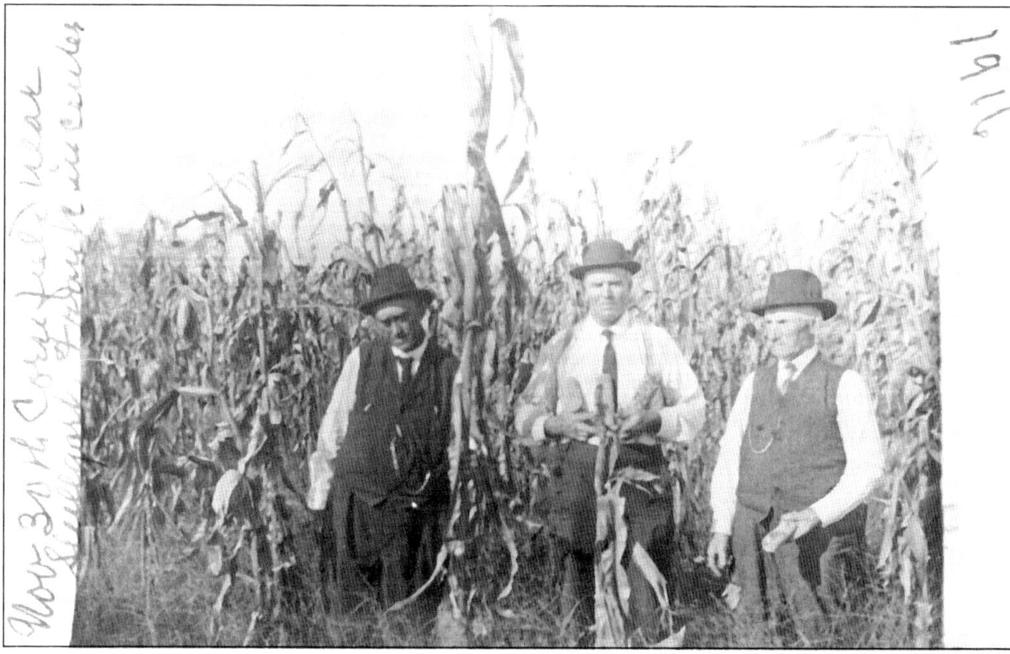

According to "Arkansas and Her Resources," a 1915 publication by the *Arkansas Democrat*, Arkansas County corn crops yielded 40 bushels per acre at the time. Maude Brierton wrote to her sister Daisy in November 1916 that the card showed "Iowa men and Arkansas corn." She went on: "This is a lovely day. We have a chicken ready to fry for dinner, kids out of school, Bennie working on cars, did a big wash yesterday so ironing is looking at me but don't think I will do it today."

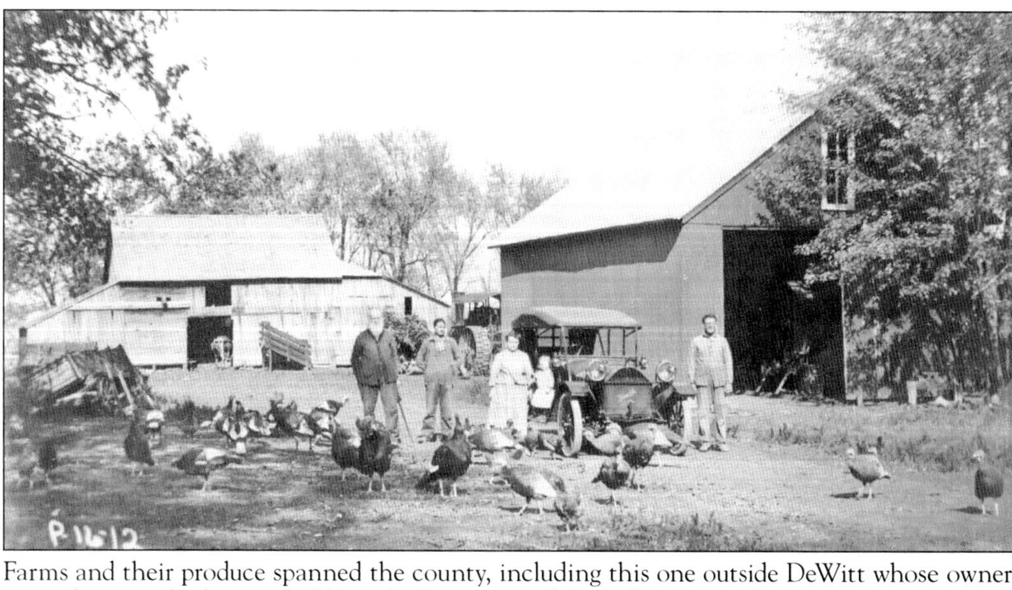

Farms and their produce spanned the county, including this one outside DeWitt whose owners were photographed around 1915 with their automobile and turkeys. The steam traction engine parked behind the barn, just over the middle man's shoulder, suggests the prosperous family also grew rice.

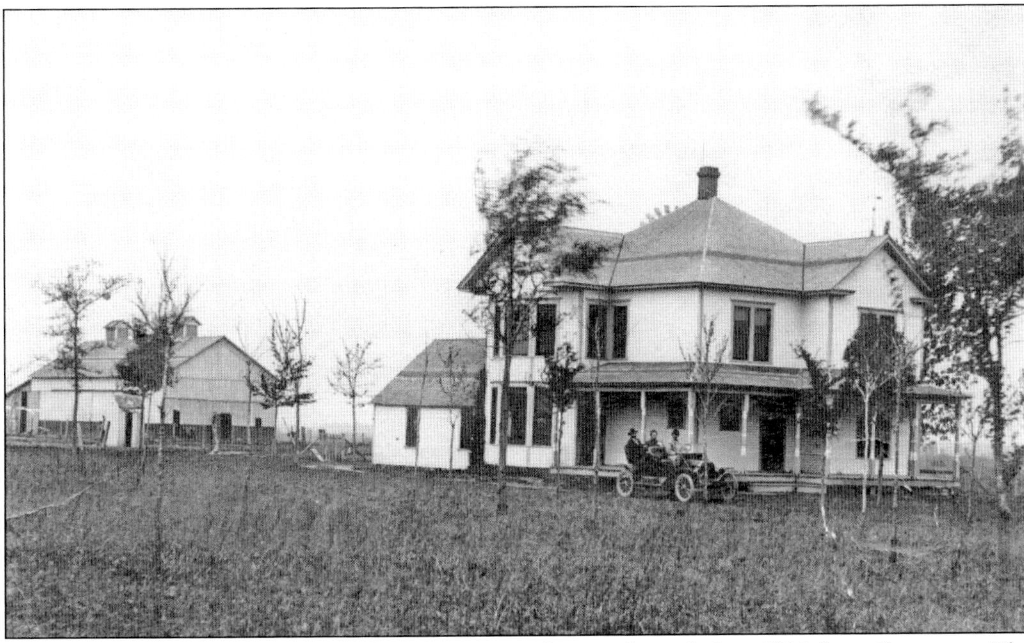

"Ohlfeldt house in Arkansas" is the caption on this card, mailed in 1911 from Stuttgart. The rambling two-story home, automobile, and fine barn imply that the family was successful at farming in Arkansas County.

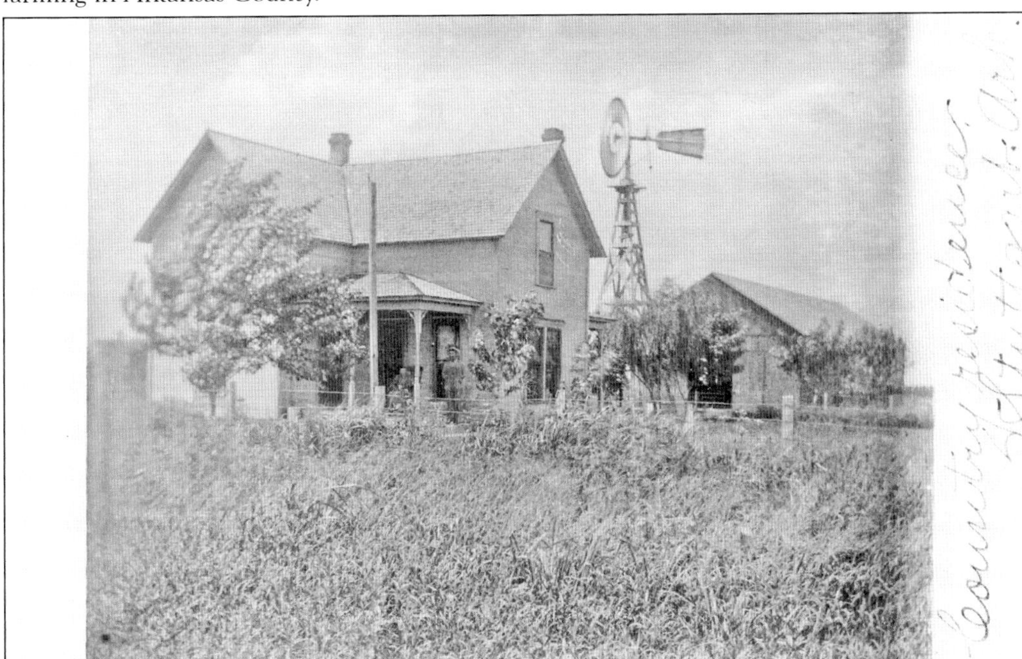

Other farmhouses were more modest than the Ohlfeldts', as in the case of this "country residence" outside Stuttgart in 1909. In another card to her sister in Illinois, Maude Brierton wrote, "We went fish frying yesterday, fried fish for dinner over fire on ground—this was a new crowd. Mrs. Moore and I took pictures of Cleve's rice field. Sent you paper tells you about fire, fire in town this a.m. but not so bad."

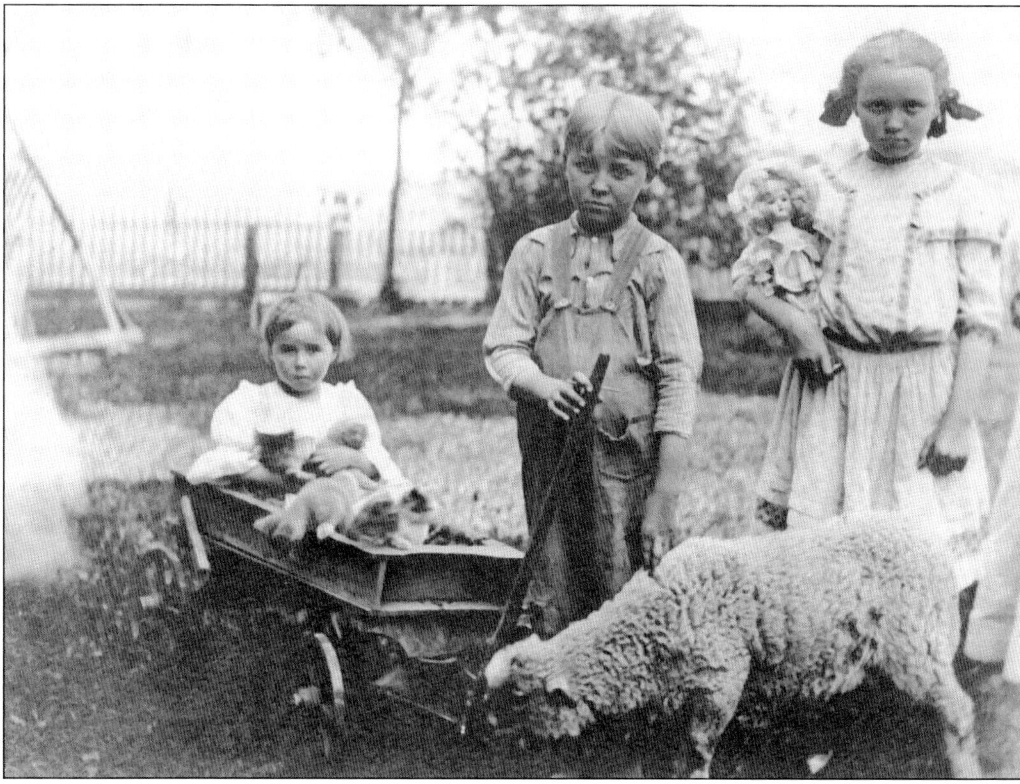

A few sheep were raised on the farms of Arkansas County, but it is unlikely that the one pictured here ended up on the dinner table. The *c.* 1910 card is labeled, "The Lenhart trio and their pets they raised on a bottle."

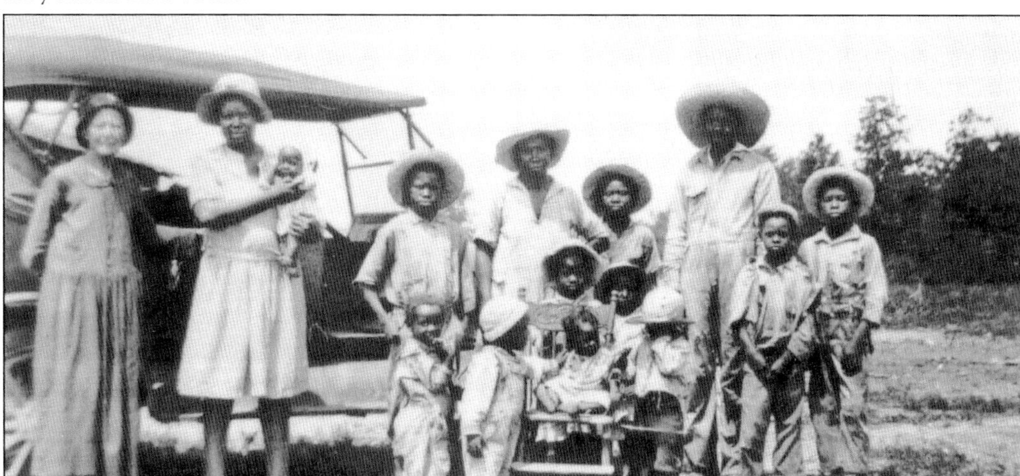

Black families lived with more modest housing and were seldom farm owners; rather, they were an integral part of the labor that produced the crops of Arkansas County throughout its history. This family consists of 13 barefoot children, all with sunhats except for the two smallest girls. They pose with Ollie Schartz (left), apparently the owner of the automobile and perhaps the employer of part of the family. (Courtesy of the Museum of the Arkansas Grand Prairie.)

Five

Outdoor Life on Prairie, Forest, and Stream

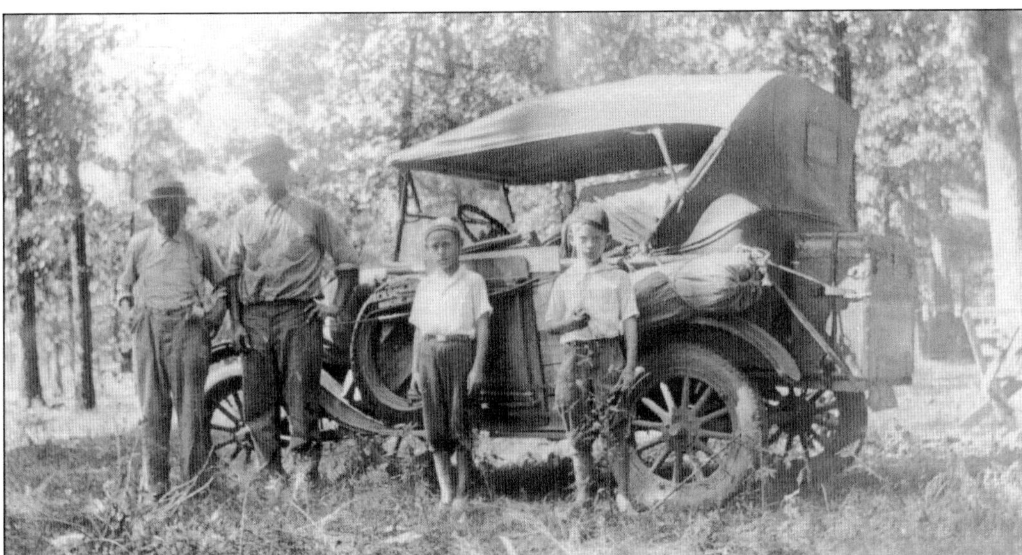

The early explorers and settlers who came to Arkansas County in the 1700s found an outdoor bonanza of wildlife ranging from buffalo, bear, deer, wolves, and panthers to vast numbers of waterfowl drawn to the rivers and bayous of the region. As the area grew into an agricultural center, its residents—with the help of the state and federal government and private organizations like Ducks Unlimited—sought to keep a balance between growing crops and sheltering wildlife. This family, camping near St. Charles around 1920 in what would later become the White River National Wildlife Refuge, surely appreciated this part of the region's heritage.

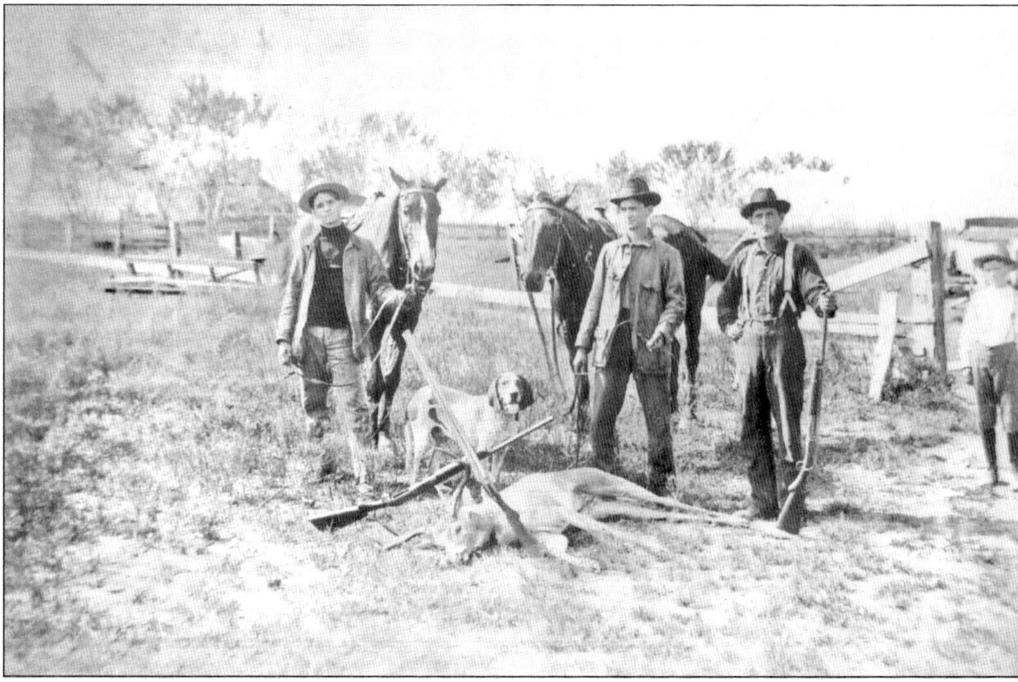

Deer abounded on the Grand Prairie and in the wooded bottomland around the streams and bayous of Arkansas County. The men above have bagged a large buck with the aid of their dog and horses about 1910. Below, hunters on the prairie around 1905 pose not only with their deer but also with a pair of pheasants suspended from a shotgun balanced between the shoulders of the center men. (Above courtesy of the Museum of the Arkansas Grand Prairie.)

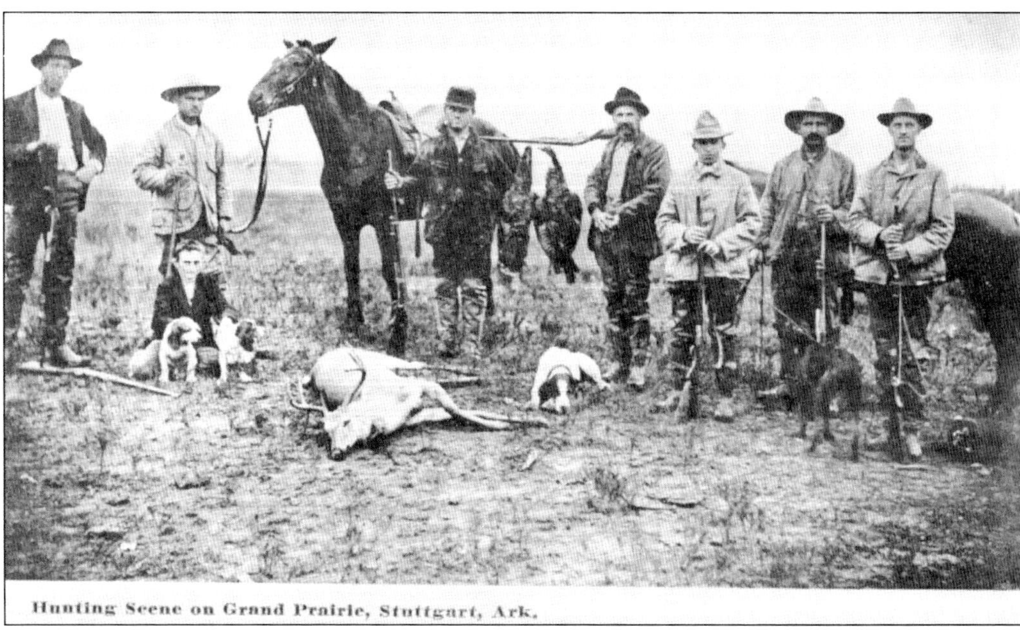

Hunting Scene on Grand Prairie, Stuttgart, Ark.

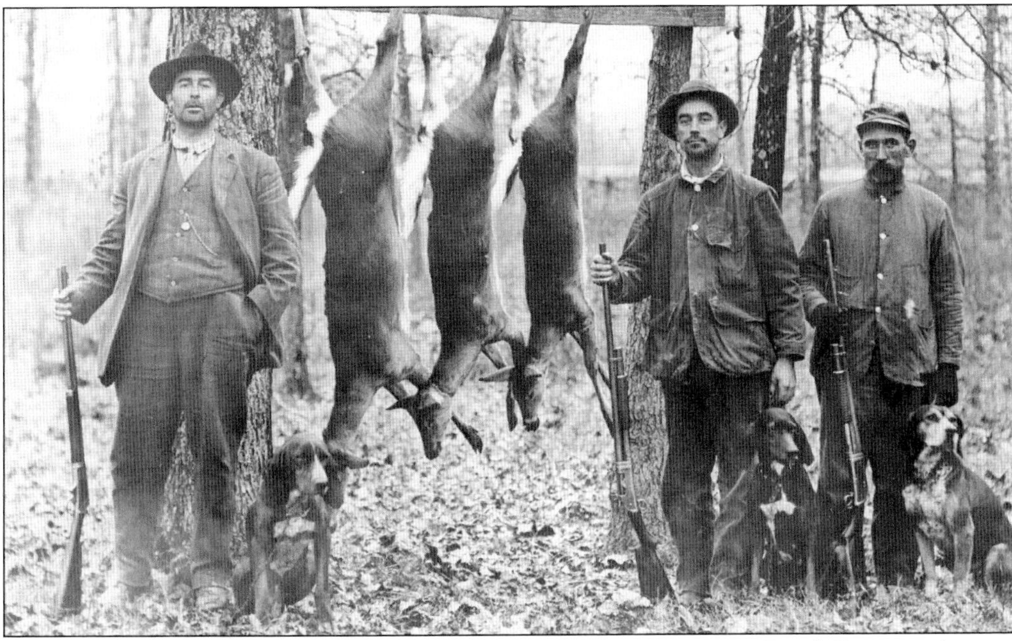

On a postcard mailed from Stuttgart as a 1910 Christmas greeting to Frank Brierton, hunters and their dogs proudly present the three deer they bagged on an expedition. Over-hunting, in the absence of limits, almost wiped out the whitetail deer in Arkansas before game management could restore the population to again make deer hunting a major state sport.

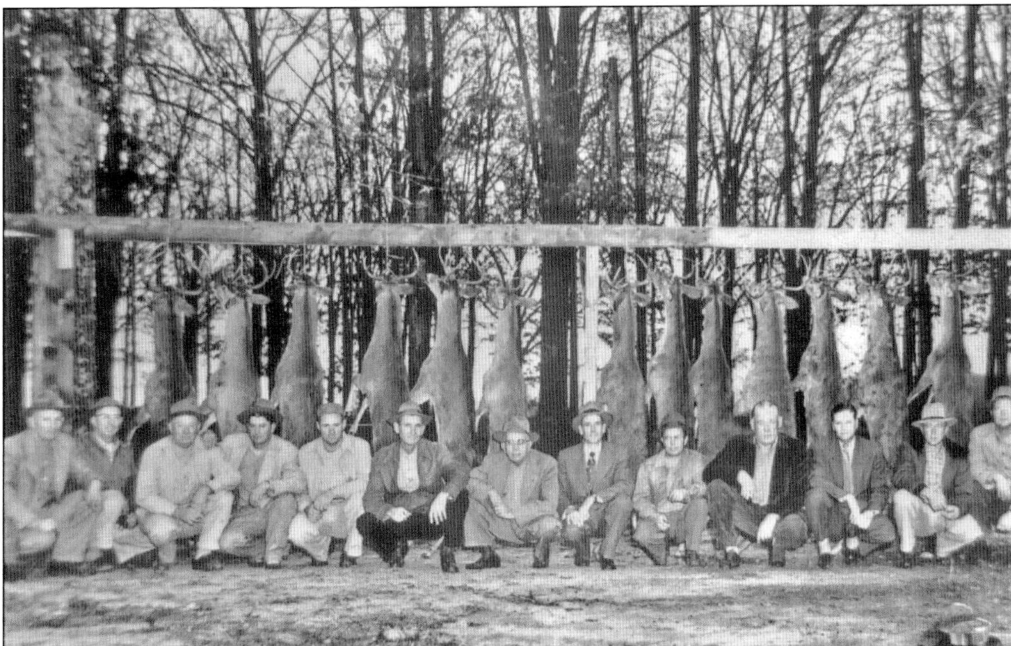

The deer are large, as is this group of hunters posing at a camp in Arkansas County in 1940. The Arkansas Game and Fish Commission was hard at work managing the state's wildlife by this time, helping to ensure that future generations would have abundant deer for hunting. (Courtesy Museum of Arkansas Grand Prairie.)

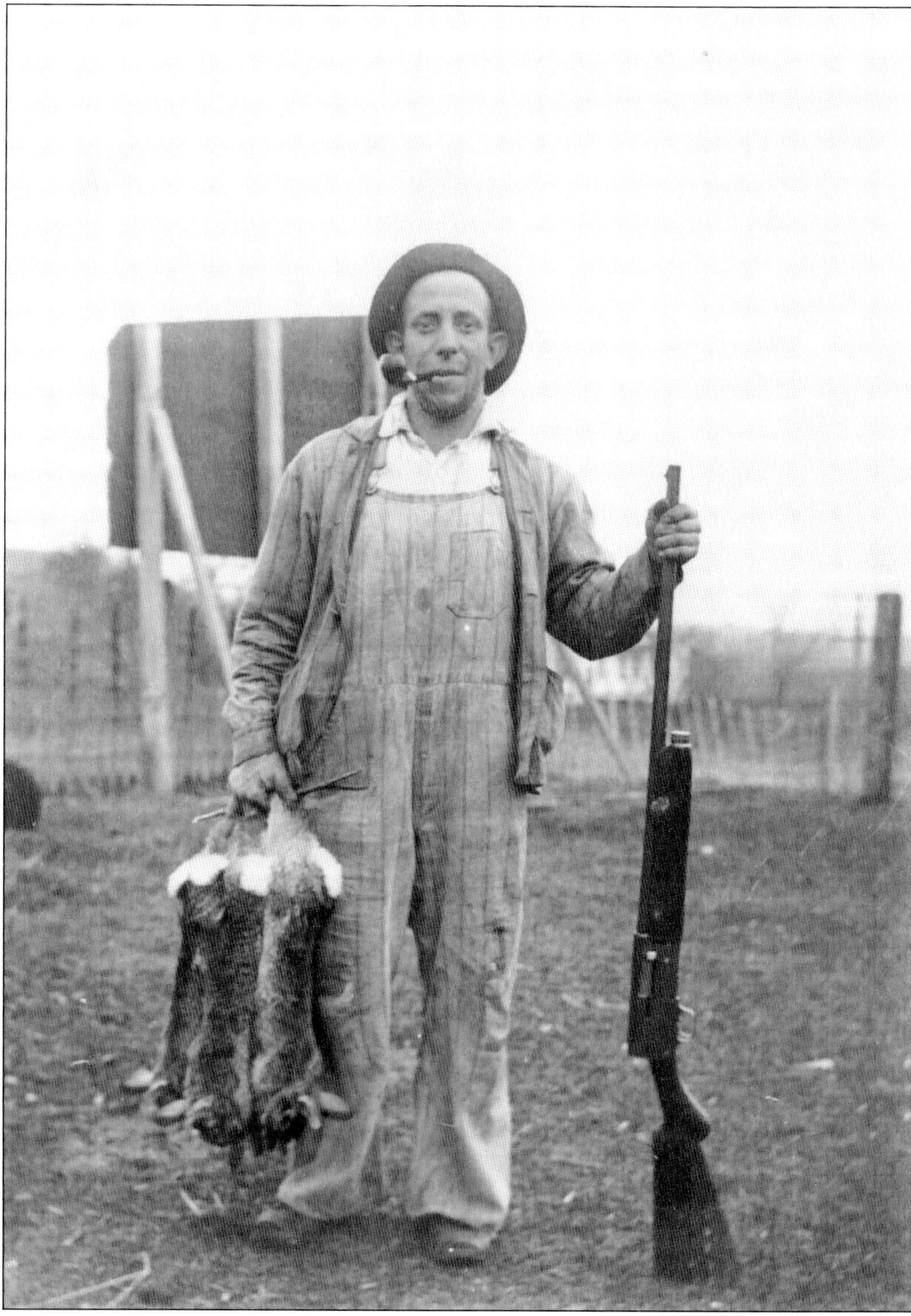

An unidentified Stuttgart man, puffing on his pipe, proudly stands with his shotgun in one hand and a fistful of rabbits in the other around 1920. While there was sport in the hunt, during this era the catch provided a key source of meat on the table as well.

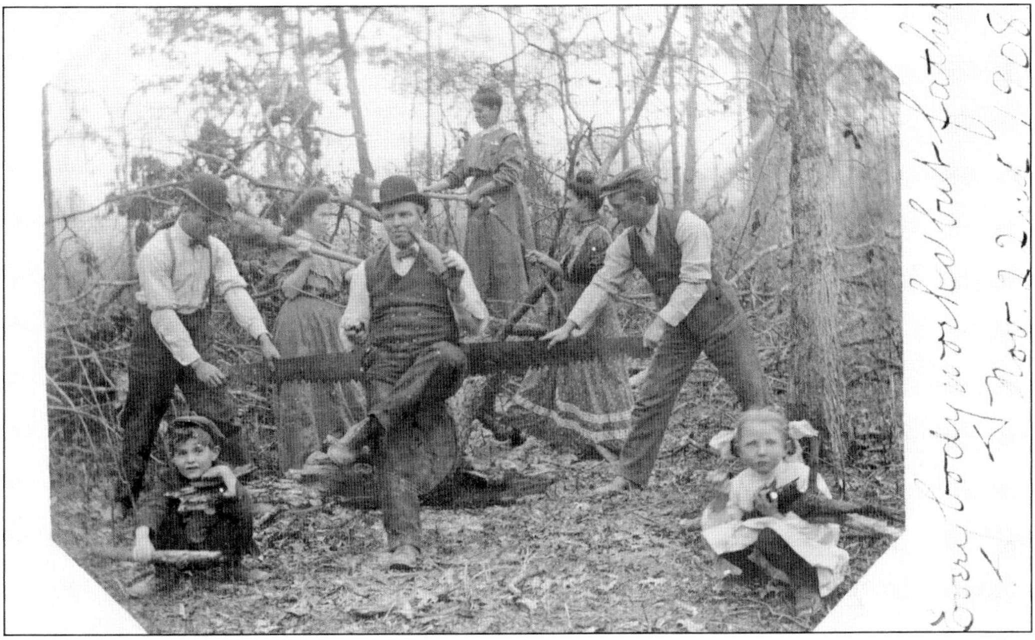

A family outing to Bayou Meto in November 1908 offered a chance to stage a comic postcard to be mailed to distant friends and relatives. "Everybody works but father" is the caption penned in the margin. The two young men are working a crosscut saw behind Father, and the women hold axes while the small children pick up wood.

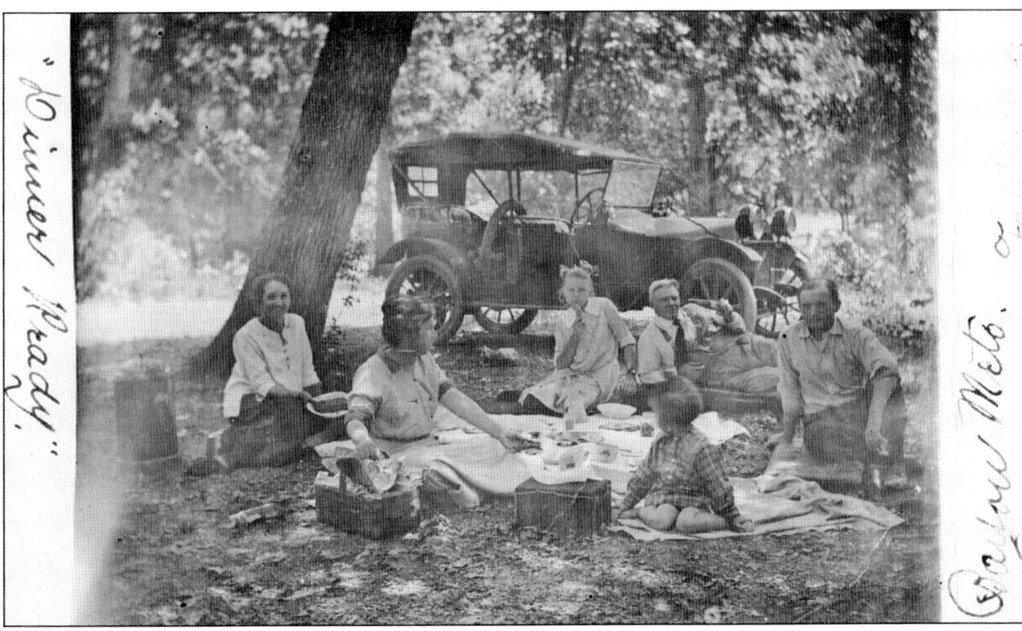

"Dinner ready" is the notation on this photograph of a Bayou Meto picnic in 1916. Mailed to a different sister in Illinois, Maude Brierton's message reads, "Frank and men left for Iowa yesterday. Rice cutting & threshing in full swing. Joe Rodman cutting ours. I got some old plates developed, will send a better one of this when I get printed."

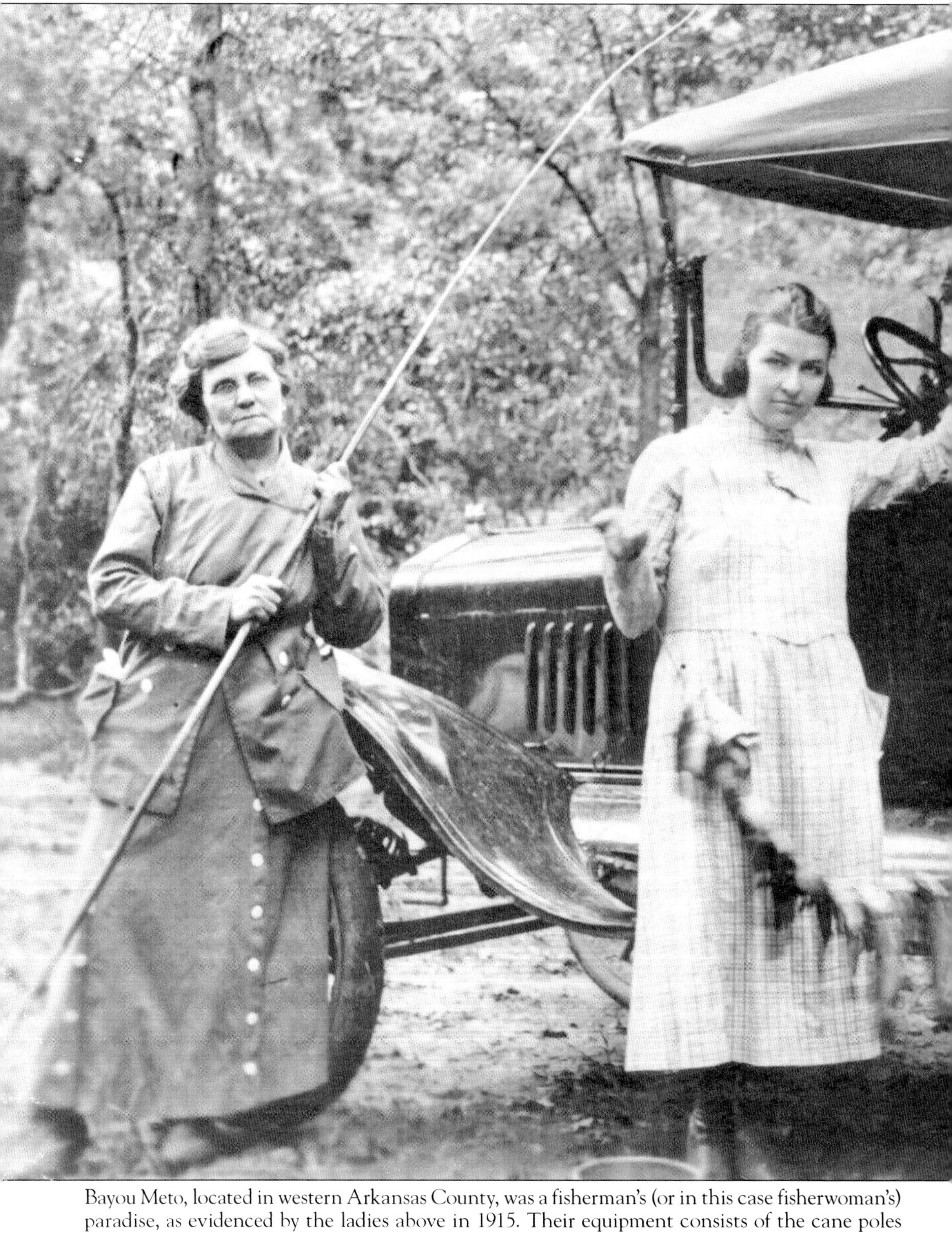

Bayou Meto, located in western Arkansas County, was a fisherman's (or in this case fisherwoman's) paradise, as evidenced by the ladies above in 1915. Their equipment consists of the cane poles

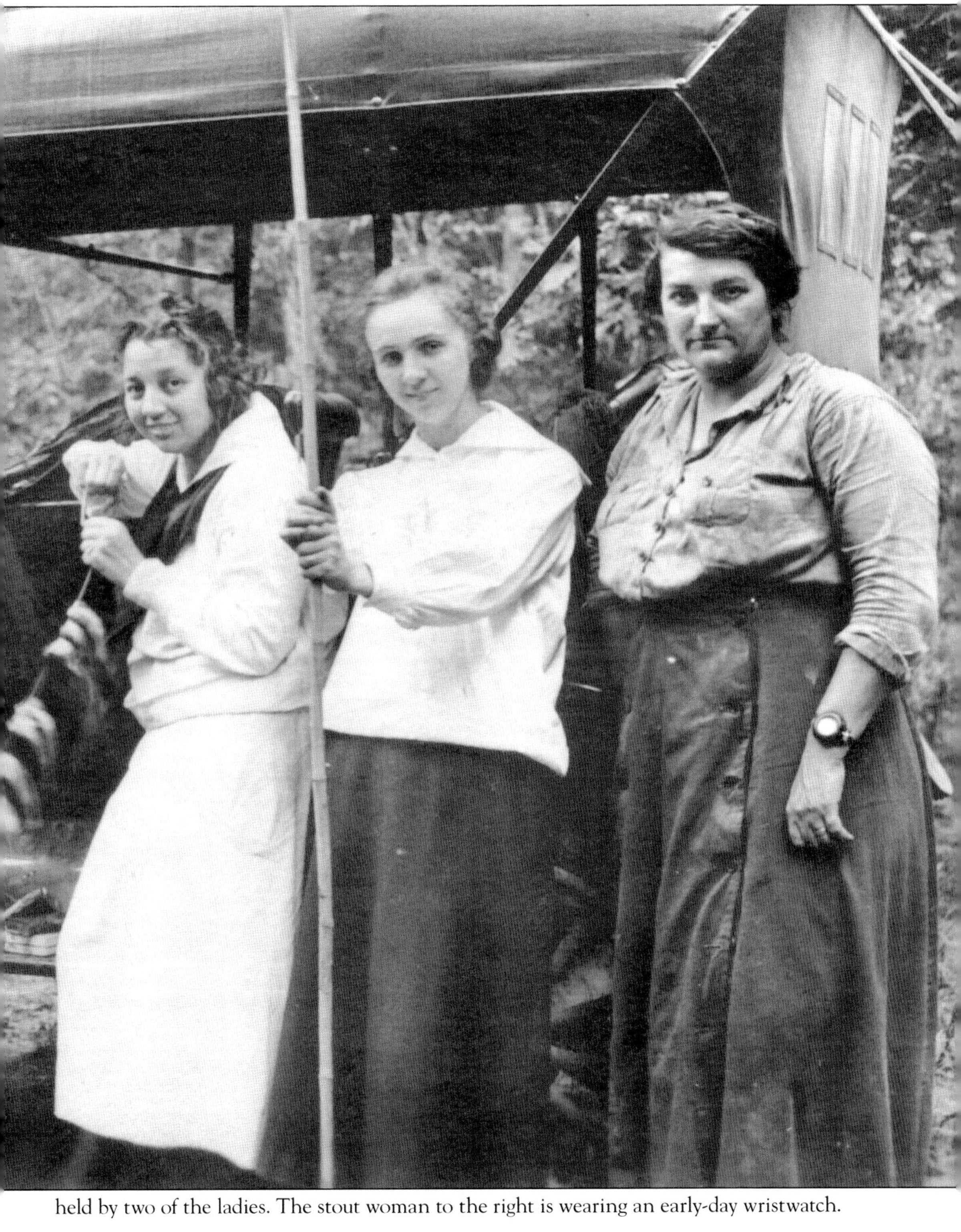

held by two of the ladies. The stout woman to the right is wearing an early-day wristwatch.

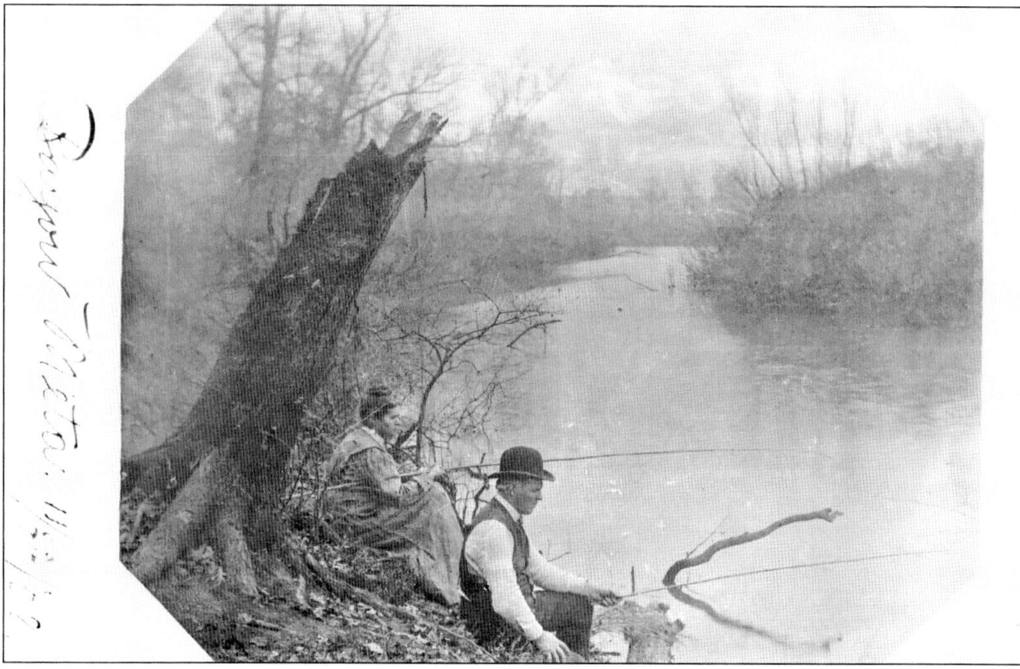

A man wearing a vest, necktie, and nice hat wields his cane pole in concentration matched by that of his wife as they fish on Bayou Meto on November 22, 1908.

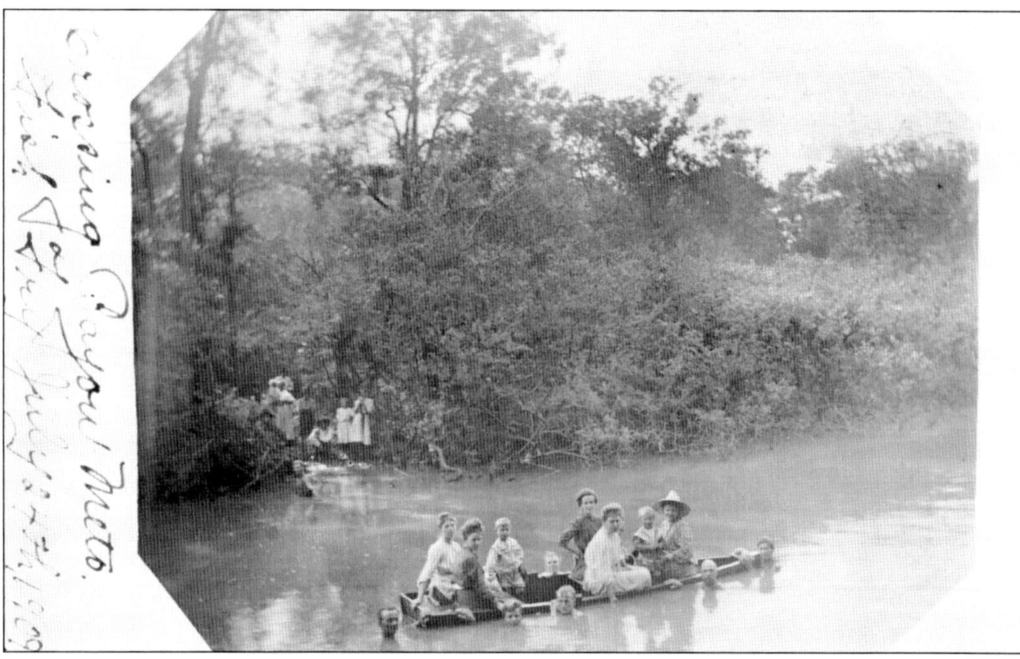

Fishing was not the only draw to Bayou Meto, for the location also offered a chance to cool off in the water. Here the Brierton family and friends are creative in their play, as 13 people either ride in or cling to the sides of their small boat. The occasion is noted to be a fish fry on July 24, 1909, possibly the same event referred to in the postcard seen on page 107.

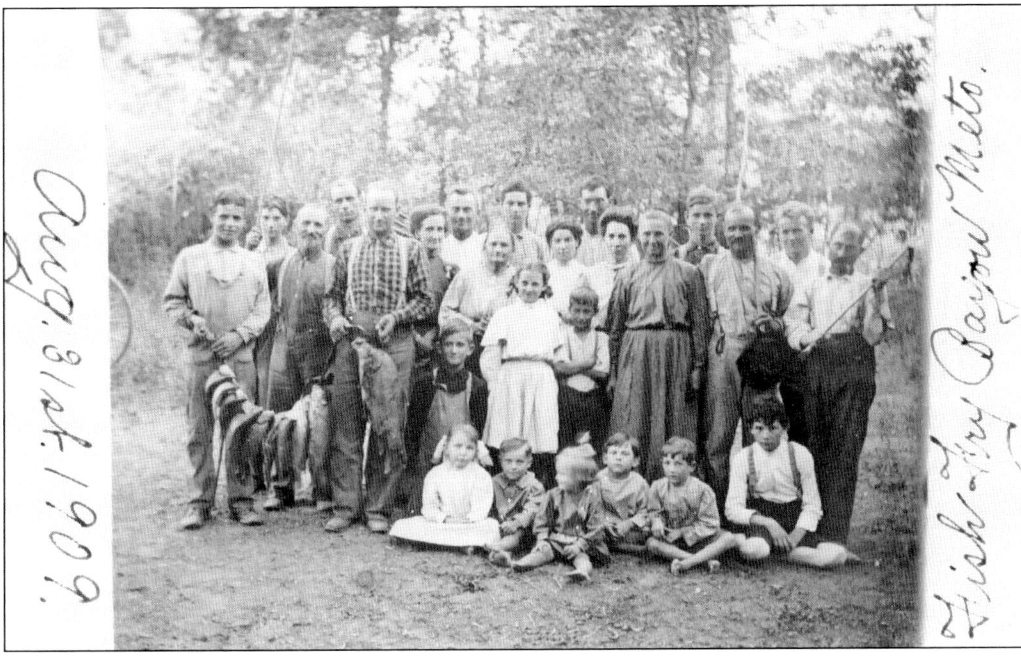

Attending fish fries at Bayou Meto was apparently a popular pastime for the Briertons and many others, as indicated by these photographs taken three weeks apart in 1909. The bounty of the waters is seen in the massive amounts of large fish displayed above, sufficient to feed a crowd of 84 people at the August 7 event. Below, the group has caught so many fish that the smaller ones are spread on the ground before them. The little girl to the right needs the helping hand of her father to hold a large fish.

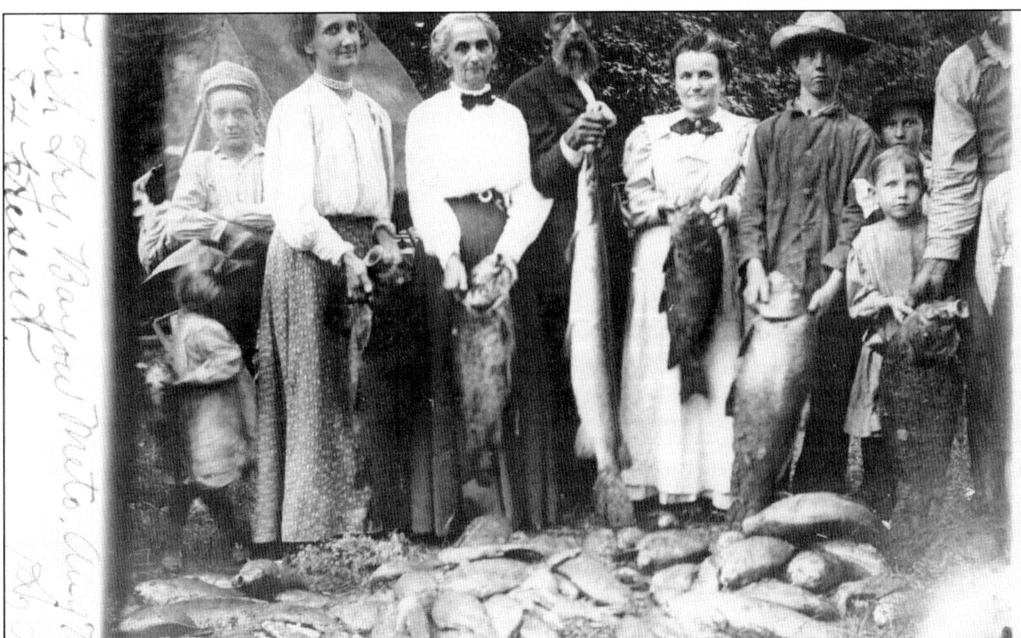

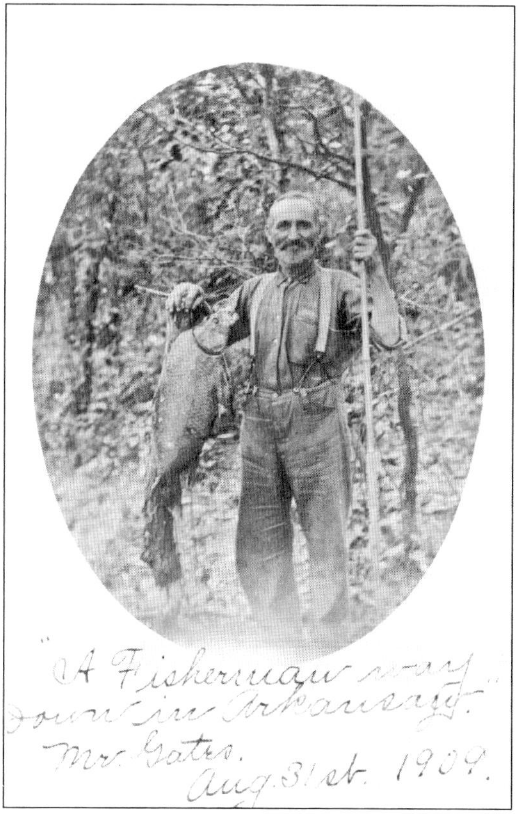

Mr. Gates, "a fisherman way down in Arkansas" and apparently a friend of the Brierton family, poses with his cane pole and a large fish he caught at the August 31, 1909, fish fry on Bayou Meto.

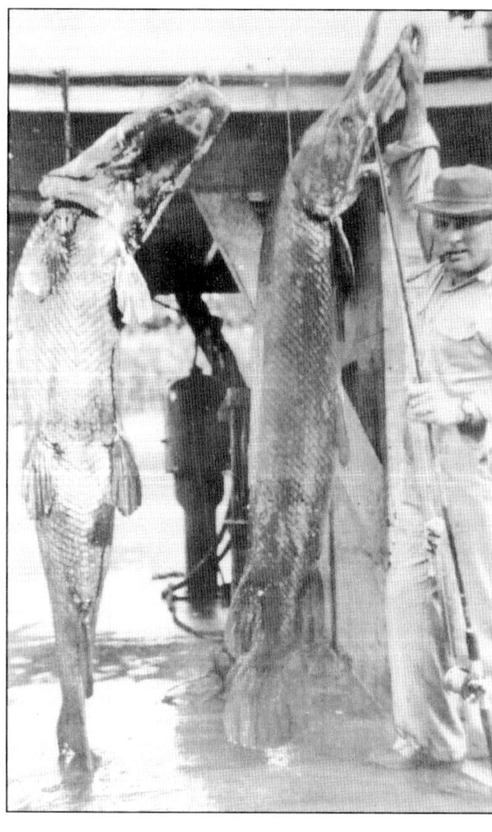

The White River, flowing on the eastern edge of Arkansas County, was home to the alligator gar, a species little changed since the age of dinosaurs. Weighing up to 300 pounds and usually landed with deep-sea tackle, the great fish were caught and then dispatched, often with a bullet. Today the giant fish are almost all gone, but game fishing in the White River remains popular.

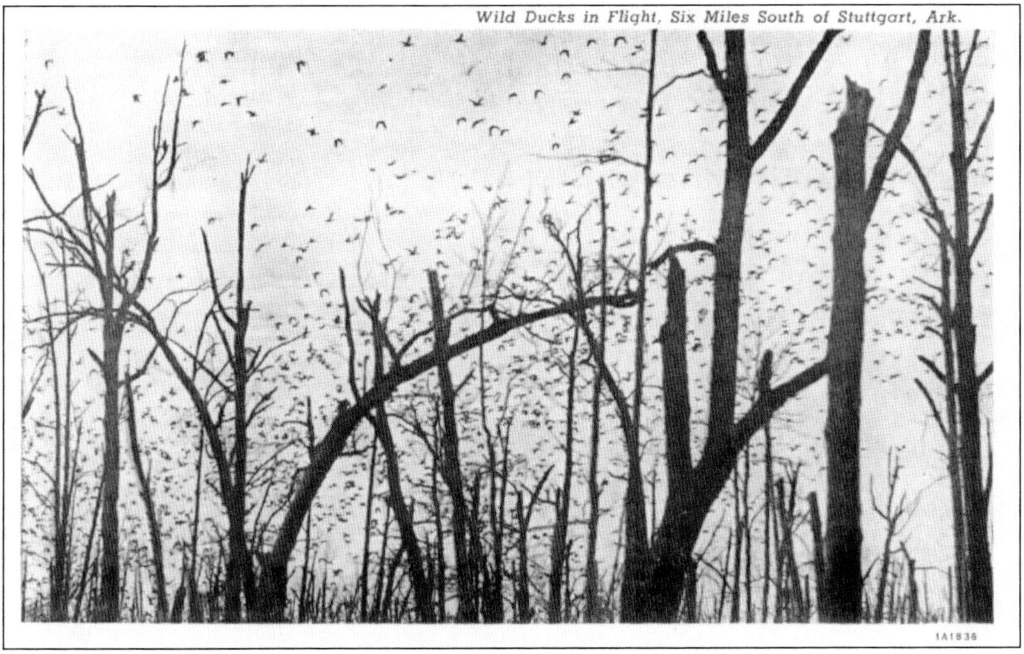

Waterfowl—and especially ducks—have put Arkansas County and Stuttgart on the world map. Ducks fly south along the Mississippi flyway in the fall, migrating to escape the winter cold. Nothing looks better to a duck seeking a place to rest and eat than the harvested rice fields and ample flooded timberland of Arkansas County. This postcard view shows the sky thick with ducks six miles south of Stuttgart in the 1940s.

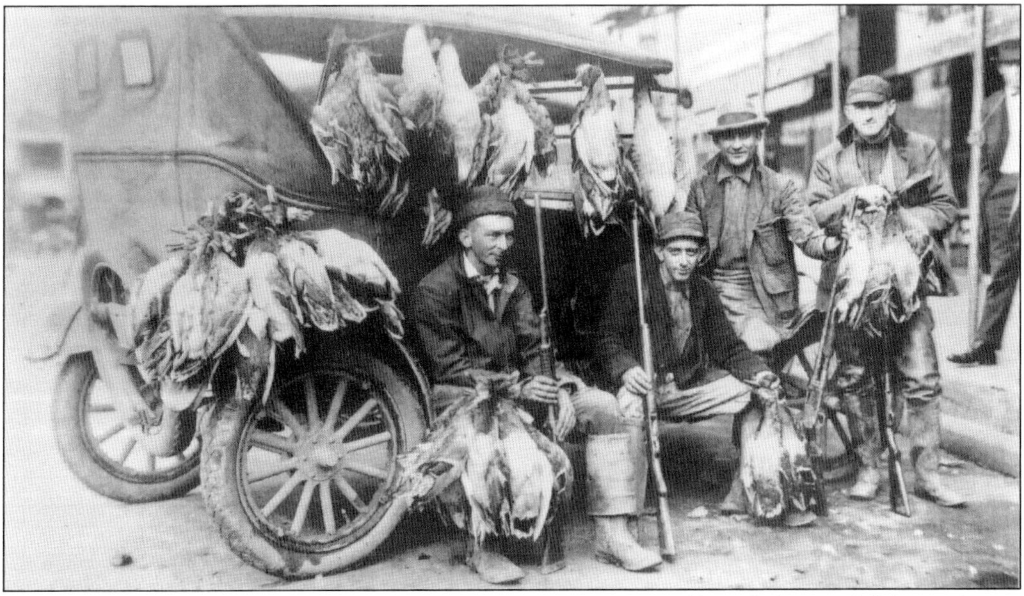

Matt Gingler, Red Wilhelm, Tex Erwin, and Christy Rittman (from left to right) have driven back into Stuttgart in 1921 to show off their morning's successful duck hunt. Daily bag limits were first set around 1916, at 25 ducks per hunter. Such controls were necessary, for in the late 1800s, market hunters were known to ship as many as 25,000 ducks at a time from a single east Arkansas lake, bound for meat markets in St. Louis, Memphis, New Orleans, and Chicago.

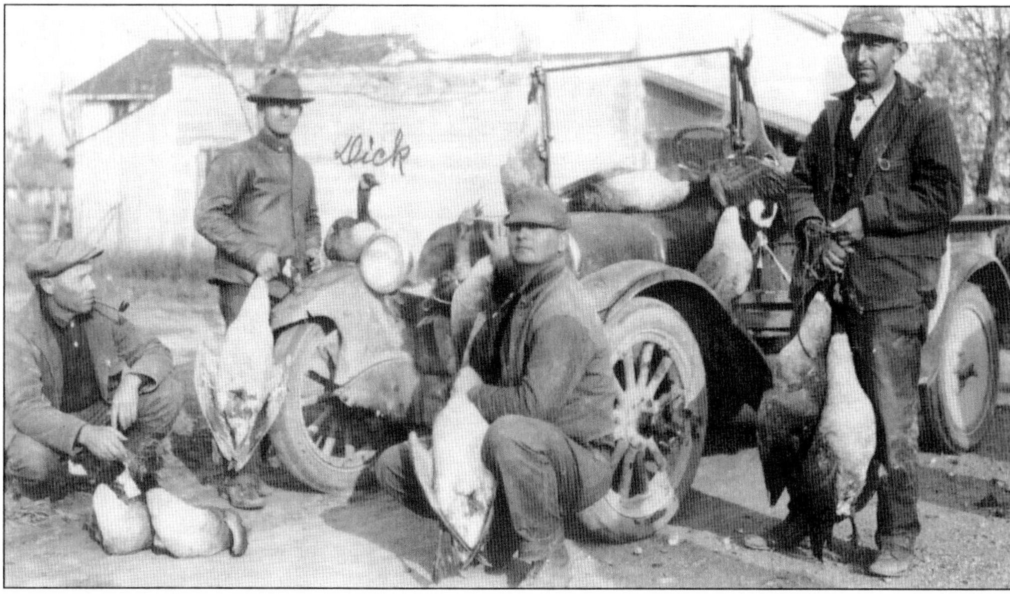

Hunters learned early on that along with migrating ducks, geese were attracted to the wetlands and fields of Arkansas County. "Fred H., Henry Voss, Will Moss and Harry Sebree" pose from left to right in Almyra in 1925 with a dozen Canada geese killed earlier in the morning.

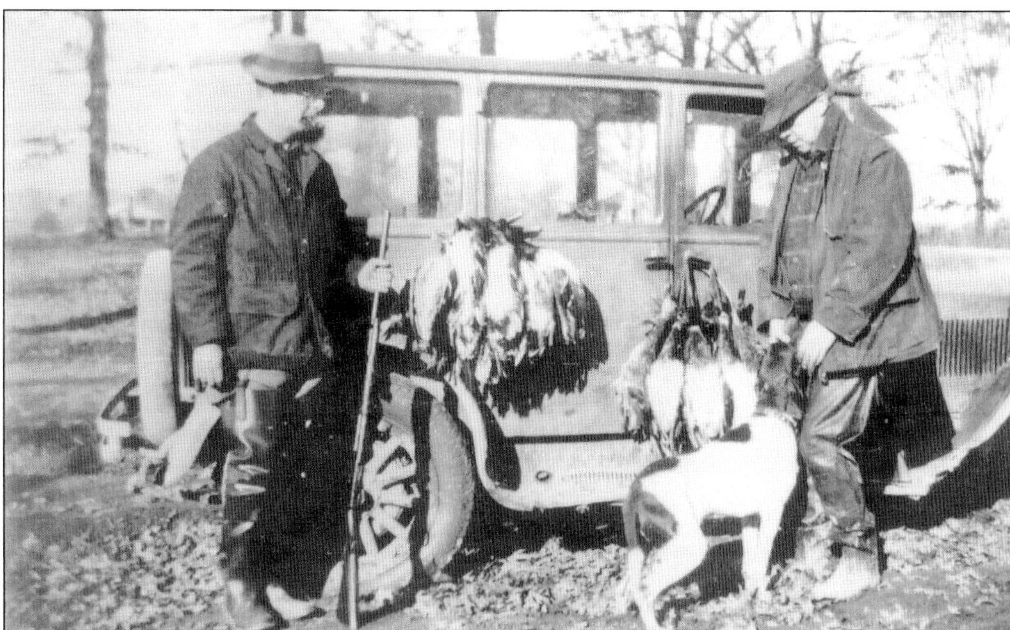

Duck hunters traveling from Little Rock in the early 1900s had a rough trip, as the road ended at Lonoke and the balance of the 70-mile distance was driven across country; the journey from the state's capital to the duck blinds was often a 12-hour trip. By 1930, when these two men stood at Cook's Lake with their limits, the roads had improved considerably.

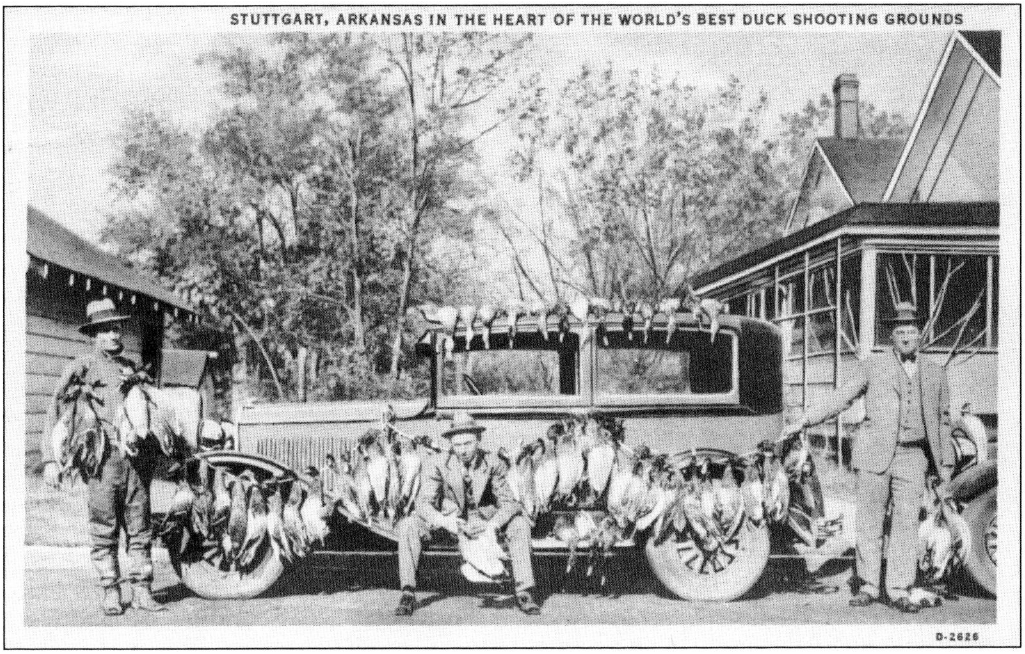

The severe drought of the 1930s dried up much of water depended on by the ducks and geese. Sportsmen, including many in Arkansas County, lobbied Congress to enact the Duck Stamp Act, which helped buy and preserve habitat to rescue the declining waterfowl populations. Benefiting from these efforts are the men seen above, who are using their car as a trophy stand, and the three men below, who stand laden with the evidence of their successful hunt in 1934. The man on the left is renowned American humorist Will Rogers, who would die the following year in an Alaskan plane crash. (Courtesy of the Museum of the Arkansas Grand Prairie.)

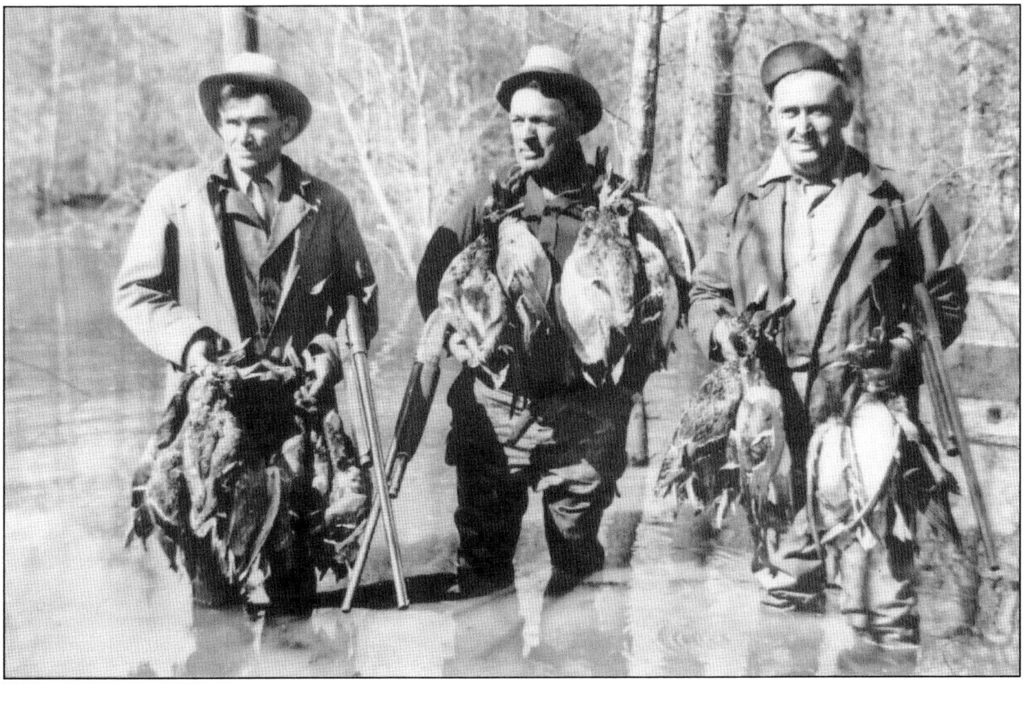

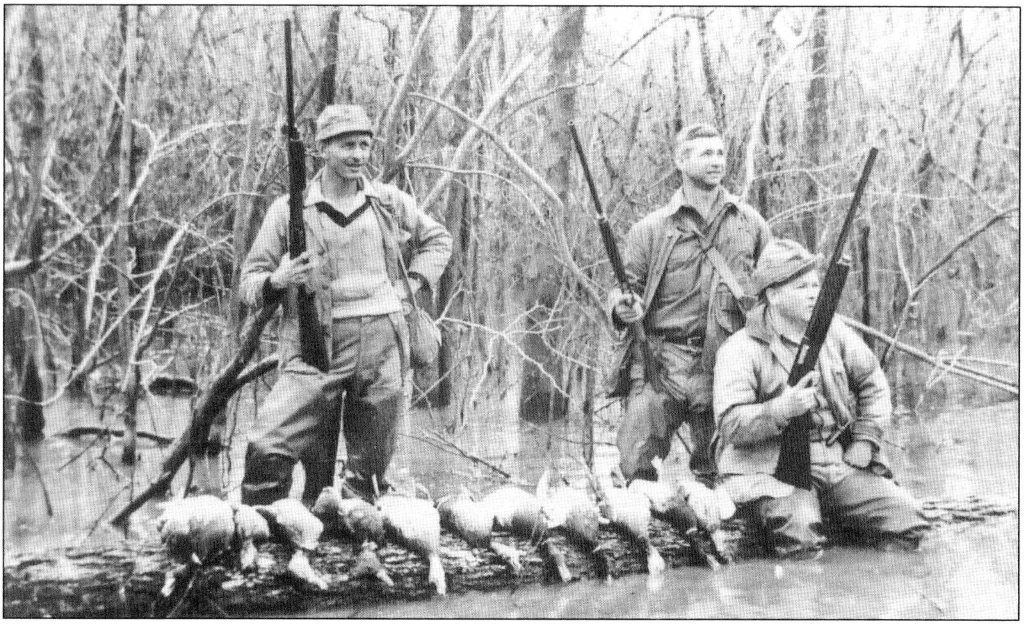

A columnist for the *St. Louis Post-Dispatch* wrote around 1940, "Much of the shooting at Stuttgart is very sporting. . . . There are many more misses than kills. To knock down a wild duck in full flight over the tops of tall trees, while the hunter himself may be standing in water up to or over his knees, is not the easiest thing to do as this city boy can testify." Hunters Ed Vinson (left), Ernest Urssey (center), and Jake Graham, seen here with a dozen ducks artfully arranged, likely concurred with that assessment. (Courtesy of the Museum of the Arkansas Grand Prairie.)

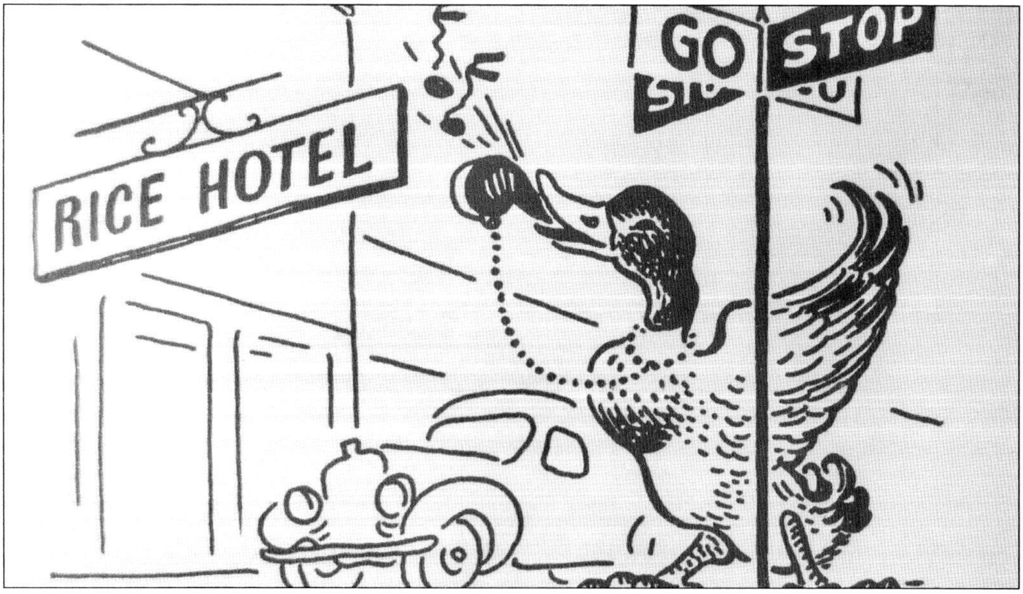

Duck calling, perhaps as much as the actual hunting, has become ingrained in the imagery of Arkansas County. The area's first official duck-calling contest was staged in DeWitt in 1935, with eight commercial duck-hunting guides vying for the prize of a hunting jacket that carried a $6.60 price tag. Thomas Walsh of Greenville, Mississippi, won by using his voice to imitate a mallard hen. This cartoon was created around 1941.

By the late 1940s, Stuttgart's ideal situation as a fall stopover for migratory ducks had cemented its reputation as the Duck Capital of the World. Crowds look on as the first national duck-calling contest is broadcast from Main Street in 1938. Time has not dimmed the event's appeal. *Sports Illustrated*, covering the competition in 2003, wrote that it presented "hour after hour of the damnedest caterwauling you ever heard." (Courtesy of the Museum of the Arkansas Grand Prairie.)

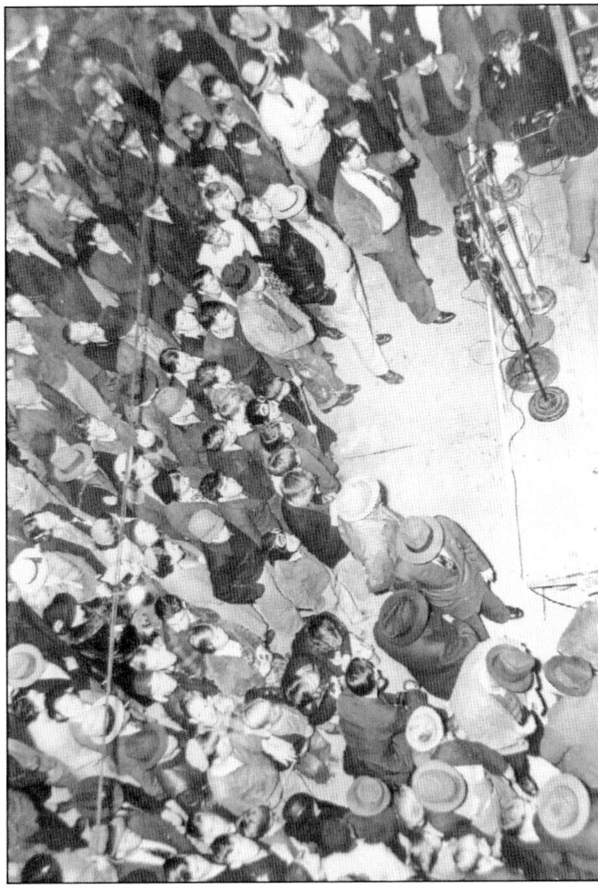

As the St. Louis newspaper columnist reported in 1940, duck hunting—as well as the calling of the ducks—could necessitate standing in knee-deep icy water for prolonged periods. That fact seemed not to have inhibited skilled callers Kenneth McCollum (left) and R. Wilhelm, shown here summoning the skyward ducks to within shooting range in the 1940s. (Courtesy of the Museum of the Arkansas Grand Prairie.)

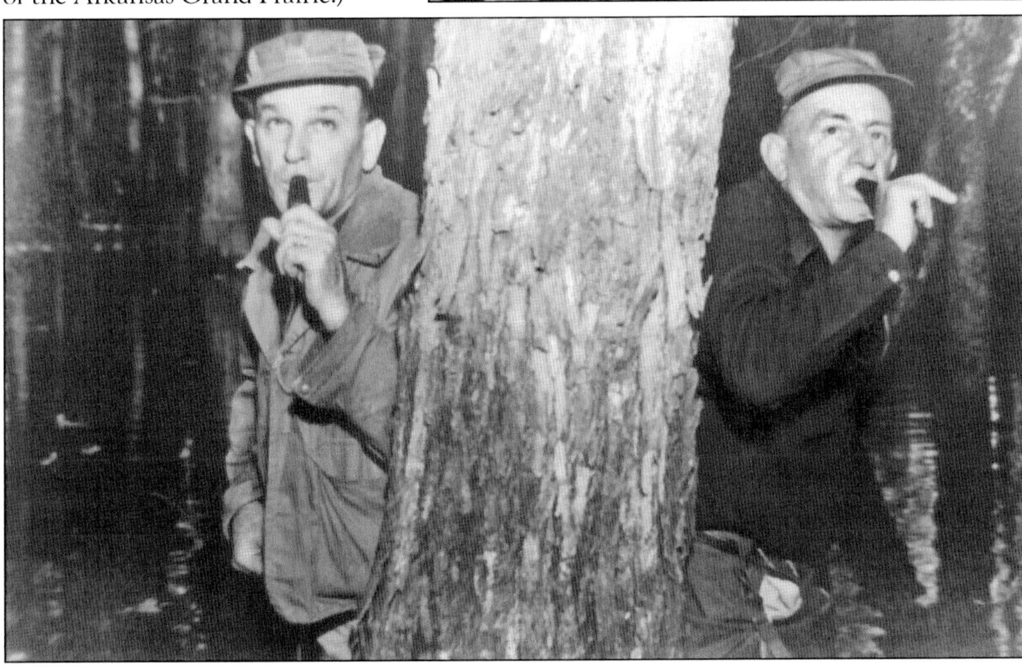

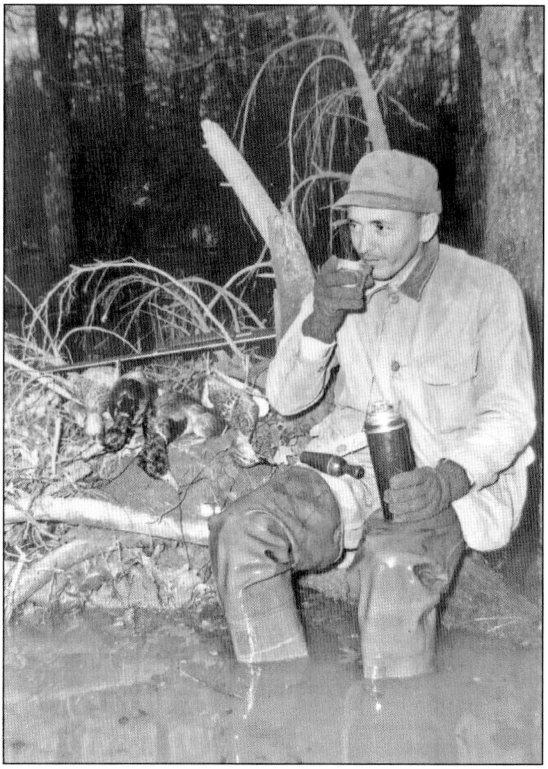

With his ducks bagged and on display to his left and with his duck call resting on his lap, a hunter finds time to warm up with coffee from his thermos. Note the waterproof thigh-high waders, enabling his feet to rest semi-comfortably in the icy waters. (Courtesy of the Museum of the Arkansas Grand Prairie.)

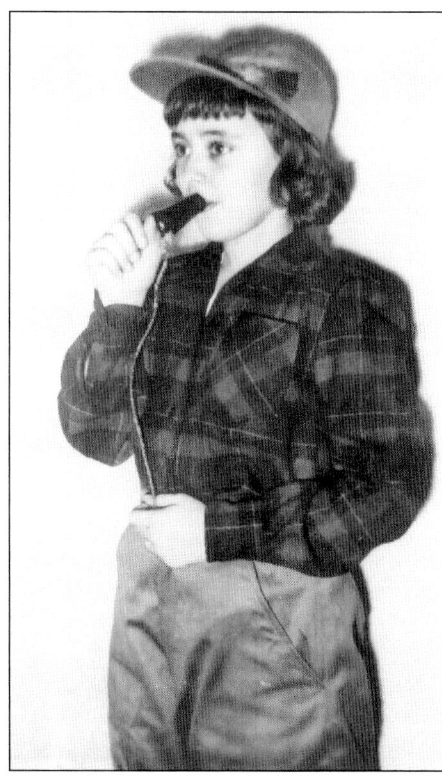

The men who had always dominated the duck-calling competition were given a hint of changing times in 1950, when 12-year-old Pat Peacock won the junior world title for calling ducks. Even then, it is doubtful that the competitors knew the determination behind the pretty girl's pose for the photographer. The next year, at age 13, Pat won the first of five straight women's world titles. (Courtesy of the Museum of the Arkansas Grand Prairie.)

In 1955, Pat Peacock won not only the Arkansas duck-calling title, but also the first of two world championship titles in a row. No contestant on earth, man or woman, could defeat the teenager from Stuttgart, Arkansas, who is pictured in 1955 with gun in hand and duck call ready, sharing a boat with hunting companion Henry Bennett. (Courtesy of the Museum of the Arkansas Grand Prairie.)

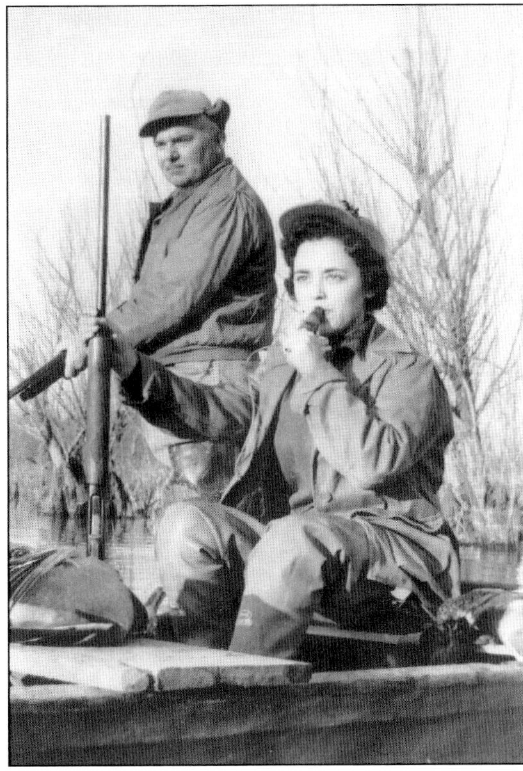

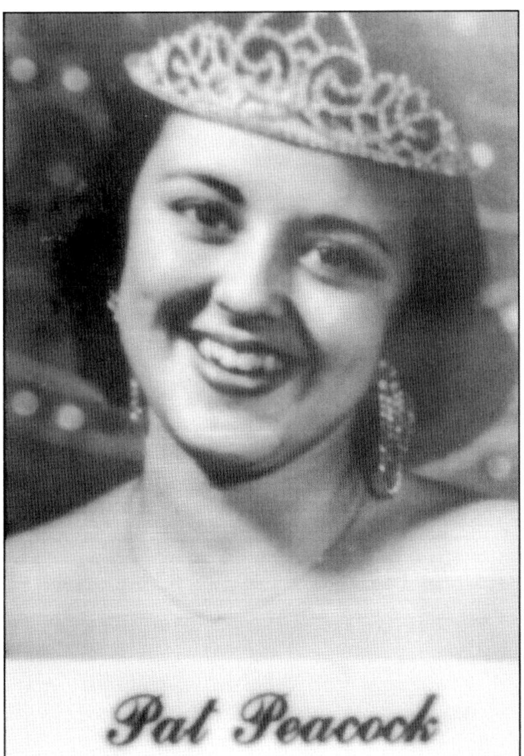

The same year that Pat Peacock won her second world championship for duck calling, she also earned the title and crown for the 1956 Rice Festival's Queen Mallard Beauty Contest. (Courtesy of the Museum of the Arkansas Grand Prairie.)

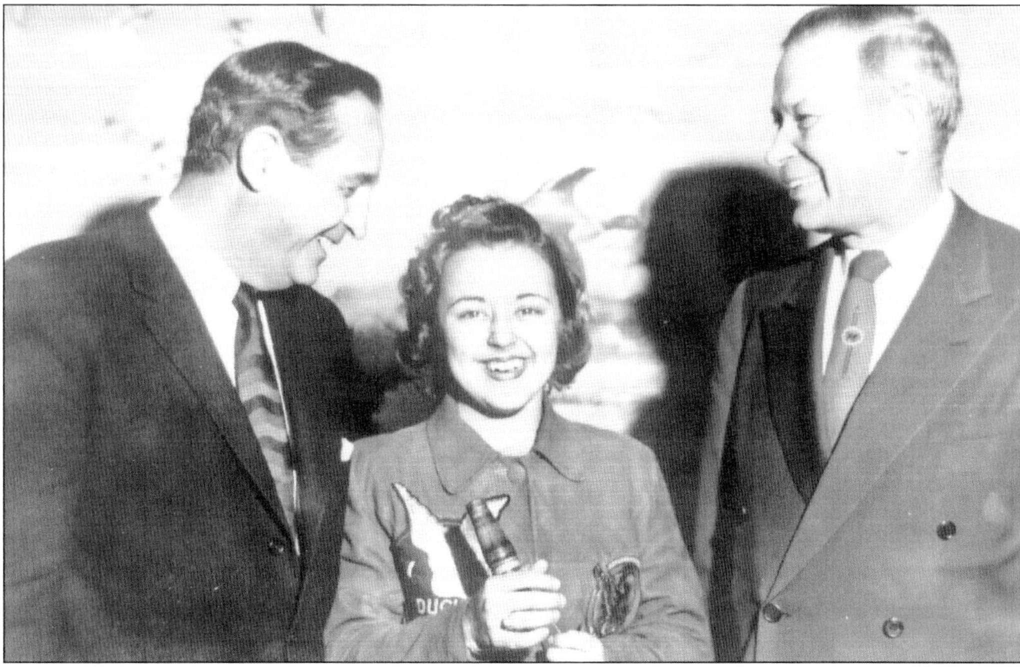

Never one to miss a high-profile event, Arkansas governor Orval Faubus (left) congratulates 1956 world champion Pat Peacock, who is beaming with her duck caller in hand. (Courtesy of the Museum of the Arkansas Grand Prairie.)

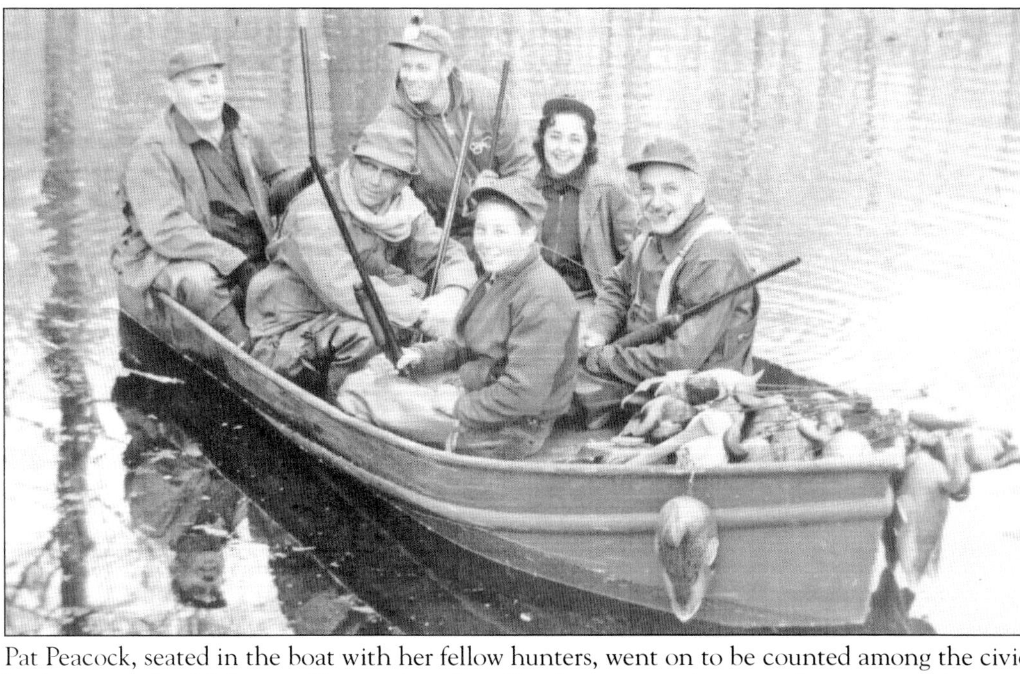

Pat Peacock, seated in the boat with her fellow hunters, went on to be counted among the civic leaders not only of Arkansas County, but also of her home state. Among other accomplishments, she became the first woman to serve on the Arkansas Game and Fish Commission. Today she works as director of the Museum of the Arkansas Grand Prairie in Stuttgart, one of the finest regional museums in the country. (Courtesy of the Museum of the Arkansas Grand Prairie.)

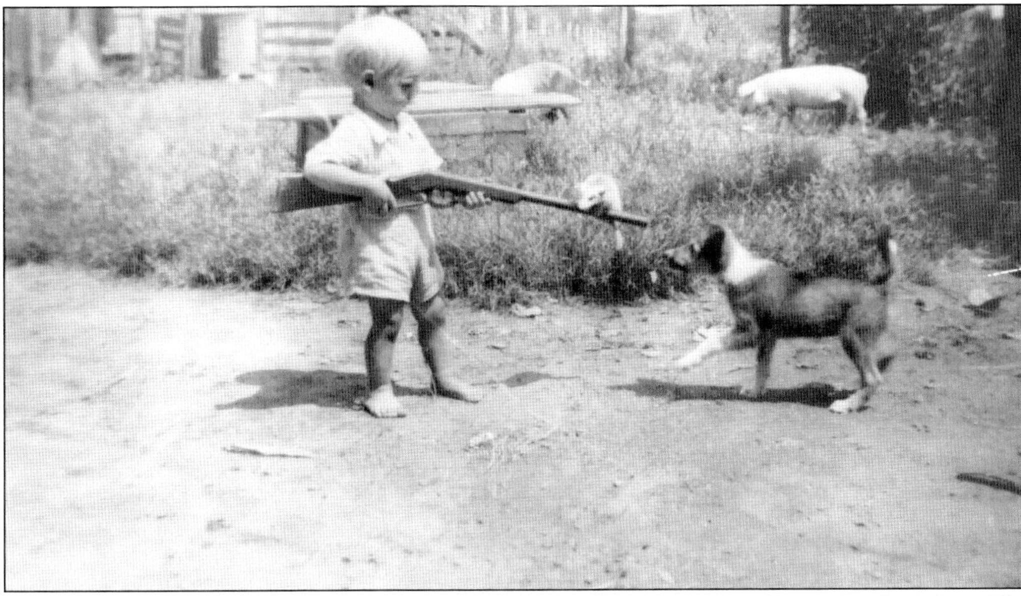

Outdoor recreation has been a part of the heritage of Arkansas County from its earliest days. The spirit of adventure is perhaps epitomized in the imagination of this small boy, pictured here on an unidentified local farm around 1920. The trophy he has bagged seems to be a young possum hanging from the barrel of his air rifle; the boy's courageous dog assists in spite of an injury.

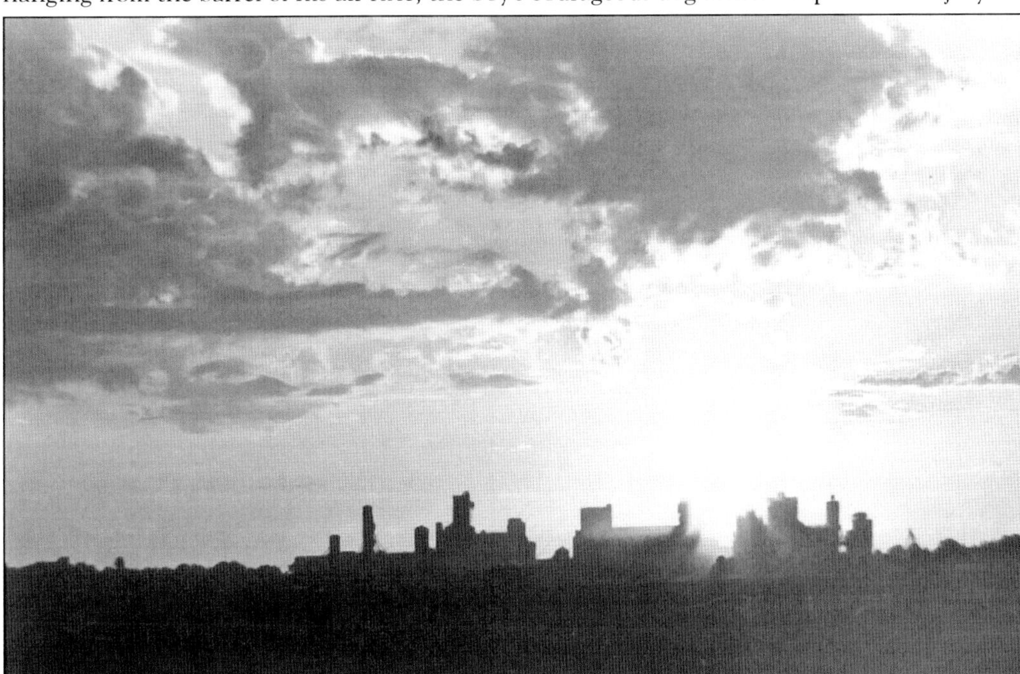

This book closes with an image of the "Castles of Stuttgart," a term for the skyline of rice mills at sunset. The people of Arkansas County—and all those across the nation who care about the balance of commerce and nature—deserve the credit for the little story we have tried to tell in the preceding pages. It is hoped that many more will continue to visit and settle in Arkansas County, for the area has much to offer anyone who is ready to appreciate its riches.